Jim Thorpe

Jim Thorpe

WORLD'S GREATEST ATHLETE

By Robert W. Wheeler

UNIVERSITY OF OKLAHOMA PRESS : NORMAN

Library of Congress Cataloging in Publication Data

Wheeler, Robert W., 1945–
      Jim Thorpe, world's greatest athlete.

      Published in 1975 under title: Pathway to glory.
      Bibliography: p. 303
      Includes index.
      1. Thorpe, Jim, 1888–1953. 2. Athletes—United States—
Biography. I. Title.
GV697.T5W47   1979   796'.092'4[B]   78-58080

ISBN: 0–8061–1745–1

7   8   9   10   11   12   13   14   15   16   17   18   19   20   21

To my mother, Dorothy Walsh Wheeler, for her prayers, inexhaustible patience, and countless hours in the physical preparation of the manuscript.

To my father, R. Warren Wheeler, who from my earliest memory instilled in me a love of history and especially of the American Indian.

To my wife, Florence Ridlon, who has helped to make me the person that I am, and whose knowledge has led me to seek ever higher goals.

Restoration of
Jim Thorpe's Olympic Awards

On February 8, 1982, my wife, Dr. Florence Ridlon, and I founded the Jim Thorpe Foundation dedicated to the restoration of the Olympic awards of Jim Thorpe and the education of the public about his accomplishments. What had previously been a labor of love over a fifteen-year period then became a full-time occupation for both of us. With a projected 2½ billion viewers slated to watch the Los Angeles Olympic Games in 1984, the timing was perfect to launch an all-out, albeit last-ditch, effort to restore the Olympic honors and, indeed, the integrity of the American Indian Jim Thorpe.

During my research for this book I was able to document three pieces of evidence that were crucial to Jim Thorpe's case. First, it was the Amateur Athletic Union, not the International Olympic Committee, as many believed, that stripped Jim of his medals. The AAU restored his amateur standing in 1973, thus making it reasonable for the IOC to follow suit and save face at the same time. Second, in 1913, Jim Thorpe was a ward of the United States government. Despite his status he was not provided with a lawyer to defend him against the charges leveled by the AAU. Third, Joe Libby, Jim's teammate at Carlisle Indian School confirmed that he, Jim, and Jesse Youngdeer were sent to Rocky Mount, North Carolina, to play summer baseball by the Carlisle coach, Glenn S. ("Pop") Warner.

These three findings, however, were only extenuating circumstances and not legally binding. We needed something more concrete. Finally, researching the general regulations of the 1912 Olympiad in the Library of Congress, my wife found what we needed. Rule 13 read: "Objections to the qualification of a competitor must be made in writing, and be forwarded without delay to the Swedish Olympic Committee. No such objection shall be entertained unless accompanied by a deposit of 20 Swedish Kronor and received by the Swedish Olympic Committee before the lapse of 30 days from the distribution of the prizes." The newspaper story that led to Jim's disqualification did not appear until nearly seven months after the games.

These facts combined with the resolutions of United States Representative James J. Howard and Senator Don Nickles and more than 250,000 signatures on the foundation's petition, enabled us to convince longtime Jim Thorpe supporter William E. Simon and United States IOC Representatives Julian K. Roosevelt and Douglas F. Roby that Thorpe's case had legal merit. The foundation's petition had been distributed by Amerian Indian organizations, the Southwestern Wax Museum, the Junior Chambers of Commerce, the Benevolent and Protective Order of Elks, and many concerned individuals.

After meeting with William E. Simon, IOC President Juan Antonio Samaranch proposed the restoration of Jim's amateur status at the October 13, 1982, meeting of the nine-member executive committee in Lausanne, Switzerland. The resolution passed unanimously, and on January 18, 1983, seventy years after Jim had been accused of professionalism, duplicate gold medals were returned to his children by President Samaranch in Los Angeles.

In 1913 the AAU had told Jim Thorpe, "Ignorance is no excuse." In 1976 the then IOC president, Avery Brundage, again told me, "Ignorance is no excuse." This time my wife and I were able to tell the IOC: "Gentlemen, with all due respect, ignorance of the general regulations for the 1912 Olympics was no excuse for illegally divesting Jim Thorpe of his awards."

ROBERT W. WHEELER

Acknowledgments

Expressions of gratitude to every individual who gave support to my research would fill an entire separate volume. There are relatives of the Conway, Ridlon, Walsh, and Wheeler families whose prayers and financial aid have facilitated the work and final publication of this book; the individuals who took time from their busy schedules to graciously receive me for interviews; Jim Campbell, formerly of the Pro Football Hall of Fame, who gave of his vast talents; the understanding friends who searched tirelessly for books; the concerned newspaper personnel and librarians who rushed off copies of old editions during the final months.

Believing that this supreme athlete deserved an honest treatment and also dismayed by the vagueness surrounding him in life and death, I determined to write his biography. I traveled more than ten thousand miles through twenty-three states, with tape recorder in hand, to interview scores of relatives, friends, teammates, competitors, and experts about every facet of the life of Jim Thorpe.

Throughout this seven-year search, many people from all walks of life made possible the continuance of my journey. To arrive at the doors of those interviewed at times necessitated hitchhiking. People who picked me up went out of their way to see that I reached my desired destination and even offered money to assist in my venture.

There were the kind townspeople who welcomed me into their homes and treated me as one of the family while I was visiting their areas.

Finally, I owe a special debt of gratitude to my thesis adviser at Syracuse University, Dr. Robert J. Rayback, whose writing and teaching abilities served as a source of inspiration and who gave ready acceptance to the controversial oral history approach for my degree.

Contents

Illustrations

Jim Thorpe

The changes of many summers have brought old age upon me and I cannot expect to survive many moons. Before I set out on my journey to the land of my fathers, I have determined to give my motives and reasons for my former hostilities to the whites and to vindicate my character from misrepresentation. I am now an obscure member of a nation, that formerly honored and respected my opinions. The path to glory is rough, and many gloomy hours obscure it. May the Great Spirit shed light on yours and that you may never experience the humility that the power of the American government has reduced me to, is the wish of him, who, in his native forests, was once as proud and bold as yourself.

10th Moon, 1833   BLACK HAWK

In the interest of scholarship you will no doubt carefully analyze all stories that come to your attention. Some ridiculous stories concerning Thorpe have been published in magazines and books and have been solemnly repeated by reliable writers such as Grantland Rice and Arthur Daley. I repeat, watch carefully what you write because more lies have been written about Jim Thorpe than about any player in football history.

October 24, 1967   COLONEL ALEXANDER M. WEYAND

CHAPTER 1

A Vigorous Youth

*Our lives were lived in the open, winter and summer.
We were never in the house when we could be out of it.
And we played hard. I emphasize this because the boys
who would grow up strong men must lay the foundation
in a vigorous youth.*

JIM THORPE

Before the turn of the last century, a star rose into prominence and radiated with so much splendor that nothing was able to eclipse it. In the late spring of 1888, this star was born not in heaven but in a one-room cabin made of cottonwood and hickory, south of the town of Bellemont in the Plains country of Oklahoma Territory. The time was six-thirty on the morning of May 28.[1]

The nine-and-a-half-pound infant, a member of the Sac and Fox tribe, was called Wa-tho-huck, which meant "Bright Path." To the world, however, he became known as Jim Thorpe.[2]

"With most Indian tribes, it is the custom for the mother to name her newborn child after a notable experience either during her pregnancy or immediately following its birth."[3] Since she gave birth to Jim shortly after sunrise, the mother's first sight upon looking out through her bedroom window was the pathway, resplendent with reflected sunlight, leading up to the house. Hence the name Bright Path.

Though he was not a full-blooded scion of his aboriginal forebears, his Indian ancestry began in 1838 on the Sac and Fox Reservation, near Fort Des Moines, Iowa. Situated far from even the periphery of anything remotely resembling settled and populated areas, the reservation served as the rendezvous for a booming enterprise, the fur trade.

3

The hardy trappers evinced courage, skill, and mastery of the conditions of their chosen life. They would not have been there if they had not responded to the attractiveness of the redolent country and found something precious beyond safety, gain, comfort, and family life. At rendezvous, the men would have rations of coffee, sugar, hardtack, and bacon. If they had meat, it was primarily buffalo: fresh, dried, or made into pemmican. Scurvy was nonexistent; in fact, the diaries of that time seldom mentioned a sick trapper.[4]

Commonly, these men married Indians from the reservation because the advantages of such a relationship became well publicized. A dependable Indian woman made an ideal helpmate and frequently meant the difference between survival or horrible death.

One of these trappers, Hiram G. Thorpe, a large-mustached Irish immigrant, took as his bride No-ten-o-quah, a member of the Thunder Clan of Chief Black Hawk. On the same reservation this great warrior, who in his younger days had fought valiantly to keep the white pioneers from taking the lands that belonged to his people, spent the last of his seventy-one years. By this time, however, the intense fire of righteousness had burned out in his proud heart.

He realized the impossibility of trying to stop the westward migration of European settlers. He therefore accepted the union between Hiram and No-ten-o-quah. In fact, to express his recognition of the white man, Black Hawk asked to be buried dressed in a military uniform given to him by Andrew Jackson and decorated with medals from President John Quincy Adams. Between his knees was to be a cane, a gift from Henry Clay.

A son, Hiram P., blessed the marriage eight years later. Although only one-half Indian, Hiram possessed no discernible Irish features. Jet-black hair topped the rich bronze skin of his face. Many elders of the tribe commented on the close resemblance of Hiram's features to Black Hawk's.

As Hiram reached manhood, the similarity transcended physical features. He became the greatest athlete on the reservation. Like Black Hawk, Hiram defeated all comers, Indian or white, in contests of strength, speed, coordination, and endurance.

In the summer of 1878, one last parallel between the two manifested itself—their consummate love of freedom. Hiram viewed life on the reservation as intolerable. From November to March the Indians needed to hunt buffalo on the plains to sustain them during these severe winter months. With assiduous attention, the infiltrating white settlers watched the Indians and severely restricted their movements. As a result, the Indians did not have the breadth of land essential for an effective hunt.[5]

The federal government under the administration of Rutherford B. Hayes, feeling its first real pangs of guilt, began making a sincere effort to alleviate the plight of the Indians. By allotting funds, the government began to help the Indian adjust to his changing environment. However, when "middlemen" or Indian agents, under whose jurisdiction this particular reservation was included, withheld vital medical supplies and used the money to increase their own salaries, it was more than Hiram could stand. Having lost his wife through diphtheria, he appealed for improvements, but to no avail. Finally coming to the realization that the situation was hopeless, he, along with his son, four-year-old Frank, daughters Fannie and Minnie, and fourteen of the Indian friends who shared his point of view, set out for Indian Territory, later to become part of Oklahoma.

Facing hunger, illness, and cold as a result of inadequate preparation by the federal agents, Hiram found his first Oklahoma winter filled with hardship. The adversities were lessened, however, when just two months after his arrival he married Charlotte View, of Potawatomi and Kickapoo extraction.

Settling in the Sac and Fox village on the banks of the North Canadian River, locally called the North Fork River, at last the Thorpes were able to live in peace. Their existence was meager, but they achieved some degree of freedom. It was not until 1887, when the General Allotment Act

5

came into effect, that the Indian reservations were broken up and individual ownership became law. The former reservation areas were laid out into 160-acre homesteads. It took twelve years of work before Hiram moved his family into a new, larger home built of land-sanded boards.

Said Art Wakolee, a boyhood friend of Jim's:

Hiram Thorpe was not too poor. Like the other Sac and Fox, he planted a wide variety of crops and raised a modest number of horses, cattle, hogs, and chickens. He always raised enough to live on during the winter: dried corn, pumpkins, beans, fruits, and meat, both wild and tame. Actually Charlotte, following Indian custom, planted and worked the field. After the men had cleared the fields by burning, the women would take over and break up the earth with digging sticks or hoes made from shells or bones. The women had to keep the crows from the corn and also harvested it. Besides their field work, the women cared for the children, made clothing, wove, and cooked. After clearing the land for farming, the men made tools and weapons, hunted, and organized the religious and political functions.

The Indians knew all about farming long before the other races came. In fact, they showed the pioneers how to plant and farm. They even furnished seed for them. When the white man arrived in Oklahoma, they were given a real welcome and a handshake of friendship. It was Indian teaching that all people were their brothers and sisters. Everyone came from the same God who created all things.[6]

It was here, tilling an Oklahoma riverbank and hunting buffalo on her plains, that Hiram and Charlotte were destined to spend their lives. Their first child, a son, was born in 1881. His name was George. Seven summers passed before Charlotte gave birth to Jim.

When Hiram saw Jim for the first time, he immediately recognized the resemblance, the same resemblance that he shared, between the child and his ancestor, Black Hawk.

Many years later, when writers were searching for something new to write about Jim, he told them, "I was born with a twin brother by the name of Charlie."[7] Surprisingly enough, Jim and Charlie were not alike in appearance. Al-

Hiram P. Thorpe, Jim's father

though Charlie's complexion was slightly darker, his hair was brown while Jim's was black. And as Jim grew he developed a prominent jaw, the result of that portion of his ancestry that was Irish. Only in size did the twins look alike.

Jim's earliest years were filled with the exuberance of youth in a world free from care.

In addition to playing the games of childhood, I spent a great deal of my time in hunting and fishing. I was always of a restless disposition and never was content unless I was trying my skill in some game against my fellow playmates or testing my endurance and wits against some member of the animal kingdom, of which there were many in that part of Oklahoma where I spent my youthful days.

I became well versed in forest lore. I particularly loved to hunt and fish. I learned how to wait beside a runway and stalk a deer. I learned how to trap for bear and rabbits, coon and possum. I used snares and steel traps, and I would catch quail in a figure-4 trap I made from cornstalks.[8]

These were the years during which Jim and Charlie were inseparable. What they lacked in similar physical features was more than made up for by their common interests. Although Jim always was the better of his twin in their games, Charlie compensated for his lack of ability with his Indian endowment, a proud heart.

During early May, 1896, just two weeks before the twins' eighth birthday, Hiram finally gave in to their incessant pleas to take them hunting. Since both were able to handle a rifle, Hiram believed the trip would be a good experience for them. But on the scheduled morning of departure, Charlie, taken sick with a fever, was unable to make the journey.

On the third and final day of the hunt, Jim was allowed to take aim at his first deer. It was a magnificent buck, and the boy brought it down with his first shot. Hiram, well pleased, promised to call the village to feast on the boy's first kill, according to the old Sac and Fox tradition. But upon their return home it became apparent that there would not be any celebrating.

Charlotte met Hiram and Jim at the door with the news

that Charlie lay dying at the infirmary in Chilocco, twenty miles away. Wasting no time, Hiram and Jim dropped off the game and hitched a fresh team to the buckboard. In a matter of minutes, the three of them were in the wagon. At last they reached the town, but it was too late. Charlie was dead.

Jim remembered:

Up to the time that little Charlie died at the age of eight of pneumonia, we roamed the prairies and swam and played together always. After Charlie's death, I used to go out by myself with an old dog and hunt coon when I was only nine years old. Often I would make camp and stay out all night. Later, my older brother, George, became my playmate and to equal him in our games I had to be strong and active. As I grew older I had other playmates in the young Indians from the neighboring reservations. As I look back at them, they were a husky crowd. Our lives were lived in the open, winter and summer. We were never in the house when we could be out of it. And we played hard. I emphasize this because the boys who would grow up strong men must lay the foundations in a vigorous youth.

Our favorite game was "Follow the Leader." Depending on the "leader," that can be made an exciting game. Many a time in following I had to swim rivers, climb trees, and run under horses. But our favorite was climbing hickory or tall cedar trees, getting on the top, swinging there and leaping to the ground, ready for the next "follow."

I swam a great deal. Indeed, I lived in the water. It is great exercise. For the development of muscle and wind I cannot recommend it too highly.

Of course, during those boyhood days, none of us were after records. Our sports were not ordered or directed. They were just the spontaneous expression of boys. And it isn't necessary that these activities should, at that age, be specially directed. They lay the physical foundation for future big performances.

During this period my habits were regular. I was in bed every night at nine — not because I had to go, but because after the day's activities I was usually tired and wanted to go. And I slept until I was called and told to dress for school. I was a sound sleeper and then, as at present, at any hour of the day I could in a very few moments fall asleep by sitting or lying down and closing my eyes. As to my meals, they always consisted of plain food—the plain meals of the average family, though I rarely ate sweets of any kind.[9]

As he grew older, these games proved to be merely pastimes for young Jim because, in 1891, Hiram was allotted an additional 160-acre tract of land. By the time Jim was nine, only a year after Charlie's death, he was expected to do a large share of the chores. With Frank off at boarding school, Jim had to feed all of the livestock and learn how to rope and break wild horses on the open plain.

Of all my activities as a boy I liked best catching wild horses on the range. My father was a ranchman and there were plenty of horses, but none of them wanted to be caught. But at ten I could handle the lasso, and at fifteen I had never met a wild one that I could not catch, saddle, and ride. That is one achievement of my boyhood days that I do not hesitate to feel proud about. It was great sport, and I know it made me strong and active and alert and helped me to quick judgment and decision. As a boy I rode horseback a great deal. I need not say it is an excellent form of exercise.[10]

The summer of 1898 marked the first time in the boy's life that Hiram allowed Jim to accompany him on a major hunting trip. At the age of ten, the small but sturdy boy was barely able to keep up the Herculean pace set by his father, usually averaging thirty miles a day.

I have never known a man with so much energy as my father. He could walk, ride, or run for days without ever showing the least sign of fatigue. Once, when we didn't have enough horses to carry all our kill, my father slung a buck deer over each shoulder and carried them twenty miles to our home.[11]

According to Wakolee,

Hiram spent countless hours teaching Jim the art of hunting. In no time Jim was an excellent marksman. He learned to shoot his prey in a vulnerable area so that it would not run away and suffer a great deal. Even though the game was plentiful he was taught to kill only what was needed for food.[12]

10

With Charlie gone, Jim and his father grew closer to one another. Every evening before the main meal, Hiram led the members of his family in prayer. He instilled in them the knowledge that all things made by God were beautiful.

They thanked him in their daily prayers for their eyes to see the beauty that He had made. They saw His power in all things. Before their meal, they first drank water because it was life. They gave thanks for food which gave them the strength to live and to learn about all things.[13]

In another sense, Jim beamed with pride as he recalled the athletic accomplishments of his father. "My father was the undisputed champion in sprinting, wrestling, swimming, high jumping, broad jumping, and horseback riding."[14] Almost every week, usually on a Saturday afternoon, the entire village gathered on a lush green pasture bordering the Thorpe homestead. All of the families brought some food for the feast later in the evening. But while there was still plenty of daylight, the menfolk engaged in the various events.

First came the long run of approximately one mile, next the running broad jump and the high jump. Finally elimination contests in wrestling would be held, with the top two facing each other to determine the winner. By this time darkness fell, and with almost the same certainty as that the sun would set, Hiram would be triumphant.

CHAPTER 2

It Is Not Always Size That Counts

In athletics, it is not always the size that counts, it is what is inside of you. Jim came to Haskell on his own. He was small for his age, so the football recruiters ignored him. It is ironic that they let the greatest of them all slip right through their fingers.

—GEORGE WASHINGTON,
Haskell Indian Junior College

At the age of six and a half, Jim and Charlie were confronted with the imminence of school, the fearsome institution of adult society, when their father enrolled them at the Sac and Fox Indian Agency School near Tecumseh.

Wakolee reports:

I knew Jim was not very happy at school. I wasn't myself and neither were any of the other children. We had a very poor school system. The teachers came from many different states and, for certification, had to pass a government test. Their salary was provided by the government. The school books were easy for the teacher but were very difficult for us.

We could not speak or understand English when we were taken there at the age of six. It took us a long time to learn our lessons in kindergarten because most of the teachers had very little patience with the Indian children. Some of the teachers were kind, while others were very mean. We got a licking many times when we could not spell a simple word. As a result, we could not learn very much because most of us were afraid of our teacher.[1]

Schooling became unbearable for Jim. He daydreamed and wished he could slip through the forest to stalk some prey or just spear bluegills beside an imaginary fishing hole. Charlie, being a better student, was not as troubled as his twin brother. If it had not been for Charlie's companionship

12

and the steadying influence of his older brother, George, who reminded him that he must strive to emulate Black Hawk, Jim would not have remained as long as he did. Besides, there was "prairie baseball!"

Jim recalled:

My first experience with baseball was at the Agency School. George gave me my first lessons and soon I was playing every afternoon. We called it prairie baseball. Teams would be chosen and the game would be played out in the field. That was the equivalent of what is called sand-lot baseball today. We were also interested in basketball, but we had no track because it was a day when track was a passé idea. Only the Indians participated in this type of activity and it was of an unofficial nature, the only regularly scheduled event being the weekly meet in front of my father's house.[2]

Wakolee concurred:

Our people were strong and healthy in the days of our old people. The Indian system of the past was better than the one we had at school. We never received any training there. That is why Jim's father trained him when he was a young boy. His dad was known as the strongest man of his time.

He taught Jim how to exercise in order to build up every part of his body. In fact, all of the young Indian men were taught the methods to keep their bodies fit and strong and clean and healthy. They were given instruction in running, jumping, wrestling, and swimming. I might add that the women also had their own health program.

I know Jim's father taught him all of the clean rules for sport and life because Jim never tried to hurt anyone in football. The athletes he played with and against loved him for his good sportsmanship. Our old Chiefs gave our instructors the authority to be strict but not to use force for fear that the good competitors would be ruined.

They were told not to create anger or hate in the young people they were teaching by using true kindness and love. Big Jim learned this and was blessed by God to accomplish all that he did in sports. He made our Indian people known by his good sportsmanship. I have seen Jim take a white football player's hand to show his friendship and love. Our people knew God, his gospels, and his

13

commandments. Jim knew he was playing with his brothers. When he lost, he offered his hand to the victor. Our people were taught that a handshake was a sign of good friendship.[3]

During the late summer days of 1896, however, a noticeable change came over Jim. Faced with the prospect of returning to school without his beloved brother, whom he had lost only three months earlier, Jim withdrew into himself and became unusually stoical for a boy of only eight.

Gradually the boy's "great leadership qualities and sense of humor"[4] began to diminish and his disenchantment with schooling increased to such an extent that he even failed to compete in his beloved prairie baseball games. Finally, he left school during the following year just a few weeks before completion of his fourth year. When he reached home, his mother was the first to meet him. The boy was surprised by her disapproving stare, because he was so elated to be back on the ranch.

Hiram hitched up the wagon and drove him right back to school, but he left him at the front door, and Jim, as soon as his father turned to go, left by the back door. Taking a shortcut that was only eighteen miles instead of twenty-three, the boy beat his father home. When Hiram found Jim waiting for him, he could not believe his eyes.

After he had learned the reasons for Jim's refusal to remain at the school—that he had not yet adjusted to the confines of the classroom or to the painful memory of Charlie's presence there—he made plans to send Jim to another school, far enough away to make it difficult for him to find his way home. During that summer, Hiram was approached by a recruiter from Haskell, an Indian school in the northeastern corner of Kansas.[5]

Haskell Indian Junior College, the fulfillment of the dream of Dudley C. Haskell, congressman of the Second District, was founded just south of Lawrence, Kansas, in the year 1884. The enrollment grew rapidly from a class of twenty-two students to a total of four hundred in only one year.

The Indian people in nearby areas were aware of the need for education for their children. In fact, one of the important features of the various treaties to which the tribes had agreed was that the government should provide schools that children might be taught the many new things they must learn. The younger chiefs of the surrounding tribes worked hard to "sell" the idea of schooling to the Indian parents.[6]

Jim arrived at the Lawrence station on September 17, 1898. At that time, the school was on a sophisticated military system. "When Jim came here," reminisced George Washington, former Haskell football great,

they drilled just like the military and even the girls wore a uniform. Contrary to widespread beliefs, our uniforms were not discards from the Army but were handmade in our tailor shops. The purpose of this type of system was an attempt to eradicate old tribal loyalties. You must realize that in those days the ancient ties were very powerful.[7]

Military drill and uniforms were abolished in 1917, reinstated in 1919, and again abolished in 1925. The drilling was colorful and useful when a lot had to be done in a very short time.[8]

It also gave the Indians, many of whom were attending school for the first time and had never been confined before, a good sense of discipline.

"Everyone enjoyed it," Washington continued:

I liked it. You had to salute and everything was neat and slick. We had to pass inspection every Saturday. Young Jim used to be very conscientious about his appearance. He was very proud of his uniform and took great pains to keep his brass buttons polished and his shoes, the first real pair he had ever owned, shined.

We had to spend four hours a day in the classroom receiving instruction in American History, Mathematics, Grammar and Composition, and a small amount of Biology. We also had to learn a trade and so an additional four hours were spent in the various shops. In Jim's instance, it was the engineering shop.[9]

A visitor to one of the academic classes preserved her impressions as follows:

When the alphabet is mastered, words are learned from the

blackboard. The teacher uses gestures, acts out, draws cartoon pictures, and, in a thousand other ways, gets across to the students the meanings of the words on the blackboard.

When all the words in a paragraph are studied, the paragraph is read in concert and then individually. The students are eager and interested and seem restless and discontented if they have not mastered each lesson before the time comes to dismiss. They are better behaved and learn as easily as any comparable group of children.[10]

According to Delaware Chief Garland Nevitt, another Haskell alumnus,

When Jim and I were students at Haskell, the total enrollment was more than a thousand, representing between eighty-five and ninety different tribes. It was recognized as a vocational school and was very strict because, although all the young people who wanted to attend were admitted, they were released if it was discovered that they weren't qualified.

Every six months meant a change of instruction in a particular trade. This cycle was kept in effect until the individual came to the tenth grade, and then the records would show where his greatest aptitude was found, whether it was a baker, painter, blacksmith, tailor, and so forth.[11]

It was here that the boy who would one day be recognized as the greatest football player in history began his lifelong love affair with the game. During the early months of his brief stay at Haskell, Jim unfailingly observed the varsity scrimmage from the sidelines.

"I can tell you about that football team," recounted Washington:

It was at its best during the time Jim was here. It was extremely difficult to schedule games because none of the universities or colleges wanted to play us. There were many standouts on the teams during those years. Ben Powell was my favorite, but the biggest star was a fellow by the name of Chauncey Archiquette. He was a huge fullback who weighed well over two hundred pounds and possessed lightning speed.[12]

It was not unusual that Archiquette caught Jim's fancy.

After watching him dominate the daily practice sessions, Jim would race back and forth across the empty turf trying to emulate his idol. Eventually Chauncey noticed the little boy and stopped to talk to him after practice one day. He was amazed at the youngster's knowledge about the game. He asked Jim if he would like to have his own football. When Jim said that he would, Chauncey took him to the harness shop and sewed some leather scraps together and stuffed the ball with rags.

Now that he had a "real" football, it was not long before Jim organized football games among his friends and, as before, began to play with enthusiasm and leadership. His ability soon outclassed his playmates so that in the period just before he left the school he was competing with older boys. He even began to try his skills at some of the other athletic contests.

He began to observe the track team. The physical director, A. A. Van, noticed the boy jumping a fence over and over again in the hurdler's style and became interested in him. But by the time he had discovered the boy's name, it was too late.

Just before completion of his second year, when he was establishing himself as a good student for the first time, Jim received the news that his father had been shot in a hunting accident and lay dying. Without waiting for the school authorities to arrange for his transportation back home, he dazedly walked out of Haskell with nothing but the work clothes he was wearing. He ran all the way to Lawrence, arriving just in time to jump a freight train.

Later that day, as the train slowed to a stop, the young stowaway was discovered and told to jump off. In the course of the ensuing conversation, Jim learned that he had boarded a northbound train instead of a southbound one. Disheartened, the boy walked all the way home, a distance of 270 miles, and finally arrived two weeks later.

He was met by his father, of all people. "I have lost much weight," Hiram said, "but the doctor said I will be back to normal in a few weeks."[13] Jim's presence was greatly appreciated by the household, and at last it seemed to Jim that he had found some measure of happiness. This was transitory, however, because the family was destined to lose a different member. This time it was Jim's mother. The sturdy Charlotte, who had never been sick a day in her life, was struck down suddenly by a severe case of blood poisoning. In one week's time she passed away and was laid to rest at the Mission of the Sacred Heart, located between Prague and Stroud, Oklahoma.

During the following months, young Jim became even more of a loner. Not even Hiram could bring him out of his doldrums. In fact, nothing was the same with any of the members of the family, including Hiram. He was not the "Big Hiram" of old in spirit, and since he was now forty-four years of age, he would never again be a dominant figure in athletics.

It was inevitable that he would lose patience with his listless brood. One day George and Jim neglected to feed the livestock and went fishing. Hiram, who had gone into Shawnee on business, returned in the late afternoon to find most of his herd scattered all over the farm. When the boys finally returned home, the usually even-tempered father gave them their first thrashing and a sound one! "I deserved it," Jim admitted later, "but I didn't feel like taking it. So I ran away from home to the Texas Panhandle and worked for a year fixing fences on a ranch and taming wild horses."[14]

The year was 1901, and Jim was thirteen years old. He was only 4 feet 11 inches tall and weighed a mere 102 pounds.[15] He missed his father very much, but refused to return until he had proven himself to be a man according to the custom of his people. When he had saved a substantial sum of money, he bought a fine team of horses and set out for Oklahoma and home.

He was met with great rejoicing. Hiram had regretted the day he lost his temper and had prayed for Jim's safe return. George had gone westward by this time, so Jim's responsibilities were great. Hiram needed him around the farm and in the house; Mary was just eight, and Eddie was three.

Jim Thorpe as a teenager

Courtesy Beth and Homer Ray

Although there was no football or track at home as there had been at Haskell, Jim was thankful that his father had not sent him back. Instead he continued his education for the next three years at the public school in Garden Grove.

19

Since the school was just three miles from home, he was able to help with the chores after classes every day.

Three years passed, and it was May 12, 1904, just a week short of the completion of the term. There was a guest at school on that day, dressed in the same kind of uniform that the Army officers had worn at Haskell. But this man was not from Haskell; he was from a place called Carlisle.

The name was not altogether strange to the boy, for at Haskell the name of Carlisle was synonymous with football supremacy and somewhat of a legend. Many of the Haskell athletes aspired to go there and play for Coach "Pop" Warner. And as Jim listened to the representative talk about Carlisle, these recollections rushed through his head.

By this time, Jim was serious about his education and had become intrigued with the principles of a new field of study, electricity. The visitor was impressed by his enthusiasm, but contrary to previous accounts, this was not the real reason the name of "Jim Thorpe" was signed to the register.[16] The truth of the matter was that "Pop" Warner was building a sports dynasty and had one of the most intricate recruiting systems of his era. He was well aware of Jim's athletic prowess and actively sought his enrollment.[17]

Jim was reared in the country between Prague and Shawnee in Oklahoma and his abilities became evident in his teens when he asked Ensley Barbour, proprietor of Prague's only moving-picture house, to play on the baseball team sponsored and managed by Barbour. In the old days of Jim's youth anyone was welcome regardless of creed, color, or age, if he could only field, catch, pitch, or bat well enough to help win games against opposing teams, and since Thorpe could easily outplay anyone with either hand in any spot on the diamond, he seldom missed a baseball game in Prague's turbulent competition with other Oklahoma towns. Fame didn't spread very far or fast in rural areas when Jim was a kid, but even so he was quite a sensation around Prague.[18]

Hiram was very much in favor of his son's going to Carlisle. "Son," he said, "you are an Indian. I want you to show other races what an Indian can do."[19]

CHAPTER 3

Carlisle Indian School

*All Indians looked to Carlisle as their University. It
was their great ambition to send their children here. To
the masses, this was the highest school, and the bids came
in by the thousands.*

—MRS. VERNA (DONEGAN) WHISTLER,
Carlisle Indian School

Lieutenant Richard Henry Pratt of the United States Army,
on November 1, 1879, formally opened the Carlisle Indian
School. This nonreservation school was located on the north-
ern edge of the town of Carlisle, Pennsylvania, in the Cumberland Valley. One hundred and forty-seven pupils were
enrolled that day.

In 1867, after a distinguished record of service with the
Union Army in the Civil War, where he held the rank of
captain, Pratt re-enlisted with the "Buffalo Soldiers," the
Tenth Cavalry, a black regiment with white officers. At
this time the "Tenth" was fighting a series of bloody battles
against the Comanches, Kiowas, Cheyennes, and other
Plains tribes.

Eight years later, Pratt was sent to Fort Sill, Oklahoma,
by General Philip Sheridan, to conduct an inquiry into al-
leged Comanche, Kiowa, Cheyenne, Apache, and Arapaho
offenses. By combining the learning experiences derived
from his association with the black soldiers and the Indian
guides, he had developed a sympathy for minority peoples.
According to Lieutenant Pratt,

Some weeks after that, under orders from the government, the
worst of the offenders at Fort Sill and at the Cheyenne and Arapaho Agency, seventy miles to the north, were sent as prisoners
of war in chains to Florida under my care and confined in old

21

Fort Marion at St. Augustine and there held during the three years 1875 to 1878. The severe circumstances of their imprisonment and their being taken so far away from their homes made these Indians almost lose hope, and that, added to the change from their free western life and its fine dry air to the close confinement within the casemates and high-walled area of the old Spanish fort in the humidity and heat of that southern climate, affected their health so that a number of them sickened and died within a few months.

In my daily anxiety and care for them I found them greatly depressed and morose. It was my custom under such circumstances to divert them, change their thought, and try to inspire them with hope and courage.[1]

It was only a matter of time before the Indians grew to respect the quiet and unpretentious gentleman. Upon his arrival at Fort Marion, his first order of business was to remove their contemptible chains and allow them free access to the courtyard.

In addition, as Pratt explained,

It also seemed best to get them out of the curio class by cutting their hair and having them wear the clothing of the white man. There was some objection by them to these changes, but by kindly persuasion it was gradually accomplished. This change to Army clothing had an unexpected feature. Soon after the clothing was issued, a number cut off the legs of the trousers at the hip, laying aside the upper part and using the trouser legs as leggings in the Indian way.

This called for immediate correction. They were formed in line and a pair of the mutilated trousers shown them. They were emphatically told that the clothing belonged to the United States Government and that it was only loaned to them so that they might dress themselves becomingly, like the people they were meeting daily, and thus rid themselves of the stare of visitors who invariably noticed every difference between them and ourselves. They must not, therefore, under any circumstances mutilate the clothing but must wear it just as the white man wore it. They yielded good-naturedly and soon became accustomed to the white man's toggery and wore it with satisfaction to themselves. I had the soldier guards teach them how to be neat in the care of their

Apache Indians as they arrived at Carlisle, 1887

Courtesy Cumberland County Historical Society and Hamilton Library Association

clothing, how to clean it and crease their trousers, keep the brass buttons on their coats and caps bright, and polish their shoes, and in a short time there was pride established in the wearing of the Army uniform.[2]

As if these innovations were not enough, he replaced white guards with Indians, who, incidentally proved to be more trustworthy. Pratt offered this explanation:

The fact that I had commanded Indian scouts during the years while serving against Indians previous to coming east had given me confidence in their good qualities, particularly when pledged to obedience. This led me, within the first six months, to request the commanding officer to allow the organization of the younger men into a company with sergeants and corporals, to loan some old guns, and to use the Indians to guard themselves.

In making this request, the doubt of the commanding officer led me to pledge my army commission for its successful results.[3]

Perhaps the highest compliment paid to Pratt was an unconscious one. General Winfield Scott, a surprise visitor to the fort, impressed by the precision of the Indian drill, asked Pratt: "What troops are these, sir?"[4]

I lived much with the prisoners. My office in one of the casemates of the old fort was always open, and they were invited and frequently visited at my home, where we talked more freely. I found among them admirable principles of life and service and many times realized that here were men who only needed proper opportunities for development in order to easily become civilized and valuable citizens. High sense of honor was not lacking.[5]

The Chiefs (Minimac, Black Horse, Heap-of-Birds, and White Horse) confided in Pratt: "We want you to teach us the way of the white men . . . we first want our wives and our children . . . then we will go anywhere you say and learn to support ourselves as the white men do."[6]

It was not long before Pratt began to realize the inadequacies of Fort Marion and the immediate environment. In a letter to the Secretary of the Department of the Interior, he wrote:

The duty of the Government to these Indians seems to me to be the teaching of something that will be of permanent use to them. Teaching them to work is one thing, but St. Augustine offers practically nothing to them in this line. They have besought me repeatedly to try to get Washington to give them the opportunity to work.[7]

Pratt's resolve to find a suitable school for his charges met with much resistance. Even after they were able to speak English, dress properly, attend the white man's church, and, most important of all, earn a living outside of the prison, they were denied admittance to white schools.

Greatly discouraged, he decided to write to a number of congressmen in Washington. However, weeks turned into months and his letters numbered in the dozens, but no replies were forthcoming. He resorted to lobbyist techniques in his ever-increasing sojourns to Washington. In order to get him out of their hair, the Department of the Interior allowed him the use of the facilities of the Hampton Agricultural School for Negroes.

During this time, General Armstrong (Samuel Chapman Armstrong, head of the school) and I had many talks. . . . I told the General my dissatisfaction with systems to educate the Negro and Indian in exclusively race schools and especially with educating the two races together. Participation in the best things of our civilization through being environed by them was the essential factor for transforming the Indian. The small number of Indians in the United States, then given as 260,000, rendered their problem a very short one. All immigrants were accepted and naturalized into our citizenship by that route and thus had a full fair chance to become assimilated with our people and our industries. Why not the Indian? The thing to be overcome in the Indian's case was a fictitious prejudice on both sides. The method we had adopted of driving the Indians away from our communities and from contact with our people and holding them as prisoners on condition was to be overcome and the Indian, as well as the white man, taught that neither was as bad as the other thought. This lesson could never be learned by the Indian or our people through the indurated system of segregating and reservating the Indians

25

and denying them all chances to see and thus to learn and to prove their qualities through competition.[8]

Finally, through the intervention of Secretary of the Interior Carl Schurz, Pratt was able to secure the abandoned Army barracks of Carlisle, Pennsylvania. The year was 1879. It had taken Pratt four long years to attain his dream. Now it was reality, and he was not going to loosen his grasp. He immediately embarked upon a western recruiting expedition.

Instead of being able to draw students from the friendlier tribes, he was forced by the Department of the Interior to approach some of the more warlike nations. The reasoning behind this procedure was the idea of keeping the children for "hostages" as insurance against future uprisings.

For one month, Pratt labored at this virtually impossible task. Initially, his success was sporadic at best, until the day of his meeting with Spotted Tail, the leading chief of the Brulé Sioux and one of the greatest lawmakers in all of Indian history. Pratt described this intensely dramatic scene in these words:

I stood up and, assuming all the dignity I could, said that the Government was about to adopt a new policy with the Indians; that it believed the Indian youth capable of acquiring the same education and industries our white youth had and this would make them equals of our youth. The Government now realized that by keeping them separate from us and on reservations remote from any material chances to learn our ways, the acquirement of our qualities was a very slow operation; that the Government believed that if they were brought among our people, placed in good schools, and taught our language and our industries by going out among our people, in a little while their children could be made just as competent as the white children. The purpose in establishing a school so far east was to bring them near Washington, where all the people could see the improvement and where members of Congress and the administrative officials of the Government could visit and witness their progress and their ability to learn.

Then Spotted Tail got up. He was a massive man with strong, purposeful features. He began by saying: "The white people are

26

all thieves and liars. We do not want our children to learn such things. The white man is very smart. He knew there was gold in the Black Hills and he made us agree to give up all that country and now a great many white people are there getting out the gold." He said that the Government had given them a reservation which took in certain points, and he named them, and that their people had gone out to live in places near what they believed the edge of their reservation and made improvements, and then the Government sent its surveyors and they were now running the lines of the reservation and these lines were a long way inside of where they had agreed with the Government they should be, and these people had to move inside, and that they did not like that.

I said: "Spotted Tail, you are a remarkable man. Your name has gone all over the United States. It has even gone across the great water. You are such an able man that you are the principal chief of these thousands of your people. But Spotted Tail, you cannot read or write. You cannot speak the language of this country. You claim that the Government has tricked your people and placed the lines of your reservation a long way inside of where it was agreed they should be. You put your cross-mark signature on the treaty which fixed the lines of your reservation. That treaty says you agreed that the lines of your reservation should be just where these young men now out surveying are putting posts and markers. You signed that paper, knowing only what the interpreter told you it said. If anything happened when the paper was being made up that changed its order, if you had been educated and could read and write, you could have known about it and refused to put your name to it. Spotted Tail, cannot you see that if you and these with you here today had been educated as the white man is educated that you might right now have all your people out there in the Black Hills digging out the gold for your own uses? Cannot you see it is far, far better for you to have your children educated and trained as our children are so that they can speak the English language, write letters, and do the things which bring to the white man such prosperity, and each of them be able to stand for their rights as the white man stands for his? Cannot you see that they will be of great value to you if after a few years they come back from school with the ability to read and write letters for you, interpret for you, and help look after your business affairs in Washington? I am your friend, Spotted Tail. I shall be near Washington. Whether you send children with me or not I shall still be your friend. You may want something done in Washington and I might be able to help you. You want to write me about it, but you must get this interpreter or the missionary to write your letter. When I get the letter I shall know it was written by someone else and will not feel sure that it tells me exactly what you meant it to tell me. Yet I will do the best I can, and try to help you, and write to you about it. Then this or some other interpreter has to tell you what I say. You cannot be entirely sure he tells you exactly what I say. Cannot you see, Spotted Tail, what a disadvantage you and your people are under? As your friend, Spotted Tail, I urge you to send your children with me to this Carlisle school and I will do everything I can to advance them in intelligence and industry in order that they may come back and help you. Spotted Tail, I hear you have a dozen children. Give me four or five and let me take them to Carlisle and show you what the right kind of education will do for them."[9]

When Spotted Tail gave Pratt five of his children, the remainder of the tribesmen followed his example. The rest of his job was all downhill and, in actuality, he ended up with 27 more pupils than his quota of 120. "Pratt just did not have the heart to say no."[10]

The next eight years were to see Pratt nearly work himself to death. His dilemma was an unenviable one. On one side he was pressured with countless requests for admission from the Indians, while on the other side he was constantly on the verge of bankruptcy because of the lack of money coming from the slow-moving Congress. If it had not been for the generosity primarily of wealthy local congregations of the Society of Friends, the school most assuredly would have failed.

After weathering this difficult beginning, however, the school was on solid footing. Through exclusive Indian labor, the facilities soon became more than adequate. During the first decade of the twentieth century, the school attained its greatest affluence, and Pratt was barely able to maintain an ambitious building program to keep up with the deluge of eager students. Mrs. Verna (Donegan) Whistler described the situation:

Thorpe as a teenager at Carlisle

Courtesy Beth and Homer Ray

When I taught there, the student body was between six and seven hundred. There was a time, several years earlier when the enrollment had reached a thousand or more. At this time, athletics were at their height under "Pop" Warner.

Students ranged in age from ten to twenty-five and were taught school subjects one-half day and worked the other half at their chosen trade. I had charge of all the vocal and piano music. Each student was taught music, the same as in public schools. Private piano instruction was given to those who elected it, and a small fee was charged and turned into a fund to be used for that depart-

29

ment. Band and orchestra were taught by a special teacher, and some of the Indians soon became good enough to later play in Sousa's band or else start one of their own.

The student body was self-governed. They were divided into troops and had their ranking officers just the same as the regular Army. You see the military life helped the Indians in discipline because no one was any better than the other. They were from different tribes and, consequently, were not allowed to converse in their native tongue while they were at school. They were required to speak English at all times. Every now and then, if there were enough of them, they would get together and start talking their language. Sometimes they would be punished for this. In 1917 we had representatives from fifty-eight different tribes; the Chippewas were in the majority.

So this system gave them a sense of order. They didn't think anything about having the same type of clothing. They had their own clothes to dress up in for socials, dances, and things like that, but when they appeared in school, they were all dressed uniformly.[11]

The entire student body participated in competitive drills on the parade grounds. Since the winning troops were presented with banners, they would vie with each other to see which would be the top unit. According to Pete Calac, class of 1916:

The boys wore cavalry uniforms, the blue jacket and light blue trousers with a blue stripe along the pant leg and we had the regular cavalry caps. Our shoes had to be shined at all times and especially on Saturday when we would have inspection. We went through the drills and had rifles and had to learn the manual of arms.

A bugle awakened us every morning at six o'clock and taps were at nine in the evening. The girls had the same schedule and also had their own inspection. Breakfast was served at seven o'clock in the large dining room which accommodated the entire enrollment. It was an older building, as were most of the structures, but they were kept in good repair by students learning to be bricklayers, masons, and carpenters. The oldest buildings were composed of brick and constructed by the Hessian soldiers. You see, Carlisle was General Washington's headquarters at one time.

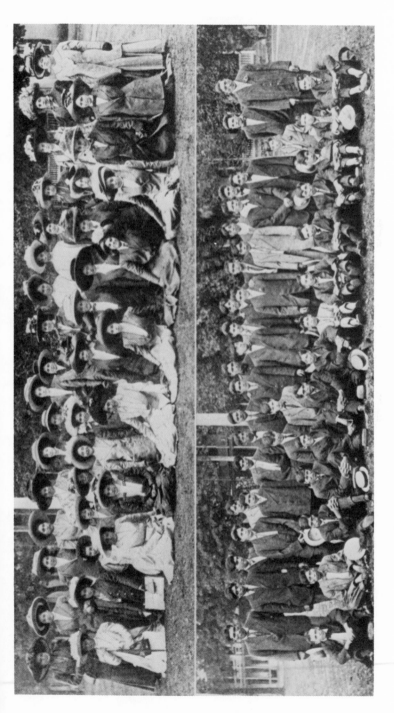

Pupils at Carlisle Indian School, 1910, after spending a term at the school

Courtesy Cumberland County Historical Society and Hamilton Library Association

The boys and girls had separate dormitories both two stories high and almost a block in length. There were two other main buildings one of which housed the children. They were little grade-school youngsters, boys and girls, alike. The other building served as the teachers' quarters.[12]

Twice each week, on Saturday and Sunday, the Indians entered the town of Carlisle. Arthur Martin, former Carlisle Athletic Department secretary, remembered:

When I was a kid (I'm seventy-six now), on Saturdays the Indians who were on good behavior were allowed to come into town. The girls went in one Saturday and the boys the next one.

On Sunday in the old days it used to be quite a sight when they would march, in perfect formation, to Church or Sunday School. The churches were always very much pleased to receive them.[13]

And Mrs. Whistler concluded:

They attended the church of the faith of their own selection, and so beforehand, they would line up, the Methodists in one corner, the Presbyterians in another and here would be the United Brethren and there are the Catholics. Each group of girls had to have a chaperone but the boys could go on their own.

Sunday evenings, everyone assembled in the school's main auditorium and all of them worshipped together. They would have a religious service presided over by a speaker of any of the various denominations in town.

This was also the time when we spoke about the scholastic side of their education. Graduation from Carlisle didn't really give them a high-school diploma but those who wished it and were permitted to come into town could attend high school or college.

An interesting survey was taken in 1914 of some four thousand students who had attended Carlisle. It showed that 94 per cent of the total were self-supporting and respected members of their communities.

All Indians looked to Carlisle as their University. It was their great ambition to send their children here. To the masses, this was the highest school, and the bids came in by the thousands.[14]

In its time, the Carlisle Indian School was unquestionably the most successful institution of its kind. Because of its existence, thousands of Carlisle graduates were able to give their tribesmen a newfound confidence in the rapidly changing American way of life, the white man's way of life.

CHAPTER 4

Glenn S."Pop" Warner

> *Carlisle had no traditions, but what the Indians did have was a real race pride and a fierce determination to show the palefaces what they could do when the odds were even. It was not that they felt any definite bitterness against the conquering white or against the government for years of unfair treatment, but rather that they believed the armed contests between red man and white had never been waged on equal terms.*
>
> —GLENN S. "POP" WARNER

When Jim entered Carlisle, June 1, 1904, he was sixteen years old, stood 5 feet 5½ inches tall and weighed 115 pounds. Too small to play on the varsity football power-house, he tried out for the tailor-shop team at, of all places, the guard position. Needless to say, he made the starting unit.[1]

The tailor-shop team was only one of many such intra-mural squads on the Carlisle campus. There was just some-thing about the game, beginning with their first moment of experience with the pigskin, that stirred the blood of the Indians.

Ironically, at one time football was banned by none other than Lieutenant Pratt, himself. Pratt wrote:

Not having had experience with football and finding here and there a victim of accidental or intended violence, I was not es-pecially pleased to encourage it. One day Stacy Matlock, a Paw-nee, one of our largest and finest young men, a foremost player, while playing with Dickinson on their field, had his leg broken below the knee and was brought in great agony to the school in a carriage. I had not gone to the game but went down to the hospital, helped lift him from the carriage to the operating table, and stood by to aid in setting the bone. This produced such a revulsion against the game that I said, "this ends outside football for us," and had outside football dropped from the school's repertoire. The broken leg was healed, and though the athletic activities of the victim were renewed without hesitation, I maintained my position.

The next year I was waited upon in the office by about forty of the foremost athletes, headed by the champion orator of the school. While they stood around my desk, their black eyes intensely watching me, the orator gave practically all the arguments in favor of our contending in outside football that it seemed possible to bring and ended by requesting the removal of the embargo. When he had finished, I waited a little and then said: "I will let you take up outside football again, under two conditions:

"First, that you will never, under any circumstances, slug. That you will play fair straight through, and if the other fellows slug, you will in no case return it. Can't you see that if you slug, people who are looking on will say, 'There, that's the Indian of it. Just see them. They are savages and you can't get it out of them.' Our white fellows may do a lot of slugging and it causes little or no remark, but you have to make a record for your race. If the other fellows slug and you do not return it, very soon you will be the most famous football team in the country. If you can set an example of that kind for the white race, you will do a work in the highest interests of your people." They all with one voice said, "All right, Captain, we agree to that."

"My other condition is this. That, in the course of two, three, or four years you will develop your strength and ability to such a degree that you will whip the biggest football team in the country. What do you say to that?" They thought that over seriously and then said, "Yes sir, we will agree to that."[2]

In 1899, football became a big-time sport at Carlisle with the coming of Glenn Scobey Warner, one of football's greatest innovators. During the seasons of 1891 through 1894, while playing for Cornell, he had established himself as one of the finest guards of his day. Being the captain and oldest member of the team, an ancient twenty-five, he was nicknamed "Pop," a name that stuck with him for the rest of his eighty-three years.

Upon graduating with an LL.B. degree, he was hired by

a law firm in Buffalo, New York. The following spring, however, found him shifting restlessly behind his massive desk as he daydreamed about the approaching football practice sessions in which teams all across the country were engaging. Finally, he accepted a coaching job at Iowa State College for the meager sum of twenty-five dollars a week.

Following a stint at the University of Georgia at a weekly salary of thirty-five dollars, he returned to Cornell as head coach in 1897. Then came the Carlisle offer two years later and there he remained until 1914, except for a three-year (1904 through 1906) hiatus at his alma mater. Warner recalled:

After thirty-six years of coaching at such widely separated and differing schools as Iowa State, Cornell, University of Georgia, Carlisle, University of Pittsburgh, and Stanford, the experiences that stand out most vividly in my memory are those connected with the Indian lads.

Carlisle had no traditions, but what the Indians did have was a real race pride and a fierce determination to show the palefaces what they could do when the odds were even. It was not that they felt any definite bitterness against the conquering white or against the government for years of unfair treatment, but rather that they believed the armed contests between red man and white had never been waged on equal terms.

"You outnumbered us, and you also had the press agents," a young Sioux once said to me. "When the white man won it was always a battle. When *we* won it was a massacre."

On the athletic field, where the struggle was man to man, they felt that the Indian had his first even break, and the record proves that they took full advantage of it. For fifteen years little Carlisle took the measure of almost every big university, with student bodies of four and five thousand to draw from; and to this day Jim Thorpe, Bemus Pierce, Frank Hudson, Jimmie Johnson, Mount Pleasant, Exendine, Lone Star, and Pete Hauser still rank among the all-time stars of football.

What added to the glory of the record was that Carlisle had only two hundred and fifty youngsters of football age, and season after season saw us going out to give battle with not more than two or three substitutes. As a consequence, almost every boy

"Pop" Warner supervising Carlisle practice on old checkerboard field, 1907

Courtesy James C. Heartwell

could play several positions, and thought nothing of being switched around.

As for kickers, every man knew what to do with his toe. Nowadays a team is lucky if there's one good leg in the lot, but it was nothing for Carlisle to have a half dozen. . . .[3]

When I went to the Carlisle school in 1899 as football coach, I had all of the prejudices of the average white, but after fourteen years of intimate association, I came to hold a deep admiration for the Indian and a very high regard for his character and capacities.

In the thousand students at Carlisle were boys and girls from seventy different tribes, many having their first contact with civilization, yet the wildest of them showed a quickness as well as willingness to learn, and gave ample evidence of courage, humor, ambition, tenacity, and all those other instinctive qualities that are blandly assumed to reside solely in the white race. Especially courage! . . .[4]

My first view of Carlisle's football material was anything but favorable for the boys who reported for practice were listless and scrawny, many looking as if they had been drawn through a knothole. . . .

My heart went down into my shoes, for I was getting $1,200 a year and felt that only an ever-victorious team could possibly justify such an enormous salary. I took my troubles to Major Pratt, the superintendent, but he just smiled when I protested that the squad ought to be trying for beds in a hospital rather than places on a football team.[5]

The most remarkable thing about the Indians was their receptiveness to new ideas. Your paleface team is usually inclined to stand-patism, but the Carlisle bunch dearly loved to spring surprises and were happiest when I came forward with something different. . . . Up to then the standard position for the offensive back was to stand with feet well apart, body leaning forward and hands resting on the knees. I figured that if sprinters could get away faster by partly supporting the weight of the body on one or both hands, it was logical to figure that backfield players could obtain the same results. The innovation was a big factor in running up the large score against Columbia [45 to 0, November 30, 1899] and soon won adoption by other coaches. . . .

Owing to the speed and daring of the Indians, I was able to work out the "body block," a new idea. Up to that time, all blocking was done with the shoulder, a method that had a good many drawbacks. In the "Indian block," as it came to be called, a man left the ground entirely, half-turning as he leaped so as to hit an opponent just above the knees with his hip, and following through with a roll, thus using his entire length. The Indians took to it like ducks to water, and when they blocked a man, he *stayed* blocked. . . .[6]

The players at Carlisle were always light in weight compared to college teams and I remember but one team that averaged as much as 170 pounds. Naturally, one would not expect power attack from boys as light as that, yet it is a fact that while spectacular tricky plays received special emphasis in the press, the Indians won most of their games by faster line charging, good blocking, and deadly tackling. Throughout my service at Carlisle I never had a team that could not consistently hit a line and make good on off-tackle plays, and the redskins were noted for their fierce and effective tackling. . . .[7]

Yet, when it comes to sportsmanship, I never want to see a finer lot of thoroughbreds than those Indians. I saw them in games against famous universities where they were slugged viciously and purposely, yet I can recall only one or two instances where an Indian repaid in kind. . . .

Once Pete Hauser had to be helped off the field during a game, and when I asked him what the trouble was, he shrugged his shoulders and said, "Same old thing. They kneed me." "Know who it was?" I demanded. "Yep," he nodded. "Well, what did you do?" I insisted, mad all over. "Didn't you say anything?" "Indeed I did, 'Pop.' Sure I said something. I said, 'Who's the savage now?'" . . .

The Indian boys gave friendship slowly, for they were a suspicious lot, but once you gained their trust, they were loyal and affectionate. I found them devoted to their race. Many a girl and boy who might have won good positions elsewhere went back to the tribe to teach and help. . . .[8]

Carlisle's lack of substitutes was always a handicap, but it never prevented the Indians from taking on all comers, regardless of size. Grantland Rice, in a comparison of early-day football with the modern, commented that "the old-timers" had only two or three games a season that called for any worry. Most of the others were "set-ups." Maybe so, but it was the ordinary thing for Carlisle to play hard games on six and eight successive Saturdays and wind up the season by traveling across the continent to do battle with some California team. I might also mention that when the Indians lost more than one game they felt like painting their faces black and throwing ashes over their heads. . . .[9]

We soon got to be a regular road team, playing most of our games away from home, and earning the title "Nomads of the Gridiron." Major Pratt, however, held that while the boys lost some time from their regular school work, the education they received from traveling and contact with college men was more than an adequate offset. . . .

No more industrious sightseers ever lived, and when we visited a strange city, it was a general thing for the players to get up at daybreak so as to take in every place of interest. Back at school, the team members always stood up in class and gave accounts of what they had seen and heard, and in this manner the stay-at-homes themselves were instructed and benefitted.[10]

"After the 1902 Virginia game," wrote John Steckbeck, "the team boarded the pleasure steamer *Alabama.* After reading the caution signs posted on each wall, medicine-man Denny [Wallace Denny, the team's trainer] donned a life preserver before going to bed and was still not satisfied until he had put on another to insure his safety."[11]

Arthur Martin maintained:

Pop was initially attracted to Carlisle by the brand of football that the Indians played. Although he witnessed in a game against Cornell, at the time that he was coaching there, a number of serious fundamental deficiencies in their game, he realized their tremendous potential and believed they could be invincible with proper coaching techniques. So when he was offered a going salary to coach at Carlisle, he accepted the job.

"Pop" was an inventor of all kinds of plays for the Indians. He used to have straps sewn on either side of the halfbacks' and fullbacks' uniforms. Then when they would line up in the backfield, the one who was to receive the ball would always be in the center. When the play started, the two men, one on each side, would grab hold of these straps and throw him through the line. Obviously the next year this was ruled illegal.

Then there was the time that he made a breast protector which he said would insure against injuries to the breast bone area resulting from blocks or falls. However, it was an oval shaped leather patch, padded up very highly so when the man put his arm across this patch, it looked just like a football. Well, with the halfbacks, the fullback, and the quarterback all having these patches to protect themselves, it looked like each one had a football tucked under his arm. They were usually the ones who were tackled and the man who actually had the ball was allowed practically free access. So that procedure was eliminated.

He would perform various types of works in the students' industrial quarters. One time I saw him hammering on the soles of some football shoes. I asked him what he was doing and he said: "The boys can't run in muddy weather because the cleats get all muddied up and they slip." So he invented what are called mud cleats which were very far apart and a little bit longer than the conventional ones.

"Pop" was a big, heavy, stout man. He was a very, very capable man as far as his knowledge of football was concerned. He wasn't rough or tough with the Indians, but he made them understand that when he said something, he wanted it done and done a certain way.

"Pop" was quite an amateur psychologist, too. He always had his hands full because the Indians tended to let up and sort of take it easy when they were ahead in a game. But when they got behind or were rated underdogs, then they would go to town. One time when we were to play a game against Dartmouth, they were putting up an end for All-America honors and he was a big fellow. So "Pop" got a small but talented Indian by the name of Vetternack, who was no bigger than I am, to play opposite him. Well, he practiced with him all week and after that game no one ever heard another word about that "All-American." This little man just went through his legs or around him and the big fellow couldn't even find him half the time. The game was played in New York and subsequently many writers were there to witness the exhibition.

But the most remarkable thing about the whole business of the Indian football team and the job that Warner performed was the number of various tribes that were working together out there. The beautiful part of it to me was the fact that he could make a cohesive unit out of them to enable them to accomplish as much as they did. There were very few of the same tribe on any one of the teams. In fact, one of the greatest centers we ever had was Nikifer Shouchuk, an Eskimo.

Once the game began, "Pop" would walk up and down the side-

41

lines. He just couldn't sit still on the bench. And in those days, it was against the rules to coach from the sidelines. The coach had to be seated on the bench before a substitute could be put in. So "Pop" would get nervous and start pacing. Eventually, he would be sent back to the bench or ordered to leave the game. In the latter instance, I would still be on the bench and would look around to the stands, where "Pop" would be, and he would make a certain motion which designated a certain play. So we would finish the game by a kind of sign language.

"Pop's" sideline maneuvers when a game was being played in the rain, however, were severely restricted. It seems that the only pair of overshoes that he owned were several sizes too large. So when the teams would be receiving dry equipment between the halves, "Pop" would be getting a tape job himself. Because of his activities off the bench, the sidelines would be so muddy that he would almost lose his overshoes with every step. Therefore, trainer Denny would have to tape the tops of them to his pantlegs to hold them on for the rest of the game.

Among my other memories was one time when I had to take a group of the players on a train ride. As a rule, "Pop" took the substitutes, or the "hot shots" as they were called, on a trip every year in payment for their hard work. So during the particular year that I'm talking about, 1911, he decided that they could go to the University of Pennsylvania game in Philadelphia. He took the varsity down on Friday and asked me to take the "hot shots" down on Saturday morning and go to the Gimbel Brothers store, who would give us our lunch as an advertising scheme. So we took the local train to Philadelphia and arrived there at about eleven-thirty in the morning. We were met and taken to a room, which they had reserved, and given our lunch. After lunch, I led them downstairs to the basement where we would catch the subway which would take us to thirty-sixth and Chestnut to the Normandy Hotel, where the team was quartered. When I went through the turnstile and boarded the train, I discovered that I was alone. I got off the train and found the Indians standing on the other side of the turnstile. I had given everyone a nickel but had forgotten to tell them how to deposit it. You see, at Carlisle they were used to riding the trolley back and forth, from the school to the town, but a conductor had been the one to collect their five cents.

On some trips the older boys would play jokes on the younger ones, newcomers on the team. They would tell them:

"Now when you go to bed tonight, put your shoes out in the hallway and a man will come along and shine them up and they will be all ready for you, in good appearance, tomorrow morning."

The first thing you know, the next morning, the shoes are all mixed up and tied in knots with the wrong pairs. They had quite a time getting them sorted out, but that was only the beginning because when they would go down for breakfast, their silverware would be all mixed up or some of it would be missing. Of course, as a rule, the boys conducted themselves very, very well.[12]

On this subject, Warner commented: "In the course of my fourteen years at Carlisle, Indian football teams covered almost the whole of the United States, and I cannot recall a hotel that was not glad to have us return. Managers often remarked to me, 'They are the most gentlemanly boys we have ever had in the hotel. They are so quiet and well behaved that nobody ever knows they're around.'"[13]

There was one man, however who did not fit into this category. As Martin told the story:

The most unpredictable Indian that "Pop" ever coached was a man named Asa Sweetcorn. One time, during the 1910 season, he was not chosen to make a road trip and became quite distressed. As soon as the team left, he came into Carlisle and began imbibing some John Barleycorn. He was making quite a commotion around the Cumberland Valley Railroad Station, which at that time, was located in the heart of town. Naturally, the local police arrested him and called up the Indian school authorities and they sent for him. But before he could be released, he had to spend the night in the local cooler. And after he got back to school the next day, the students had quite a laugh, saying that Sweetcorn was now canned.[14]

Former competitor Hyman Goldstein reminisced:

Yes, "Pop" was an outstanding man and a good friend of mine. "Pop" was always working new plays and switching formations. The Dickinson College team, of which I was a member, would be out there practicing with the Indians and he would be constantly changing them around. Then in the evening, he would come into the town and go into the chocolate shop where he and our coach, Si Pauxtis, would get together and gather up all the salt and pepper shakers and place them on the table and do this and do that and move them around.

After several hours of this, "Pop" would stand up and take a breather and go down to the bucket shop to check the latest readings of the stock market. Unlike today, the stock investors were not looked upon very highly and "Pop" was forever sneaking in there without Mrs. Warner's knowledge.[15]

Warner was even shrewder on the football field, where his favorite play was the hidden ball trick. The Indians were playing at Harvard on Saturday, October 31, 1903. Warner's own account stated:

Trick plays were what the redskins loved best. Nothing delighted them more than to outsmart the palefaces. There was never a time when they wouldn't rather have won by an eyelash with some wily stratagem than by a large score with straight football.

I don't think any one thing ever gave them greater joy than when we worked the "hidden ball" or "hunchback" play on Harvard. Carlisle's speed scored five points almost at the outset, and it was up to the Crimson to kick off. The ball sailed far and high down the center of the field, and was caught on the five-yard line by Jimmie Johnson, our little quarterback who was an All-American that year.

The Indians gathered at once in what now would be called a huddle, but facing outward, and Johnson quickly slipped the ball under the back of Charlie Dillon's jersey. Charlie was picked as the "hunchback" because he stood six feet and could do a hundred yards in ten seconds. Besides, being a guard, he was less likely to be suspected of carrying the ball.

The stands were in an uproar, for everybody had seen the big lump on Dillon's back but the Harvard players were still scurrying wildly around when Charlie crossed the goal line. One of his mates jerked out the ball and laid it on the turf and, as I had warned the referee that the play might be attempted, he was watching carefully and ruled that the touchdown had been made within the rules.[16]

Another chapter from Dillon's colorful eight-year varsity career happened in 1899. Confined to the school infirmary, he slipped out to attend practice.

"What are you doing here?" demanded Warner. "I thought you were too sick to play."

"I am feeling fine," lied the Redskin. "Only got a little pleurisy."[17]

"But aside from the trickery," concluded Goldstein, "they were the best team in the country. So I guess my greatest thrill in sports occurred when we held Carlisle zero to zero at the end of the first half in our 1911 game."[18]

Andy Kerr, another close associate of Warner's, describes his friend:

My preceptor and greatest friend was "Pop" Warner. I had the pleasure of telling him year after year what a great contribution he made to any success I may have had in football.

I consider Warner to be the greatest creative genius in American football. Most of us coaches are imitators but "Pop" was an inventor. He could have been an inventor of a lot of things.

My own feeling is that he would have been a marvel in any type of profession in which he was engaged. He could have been a mechanical expert. I've seen him take an automobile completely apart and put it back together again. He was always tinkering with our equipment, at that time, to make it better. He was responsible for turning out the best protection for injured knees, that actually was an improvement upon the type of knee braces the surgeons developed. I know that by the time I came to Colgate, the "Warner brace," or "wooden leg," as the players named it, was widely accepted.

In his latter days, he did a lot of whittling. He would carve out a cane and then at its head he would insert a marble with three or four strips of wood, making a little cage for it. Then he would defy you to tell him how he did that.

One of the things that has never been mentioned in connection with "Pop" was his outstanding ability as an artist in oil and water colors. A great many of his paintings have been on exhibition. Around "Pop's" time at the University of Illinois was the fine football coach, Bob Zupke. He had two ambitions in life, outside of being a great coach. One was that he could be a better after-dinner speaker than Knute Rockne and the other was to be a better painter than "Pop" Warner.

One of "Pop's" plays was to line up the quarterback over the center and place the two guards in the backfield. So with the four backs, there was a total of six men in the backfield. This was called the "guards back" formation. That created too much momentum and was not allowed. The next year "Pop" set one lineman back, a tackle, but still there was too much momentum. Finally, the rules were changed to read that seven men had to be on the line of scrimmage.

"Pop" then decided to abandon the T-formation in favor of his new invention, the Z-formation. We know it as the single wing. However, he found out with that formation it was difficult to run to the short side because the tackle could not be blocked very effectively. We could block the tackle on the long side by using the end and the wing back. So "Pop" said, "All right, if we block the long side tackle that way, let's block the other side." Then he put another back up on the other side and that was how he developed the double-wing formation. "Pop" soon became the greatest advocate of the double-wing.

The first formation was very tight. It was used basically for runs and then as the forward pass became more important, it was loosened up. First one of the ends was split and the passer was back about five yards and then both ends were split. Today it is called the double-slot formation because the backs are in that slot between the end and the tackle. Using this basic idea, the two things in which I excelled were the use of the lateral pass and the development of the screen pass.

"Pop" handled men wonderfully. He was not the hard taskmaster type, but an easygoing boss. He knew football so well and he was so fine a coach that he had the confidence and respect of the men and could get from them their very best efforts. He was so far advanced in the things he had developed that the men in his squad recognized him as an expert, and for that reason they were willing to give him their best efforts.

In the early days of football, the coaching was never done by one man on the major teams but "Pop" himself was definitely a one-man coach at Carlisle. He did not have an assistant, although occasionally a Yale graduate would come up and help him a little bit. Not only was he the football coach but the athletic director and track coach as well. As a matter of fact, "Pop" didn't really have a full football staff until he went to Stanford University in 1924. At Pittsburgh I was the backfield coach and there was a line coach and that was all.

In regard to his career at Carlisle, I don't believe that he had to change methods with the Indians. He told me the story of how his whole outlook on coaching changed. It seemed that one year not long after he had arrived at Carlisle, a large group of his players suddenly quit the team. "Pop" met one of them on the campus and said, "You haven't been to practice in two days! Where have you been?" "I'm tired of coming out to practice every day and listening to your swearing every time I make a mistake. I've had it!" the boy replied. "Pop" thought for a moment and promised, "If you will come back on the team, I will never swear at you or anyone ever again."

And in all my experience with "Pop," I never once heard him swear at a player. He was always within bounds, within limits, with anything he said on the field. He had learned his lesson well that one could not handle men, Indians or white men, if too rough speech were used.[19]

CHAPTER 5

Nobody Is Going to Tackle Jim

I had a pair of overalls on, a hickory shirt, and a pair of gymnasium shoes I had picked up in the gym that belonged to someone. I looked like anything but a high jumper. The track athletes snickered a bit as the bar was set for me. I cleared the bar on my first try and, laughing at the astonished group of athletes, went down to the lower field for the game.

— JIM THORPE

While Jim had hoped to learn the trade of an electrician, such a course of study was not offered at Carlisle. And so it was decided that his strongest aptitude was to be found in tailoring. He began his studies in earnest, but once again death was to strike down another loved one. This time it was the love of his life, his father. The great man's life was claimed by septicemia, incurred during a hunting expedition, just four years after Charlotte's death. The boy was pained greatly and could not even return home for the funeral because of the slow modes of travel at that time.

Since his brother's death and then his mother's, Jim had become uncharacteristically silent and unable to mix well with new companions. And with the passing of Hiram, he became worse.

The authorities at the school were concerned with the well-being of the young boy and decided that living with a volunteer family, a member of the Society of Friends, would be good therapy for him. This "outing system" was the most important facet of the school. In the words of Lieutenant Pratt, "It enforced participation, the supreme Americanizer. Preventing participation stops Americanization. The native Americans have been, without exception, most harshly and by many devious demoralizing devices excluded from participation in our American family."[1]

Mrs. Whistler described the system:

Established in 1880, the "outing system" enabled the boys and girls to be placed in homes in Pennsylvania, New Jersey, and New York as domestics and paid a prevailing wage for their service. This was usually during the summer, but on special requests those with good records could remain as long as two years providing they continued their studies. The patrons were obligated to follow certain rules and regulations and were asked to treat the students as members of their household.[2]

Closely related to this program was an opportunity for apprenticeships that would enable the boys to learn a skilled trade.

At one time, nineteen boys were sent to the Ford Motor Company plant in Detroit as apprentice machinists. Mr. Ford was so pleased with their work that he asked for as many as would come. I don't know how many there are now but at one time, there was a little colony of Indian boys and their wives located there, who were products of this school.[3]

In addition, Warner, who had recognized Jim's potential talents all along, believed that this could help to accelerate the boy's bodily development and gave his assent. Thus on June 17, 1904, after only two weeks at Carlisle, Jim arrived in the small town of Somerton, Pennsylvania, and lived at the home of A. E. Buckholz. His task was to cook all the meals and keep the house in order. For these duties he received his room and board and five dollars a month, which was sent to Carlisle and held in trust.

All the white families who took part in the "outing system" were thoroughly checked for their general character and integrity. Therefore it was rare for an Indian youth to be mistreated. Jim's home was ideal in this respect, for he experienced a great deal of kindness. Yet it soon became apparent that this was not the type of work for an active sixteen-year-old boy. Mr. Buckholz, not wanting to lose such a helpful boy but more interested in Jim's welfare, requested a transfer.

The following March, Jim was allowed to leave and enter the employment of James L. Cadwallader in Dolington, Pennsylvania. Jim stayed from March 31 to July 1 and did various gardening tasks. After this beginning experience, he was recommended for the more demanding position of foreman for the Indians on the farm of Harby Rozarth in Robbinsville, New Jersey. This job lasted from September 15, 1905, to April 8, 1907. It was here that his monthly salary rose to eight dollars.

Jim returned to Carlisle in 1907. He had grown to 5 feet 9½ inches and 144 pounds and was his old self in his dealings with the other students, once again displaying his leadership qualities.

Marianne Moore, one of Jim's teachers, reflected:

> In the classroom, he was a little laborious, but dependable; took time—head bent earnestly over the paper; wrote a fine, even clerical hand—every character legible; every terminal curving up —consistent and generous.[4]

For all his athletic genius, Warner needed help in order to fully recognize the potentialities the nineteen-year-old Sac and Fox possessed. He received it on April 28, 1907.

Jim himself tells the story:

> Late one afternoon in the spring of 1907, I was among a group of tenderfoot football players crossing the upper track field on our way to the lower field where we would play a twilight game with one of the scrub teams on campus. I happened to notice that some of the members of the varsity were practicing the high jump.
>
> I stopped to watch them as they went higher and higher. After awhile they had the bar set at five feet nine inches and none of them could jump over it. They were just about ready to call it a day when I asked if I might try it.
>
> I had a pair of overalls on, a hickory shirt, and a pair of gymnasium shoes I had picked up in the gym that belonged to someone. I looked like anything but a high jumper. The track athletes snickered a bit as the bar was set up for me. I cleared the bar on

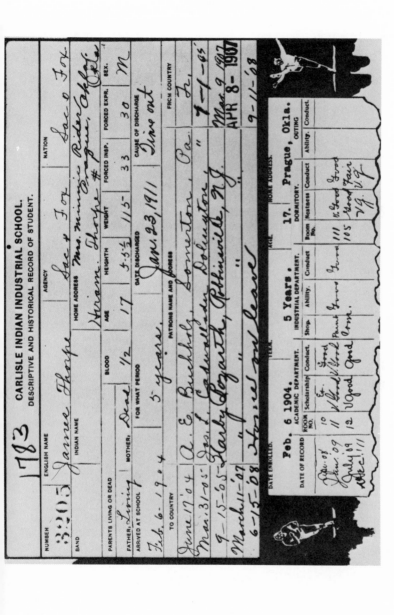

Jim's academic record at Carlisle

Courtesy Allan Peterson and Charlotte Thorpe

my first try and, laughing at the astonished group of athletes, went on down to the lower field for the game.

A student named Harry Archenbald, who had seen me take the jump with so little effort, reported the incident to Coach Warner. Next day, he sent for me.

"Do you know what you have done?" "Pop" asked.

"Nothing bad, I hope," was my reply.

"Bad," growled the coach. "Boy, you've just broken the school record! That bar was set at five feet nine inches!"

I told "Pop" I didn't think that very high, that I thought I could do better in a track suit. "Pop" told me to go down to the club-house and exchange those overalls for a track outfit. I was on the track team now.

He said, "You might want to coach someday and if you do, you must know something about track."

I replied, "I believe coaching would be a good vocation. I'll come out tomorrow."[5]

Warner wanted to groom Jim and sharpen his raw skills. Albert Exendine seemed to be the ideal man for the job. He had recently been ruled eligible for only one more year of varsity competition under the new four-year-maximum rule. Besides this, he held nearly all of the track and field records at the school.

Under Warner's supervision, Exendine put Jim through a rigorous training schedule. The climax of the season occurred at Harrisburg, where the Pennsylvania Junior College Interscholastic Meet was held. Jim dominated the field and in the process demolished every last one of Exendine's records. Albert commented, "I later found out it was no accident."[6]

The slender Thorpe, at the urging of a part-time assistant football aid, Frank Newman, eagerly tried out for a place on the varsity football team the following September. Newman had remembered Jim for his running and kicking ability shown on the tailor's team and had offered him the invitation without thinking it necessary to inform Coach Warner.

Wallace Denny laughed to himself when Jim stood before him and asked to be suited up. Surely, he thought, here was

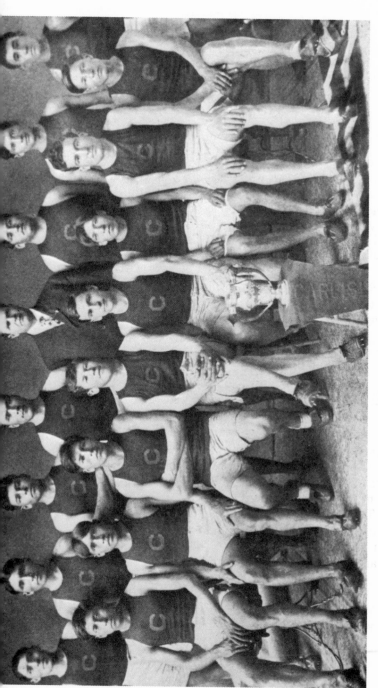

Carlisle track team, 1909. Thorpe fourth from left, front row; Tewanima sixth from left, front row; Exendine fourth from left, back row; Warner fifth from left, back row

Courtesy Cumberland County Historical Society and Hamilton Library Association

a track star, but not football. This was a sport for big fellows, and a man of Thorpe's stature would take a fearful beating.

"Well," Jim said, "what about it?"

"What about what?" said Wallace.

"My uniform! Where is it?"

"Go away and come back when you have some meat on your bones. You're too light and too skinny. What do you want to do, get yourself killed?"[7]

Finally, Jim got his "uniform," an old tattered suit that was full of holes and at least two sizes too large. When Jim trotted out onto Indian Field for the first time, he was met by a furious Coach Warner.

"What do you think you're doing out here?" yelled "Pop."

"I want to play football," replied Jim.

"I'm only going to tell you once, Jim, go back to the locker room and take that uniform off! You're my most valuable trackman and I don't want you to get hurt playing football."

"I want to play football," repeated the determined Thorpe.

"All right if that's the way you want it."[8]

Warner thought that he could outsmart the Indian by assigning him to kicking practice and thereby avoiding any possible contact. But Jim had other ideas and wanted no part of this. Day after day he would pester "Pop," until after two weeks the coach could stand it no longer. Losing his temper, Warner threw Jim a ball and bellowed: "All right! Give the varsity some tackling practice!"[9]

"Up to that time," remarked Jim, "my hands had never gripped a real football."[10] Nevertheless, it soon appeared that he had been born with one in his hand. Without the slightest form but with "the grace and power of movement that promised great things,"[11] he upended some would-be tacklers as if they were bowling pins and simply outran the rest, leaving them lying on the turf hugging air pockets.

"Pop's" ever-present cigarette had fallen from his lips by the time Jim had completed his run. His mouth was opened wide in amazement.

Finally recovering his composure, "Pop" yelled at Jim,

"You're supposed to give the first team tackling practice, not run through them!"[12]

Jim's broad grin quickly faded, and with a boy's feeling of hurt pride at failing to receive just praise, he firmly declared to Warner, "Nobody is going to tackle Jim!"[13]

Warner, now believing that the upstart should have some of the cockiness knocked out of him, took another ball and slammed it into Jim's midsection. "Let's see you do it again," he said.[14]

Then Warner, whose complexion was by now a bright crimson, turned on his men and screamed: "Get mean! Smack him down! Hit him down so hard he doesn't get up! Who does he think he is? This isn't a relay race! This is football! Hit! Hit! Hit!"[15]

With a deceptive burst of speed, Jim streaked past the first group of onrushing linemen. Now, in stride, tacklers began to hit him, but it was no use. They "bounced off and shriveled up behind him like bacon on a hot griddle."[16] Jim crossed the goal line and did not stop running until he flipped the pigskin to Warner and solemnly repeated, "Nobody is going to tackle Jim." "My," Jim overheard "Pop" say to Denny, "he is certainly a wild Indian."[17]

Jim, needless to say, immediately graduated to the varsity. But with only a fortnight of formal football training under his belt, he was relegated to the bench. As an open-field runner, he was incomparable. However, without such contrivances as platoon systems or specialists, he needed time to learn the intricacies of defense as well as offense. Even on offense, interference was meaningless to him and was infrequently used at best, and almost never effectively. And with Warner's "iron man" schedule of first-rate opponents, the "breather" games were few and far between.

Besides, the year was 1907, and this Carlisle team was one of the greatest elevens in intercollegiate history. According to Warner: "With the exception of the unbeaten Pitt team of 1916, it was about as perfect a football machine as I ever sent on the field. . . . The boys clicked into shape

Carlisle scrimmage, 1908

early in the season, and the very first game [against Lebanon Valley College, September 21, 1907] convinced me that a big year was ahead. Our opponents came from a small college nearby, and later on it was reported to me that the Pennsylvania Dutch coach made this stirring plea to his men:

"'Now poys, I vant you to show dose Indians dat you are yoost as good as dey are. Watch vat dey do to you and den you do de same ting to dem, only harder.' Despite the coach's oratory, Carlisle won by a huge score [40 to 0]."[18]

It is not surprising that young Thorpe did not log very much playing time. The strong starting team was comprised of Albert Exendine and William Gardner at the end positions; Emil Hauser (Wauseka) and Antonio Lubo (the Wolf), the tackles; Samuel McClean (Man-Afraid-of-a-Bear) and William Winnie, the guards; Little Boy at center; Frank Mount Pleasant at quarterback; Albert Payne and Fritz Hendricks, the halfbacks; and Peter Hauser, the fullback.

They soundly defeated three of the top teams in the East: Penn State, 18 to 5; Syracuse, 14 to 6; and Pennsylvania, 26 to 6. The newspaper accounts of the games suggest the incredible odds that the Indians faced and the way they played in order to achieve victory:

Williamsport, Penn., Oct. 5—Redoubtable Pennsylvania State College, with six fancy coaches and a beefy eleven, bit the dust here today at football before the Carlisle Indians, 18 to 5. The redskins, averaging ten pounds less that State, wiped out their accidental defeat here by State last year with a wealth of marvelous plays. State's day was brief. She was simply outclassed.[19]

Buffalo, N.Y., Oct. 12—Outclassed and outgeneraled, the big eleven from Syracuse was defeated by the Carlisle Indians before 8,000 people here this afternoon by a score of 14 to 6. The game was fast and furious from the beginning. The field was sticky from the rain of over night, and several times the runner missed his footing where there was a chance for a big gain. The forward pass was used with effect by both teams.[20]

Philadelphia, Oct. 26—Playing the most remarkable football ever witnessed on Franklin Field under the new rules, the Carlisle Indians humbled Pennsylvania this afternoon 26 to 6 in the presence of 20,000 spectators, the largest attendance of the year in this city. The day was perfect for football. The Indians scored 16 points in the first half while the Quakers failed to tally until near the end of the contest. . . .

The entire Indian team played magnificent ball. . . . All of the Indians tackled like fiends, Penn being unable to gain through their line, around the ends or run back on punts. . . . Penn was defeated after the first five minutes of play. The Indians just swept them off their feet. Not only did Penn play poor football, but they lost their heads. They could gain at no point. . . .[21]

Before their meeting with Carlisle, Penn State had scored 159 points and had allowed none, Syracuse had outscored her opponents 42 to 17, and Pennsylvania had demolished her adversaries to the tune of 179 to 10!

After this last victory, the Indians assumed a careless attitude against their next opponent, the Tigers from Princeton. This reckless tendency would prove to be a continual pitfall throughout the years, and prevented Carlisle from ever having a perfect season. They became so emotionally keyed up for an important game that, after the victory had been achieved, the necessary unwinding process would still be evident the following Saturday. In any event, they lost to a poor Princeton team on a muddy field.

"Tigers Humble Indians. Polo Grounds' Greatest Crowd Sees Princeton Beat Carlisle," blared the *New York Times'* headline.

Drenched in a downpour of rain that fell constantly throughout the game, a crowd of nearly thirty thousand persons, fully half of whom were collegiate enthusiasts, watched Princeton and the Carlisle Indians fight out their first contest on the gridiron in a half dozen years at the Polo Grounds yesterday afternoon, saw Princeton win an unexpected victory over the vaunted Indian eleven by the score of 16 to 0. . . . Carlisle, on the other hand, fell from the high estate which it had attained in its game with Pennsylvania and played a headless game which failed to do justice to its real strength.[22]

Incidentally, the Indians never performed at their best on a rain-soaked playing surface. As early as 1905, for three straight days before a game with the Canton Athletic Club, a group of Canton fans fire-hosed the playing surface, there being no rule against it.

"Pop" explained:

What may have helped to create the impression that the Indians lacked gameness was the way they let themselves be affected by adverse weather conditions. If the field was a sea of mud, or if snow fell, or if an icy wind was blowing, the redskins had a tendency to play listlessly and halfheartedly. This however was not due to lack of courage but to their aboriginal point of view, they played entirely for pleasure not having "I'd die for dear old Rutgers" tradition, and as Little Boy, a big center once said to me, "Football no good fun in mud and snow."[23]

Nevertheless, the season ended in a blaze of glory with wins over the perennial frontrunner Harvard, 23 to 15, a strong team from the University of Minnesota, 12 to 10, and 18 to 4 over what many experts believe was the University of Chicago's greatest squad, coached by the former grand old man of American football, Amos Alonzo Stagg. Warner admitted:

Few things have ever given me greater satisfaction than that Chicago victory. Stagg's team undefeated to then, was laying claim to the championship, and sports writers refused to concede that poor Lo had a chance. The game, in fact, was to be a field day for the great Wallie Steffen, famous for his twisting, dodging runs and educated toe, and all Illinois gathered for the spectacle. I remember that Carlisle's share of the gate was $17,000, an almost incredible sum in those days.

Steffen did kick one field goal, but that was his only pretense to glory. Gardner and Exendine were on him everytime he tried to run back a kick.[24]

The descriptions of the final three games were reported in the *New York Times:*

"Speedy Indians Crush Harvard. Crimson Eleven is Outplayed at

Every Point by the Redskins. Brilliant End Running, Carlisle's Offense Irresistible."

Cambridge, Mass., Nov. 9—Harvard was scalped by the Indians this afternoon in the fastest game seen in the Stadium this fall, Carlisle quitting the field victors, 23 to 15. The offense of the Indians was well nigh irresistible, and the Crimson line was completely demoralized, the redskins having possession of the ball nearly all the first half. . . .[25]

"Carlisle Beats Minnesota."
Minneapolis, Minn., Nov. 16—Carlisle defeated Minnesota on Northrop Field this afternoon, 12 to 10, in what proved to be the most spectacular game of football ever played in Minneapolis . . . clever trick plays and beautifully executed forward passes. . . .[26]

"Indians Fast Play Routs Chicago. Western Champions Completely Outplayed by the Carlisle Eleven."
Chicago, Ill., Nov. 23—The Carlisle Indian football team defeated the University of Chicago eleven here today in a fast, desperately fought game. The score was 18 to 4. . . .
In almost every department of the game, especially in line play, the Indians had the better of their rivals. Chicago, having won the championship of the college conference of the Middle West, was expected to give the Eastern players the hardest kind of a battle. But these hopes were proved vain.[27]

All told, the Indian unit rolled to a 10–1 season, outscoring their opponents, 267 to 62.

Contrary to previous writings, Jim saw his first action in the Syracuse encounter and in four contests thereafter. Hendricks, called on for numerous plunges at the line, absorbed a fearful beating against the Orangemen, and midway through the second half Jim was sent into the game at the right halfback position and played flawlessly, if unspectacularly.[28]

After the exact midpoint of the season, in which Bucknell invaded Indian Field on October 19, the student newsletter, *The Arrow,* carried a description of the game and mentioned Jim's name for the first time. According to the story, Jim received the second kickoff of the game and was in the

Thorpe as a young man

process of making a long runback when he fumbled the ball near the goal line. However, a teammate, Theodore Owl, picked up the loose pigskin on the bounce and carried it the rest of the way for a touchdown. The final score of the game was Carlisle 15, Bucknell 0.[29]

The rest of the schedule was to find "the anxious Thorpe"[30] spending most of his time on the bench as Albert Payne's understudy. Payne, the great but often injured backfield ace, was spurred to new heights by the presence of the talented youngster. Even so, Jim did manage to relieve Payne in the Pennsylvania game and start in the Princeton and Minnesota contests.

After the Minnesota game, Exendine commented that, "Jim gave a good account of himself."[31] And an article written by his dormitory friends, which appeared in *The Arrow,* expressed their pride in his performance "out west."[32]

"There was no free substitution in college or pro ball in those days," observed Jim Wood, a superb guard and tackle for nine years in the professional ranks with the Rochester Jeffersons.

Later in the pros, we never had more than five or six extra players and these very rarely at best, saw action. The ones that did had already made it a point to make friends with the captain who was in charge of substitutions.

One thing I know for sure, football will never see another Thorpe. The two or more platoon system produces defensive players who don't know how to carry the ball or famous offensive stars who don't know how to block or tackle. There's been only one all time, All-American football player and his name is Jim Thorpe.[33]

CHAPTER 6
Natural Athletic Talent

. . . with time running out, late in the second half, the score was tied nothing to nothing and the crowd was screaming itself hoarse: "We want Jim! We want Jim!" they chanted.

At long last, "Pop" tapped Jim on the shoulder and sent him in. What followed was the single most dramatic play I have ever seen in sports. Jim took the very first hand-off and blasted into the line with the loudest crash I've ever heard. When he was able to continue into their backfield, I couldn't believe my eyes! He didn't use one block on his way to the goal line seventy yards away while all the time he kept hollering, "Out of my way! Get out of my way!"

—CHIEF FREEMAN JOHNSON,
Grand Sachem of the Senecas

"If you can clear the high jump bar at 5 feet 10½ inches, I'll take you to Philadelphia to compete in the Penn Relays,"[1] Warner promised the high-jumping contingent of the track team. One man qualified, Jim Thorpe. He jumped 5 feet 11 inches.

The year was 1908 and it was springtime. Once again, Jim was turning his enormous energies to track and field. At Philadelphia, he jumped 6 feet 1 inch, his greatest effort up to that time. But it was only good enough for a tie for first place with an entrant from Indiana. An official flipped a coin to determine the winner. Jim won the toss and his first major gold medal. He also competed in the high hurdles for the first time and finished third.

Beginning to find himself, Jim went wild against Syracuse in a dual meet the following Saturday. He captured five firsts and a second as the vaunted Orangemen were humiliated. He won the high and low hurdles, the high and broad jumps, and in the shot put conquered the great Thor, who out-weighed him by fifty-two power-packed pounds. He was runner-up in another event filled with brawny contestants, the hammer throw.

Later, at the Pennsylvania Intercollegiate Meet at Harris-burg, Jim placed first in all five events in which he partic-ipated: the hammer throw, the high and low hurdles, and the high and broad jumps.

The climactic ending of the season found Jim gaining top honors with his typical monotonous ease. At the Middle Atlantic Association Meet at Philadelphia Jim walked away from the cream of the college athletes, again winning the five events mentioned above. Warner remembered that year well:

In the spring I tried him out in hurdling and jumping, and almost at once he became the star of the team. There seemed nothing he could not do, and whenever we needed points to win a meet, I would wait until Jim finished on the track and then throw him in the weight events. The 100-yard dash, the 120- and 220-yard hur-dles, the broad and high jump were his specialties, but he could also throw the hammer and put the shot with the best.[2]

After the track season, Jim finished out the term and headed for home at the beginning of summer vacation. Al-though the call of his homeland in Oklahoma was too power-ful for him to ignore, he realized that only sadness awaited his return there.

Before long, he grew impatient to go back to the comfort-ing atmosphere of Carlisle. Returning to the school nearly a full month in advance of the opening day of the new term, he began to train in earnest for his first truly great football season.

Working diligently day after day, he was in superb con-dition when the time came for "Pop" to blow the first whistle for fall practice. The date was the first of September and the workout was a brief one. But this was no indication of things to come, because the four-year eligibility rule was now in effect. This resulted in the immediate departure from

Thorpe winning gold medal in 220-yard hurdles, Harrisburg Track Committee Meet, 1909

Courtesy Beth and Homer Ray

the varsity roster of Exendine, Mount Pleasant, and Lubo, all great stars. Their loss was a burden that fell heavily on the shoulders of the returning regulars, Wauseka, McClean, Little Boy, Hauser, Hendricks, Payne, and Winnie. However, this team, which was to finish the season with ten wins, two defeats, and one tie was not to be led by any of these stalwarts. The man of the hour was Jim Thorpe.

"I never had to do much coaching with Jim," Warner admitted. "Like all Indians, his powers of observation were remarkably keen, developed as they were through generations. The younger players always watched the older ones and they were quick to catch on. I guess the Carlisle Indians provided me with the easiest coaching job I ever had."[3]

The first three games of the season were nothing more than glorified warm-up drills, all played on Indian Field. Conway Hall, the preparatory school for Dickinson was the first to fall, and fall they did, 53 to 0. Then came the Lebanon Valley College encounter that ended with a 35 to 0 score in favor of the Indians. Finally, Villanova succumbed 10 to 0.

Although the records for these games were poorly kept, Chief Johnson, an eyewitness, vividly recollected them:

Those opening three games of 1908 were the only ones played on our home field at Carlisle. The reason being, we had to take the games when we got them. We never received official recognition or anything like that because we were neither a college nor a university and so if we wanted to play the big schools it was always on their terms and at their stadiums. And so you can bet all of us students attended the few home appearances of our team.

Against Conway Hall, Jim Thorpe was the whole show. The funny part of it was he might not have seen any action at all if Al Payne had not had the wind knocked out of him. "Pop" pulled him right out because he didn't want to risk a serious injury in so early a game.

Once Jim got in, did he ever go to town! He ripped off five touchdowns from beyond the mid-field stripe and threw for another score on a thirty-yard pass to Pete Hauser. All this he did in the first half! "Pop" took pity on them and didn't play Jim for the rest of the game. It was the same story against Lebanon Valley when Jim again played only half the game.

To the dismay of the crowd at the Villanova game, it looked as if "Pop" was never going to let Jim play. However, with time running out, late in the second half, the score was tied nothing to nothing and the crowd was screaming itself hoarse: "We want Jim! We want Jim!" they chanted.

At long last, "Pop" tapped Jim on the shoulder and sent him in. What followed was the single most dramatic play I have ever seen in sports. Jim took the very first hand-off and blasted into the line with the loudest crash I've ever heard. When he was able to continue into their backfield, I couldn't believe my eyes! He didn't use one block on his way to the goal line seventy yards away while all the time he kept hollering, "Out of my way! Get out of my way!"

The drama of the game was heightened when "Pop" took him out knowing that he couldn't be put back in but Villanova's back was broken and didn't pose a threat the rest of the game.[4]

On Saturday, October 3, the "real" schedule began when the Indians took the field against the Nittany Lions of Penn State at Wilkes-Barre, Pennsylvania. Fierce line play and vicious tackling was the order of the day, which resulted in sloppy ball handling and numerous fumbles. It was on this day that the soon-to-be-celebrated toe of Jim Thorpe first came into prominence. Three times his powerful leg swung into the ball and three times it split the uprights. State's only score of the game came on a blocked Balenti punt. The final score was: Carlisle 12, Penn State 5.[5]

Syracuse, the Indians' next opponent, was a squad which boasted a scoring advantage of 66 to 5 over its competition before the game. Another capacity crowd of 8,000 witnessed the action in Buffalo, and the headline proclaimed the event, "Indians Again Beat Syracuse."

Buffalo, N.Y., Oct. 10—For the third consecutive time in three years the Carlisle Indians defeated the heavy Syracuse team this afternoon. The score was 12 to 0. Carlisle depended upon Thorpe for her scorings. He made three pretty goals from placement, two in the first half and one in the second. The game was a very open one, the Indians resorting to many startling trick plays that netted never less than twenty yards. Thorpe, Hendricks and Payne had no difficulty battering holes in the heavy Syracuse line.[6]

According to John Steckbeck's account,

Pop Warner had plenty to do with the victory at Syracuse. He had bemoaned the fact that his warriors were injured and tired. Proof of this was the appearance of the Indian team on the field. They had bandaged fingers and heads. Their practice before the game was non-energetic. Painful, reluctant limping on the part of most of the Indian squad left the impression that the Syracuse team would have a field day. But when the ball game started all evidence of fatigue and injury faded. Speed, speed and more speed was shown. Several thousand fans witnessed the unbelievable, as the Indians trounced their opponents, 12 to 0. The ease with which they ran their plays and the complete confidence they displayed had more to do with the victory than anything else.[7]

The next Saturday found the Indians watching a football game from the sidelines! Since Susquehanna University had called off their game with Carlisle, Warner decided to treat the entire squad to a game between Pennsylvania and Brown at Philadelphia.

This unusual occurrence, a cancellation, proved to be a blessing in disguise. The October 24 game against Pennsylvania, the national champions, was in Thorpe's words "the toughest game in my twenty-two years of college and professional football."[8]

That year, Penn not only was stacked with All-Americans, William Hollenback at quarterback (first team), H. W. Scarlett at end (first team), D. W. Draper at tackle (third team), and A. C. Miller at quarterback (third team), but also was thirsting to avenge the humiliating 26 to 6 thumping received at the hands of Carlisle the year before. James C. Heartwell quotes Jim:

Bill Hollenback of Penn, no one was in a class with him as a tackler. I could sidestep a lot of others or fake them into making foolish dives. But not Bill. When he came at me, I knew it was just a question of how hard he'd hit me. When he did hit, it was like being struck by a battering ram. If Bill didn't pulverize or half-paralyze the man he hit in a head-on tackle, the man had a shaky feeling for the rest of the game. I know. I was among Bill's victims.[9]

In seven previous games, Penn had rolled up 104 points to the incredibly low total of 4 points for her opponents. And this time the Indians were really hurting! Pete Hauser, Hendricks, Winnie, and Kelley were unable to play because of serious injuries.

When the final whistle was blown, the two teams staggered off the field with a 6 to 6 tie behind them. In retrospect, one might decide that the Indians had had "Lady Luck" on their side, but a close analysis of the statistics indicate that it was the other way around.

First downs:	Carlisle 8,	Penn 6
Yardage gained:	Carlisle 272,	Penn 196
Fumbles lost:	Carlisle 1,	Penn 5

The newspaper account, with the headline, "Indians Tie Old Pennsy's Eleven. Paleface Collegians Narrowly Avert Defeat at Hands of Carlisle Redskins," described the event:

Philadelphia, Penn., Oct. 24—The University of Pennsylvania and Carlisle Indian Football teams played each other to a standstill this afternoon, the final score being 6 to 6. The biggest crowd that ever saw the annual game between these teams was present, 26,000 in all, taxing the capacity of Franklin Field to the limit.

Pennsylvania scored her only touchdown by carrying the ball from mid-field and over the Indian line in four plays. Quarterback Miller went around the Indians' end for ten yards and then Reagen made a quick kick which Braddock recovered for Pennsylvania on the Indians' 6-yard line. It required only two plays for Manier to take the ball over the line for the touchdown. Scarlett kicked the goal. In the second half Balenti and Thorpe were the stars in the making of the Indian touchdown. Balenti ran back one of Hollenback's punts for twenty-five yards to the Quaker's 40-yard line. On the next play, Thorpe worked his way through the Quaker forwards and without interference started for the Quaker goal. He got by all the Pennsylvania backs but Reagen, who caught up with the flying Indian on the 5-yard line. Thorpe literally threw himself over the line for the touchdown and then kicked a very difficult goal, tying the score.

For the remainder of the half, the Pennsylvania team was on the defensive. The Indians started another series of line plunges and carried the ball by straight football fifty yards before a fumble by Gardner lost it on the Quaker's twenty-yard line.[10]

In another battle of unbeaten teams, Carlisle emerged with a victory; the victim was Navy. The Indians' unbeaten skein now stood at seven for the year and snapped the Middies', which was also seven. In doing so, the Indians nearly tripled the total scores of the seven preceding Navy opponents, who had been held to six points as opposed to the 141 points compiled by Navy.

The most serious problem that faced the Indians before game time did not seem to be their awesome opponent. Rather, Coach Warner was troubled over the condition of Thorpe's right ankle. Not wanting to aggravate Jim's painful injury incurred the previous week, Warner turned the kicking chores over to Mike Balenti. With the Indians leading by only one field goal, four points, at the half, Jim tested it out on the opening kickoff when play resumed. It was no use! However, as "Pop" explained, the Indians' great versatility quickly took up the slack:

The Indians came closer to being athletes in the real meaning of the word than any other group that I ever knew. Most of our so-called athletes are merely specialists, able to do only one thing; but the Redskins took in the whole field of sport, nearly all of them excelling in three or four different games.[11]

With the headline, "Little Indian's Boot Downs Navy Eleven. Gloom Among the Sailors," the account in the *New York Times* said:

Annapolis, Md., Oct. 31—The Naval contingent is disheartened tonight over the first defeat of the season. It was inflicted by the Indians from the Carlisle school, and the score was 16 to 6.

Every one of the sixteen points was made by Balenti, the little Indian quarterback, who lifted four field goals from placement accepting every opportunity he received.

The game was a bitter one for the Middies to lose. It was the first defeat of the season, the Harvard game of last Saturday being a tie and the first time that the Indians have ever won in Annapolis. There is some consolation, though not much, in the fact that the Navy goal line was not crossed, but the fact that they were out-generaled and outplayed is a bitter dose to the Navy contingent. It is felt here that the team had been brought to a high pitch for the Harvard game and that there has been some reaction. Nevertheless, the confidence in the team is unabated.[12]

The following editorial, which appeared in a local Philadelphia paper, was written two days after the game:

The Indian team, if not the best in America, has a most distinguishing factor; it is always fit. At one stage of the season, Yale, West Point, Harvard, or Princeton might defeat the Indians. It is nearly always necessary for each of these teams to be at their best when they meet the Indians, but the Indians can always in any season beat almost any team at any time in the season. The Indians display the most remarkable form and football prowess.[13]

The Carlisle bubble finally burst when the redmen journeyed to Cambridge to take on the mighty Crimson, who had scored 105 points in seven games to eight for her outmanned opponents. "Harvard Crushes Carlisle's Line. Crafty Indians Outplayed in Everything Except Handling Punts."

Cambridge, Mass., Nov. 7—Harvard routed the strong Carlisle football team this afternoon on Soldiers' Field, winning 17 to 0.

The first touchdown came within sixteen minutes after the opening of the game. Harvard had the wind in its favor and Cutler booted the ball for the Crimson and kept it well in Carlisle's territory. Cutler finally caught an Indian punt on the Harvard 35-yard line, and plunges by the Harvard backs carried the ball to the Carlisle 46-yard line. Here Cutler made an onside kick, which McCay picked up on the 22-yard line. On the next play Corbett burst through right tackle, and, evading Balenti, scored a touchdown. McCay missed the goal.

The next touchdown was made in very much the same way. Cutler caught a punt in midfield, and then the Harvard backs tore through the Indian line to the five-yard line. Here Leslie relieved

71

Corbett, and, aided by him, White carried the ball over the line. McKay kicked the goal.

In the second half Harvard twice had the ball on Carlisle's one-yard line, only to be set back 15 yards for holding. Finally they worked it back again, and Leslie carried it over for the last touchdown. McKay kicked the goal.

The Indians got the ball on Harvard's 17-yard line in the second half, and Thorpe tried for a field goal, but the whole Harvard line was down on him, and McKay blocked his kick. Then a fine run by Thorpe gave Carlisle the ball on Harvard's 8-yard line for a first down, but Harvard braced and held for downs.

White, Corbett, Leslie, Cutler, Browne, McKay, and Fish played a star game for the Crimson. Little Old Man, Thorpe, and Balenti were Carlisle's best men.[14]

The way that Carlisle "got the ball on the seventeen-yard line in the second half" was by Thorpe's throwing a perfect bullet to Hendricks, who lateralled the ball to Wauseka. The picture play covered fifty-five yards. And the "fine run by Thorpe" that "gave Carlisle the ball on Harvard's eight-yard line for a first down" was a brilliant sixty-five-yard gallop![15]

The Indians were very fortunate to win their next game. Not only were they still nursing their damaged pride after the debacle with Harvard, but also the playing surface for the game against Western Pennsylvania was in deplorable condition. Rain had been falling steadily during the previous evening and into the day of the game. Most of the Indians felt like going back to Carlisle before and during the game. They almost should have, because they were extremely lucky to escape with a narrow 6 to 0 victory. It was Thorpe who went off right tackle late in the game and virtually slid down the field for the winning tally.[16]

Warner's exhausted warriors tasted their second defeat of the campaign against the University of Minnesota, and the newspaper headline declared, "Carlisle Redskins Downed. Minnesota Beats Them at Their Own Style of Open Play."

Minneapolis, Minn., Nov. 21—Showing their best form this season and the best exhibition of the "open game" seen on Northrop Field this year, Minnesota completely outplayed the Carlisle Indians at their own game today and won by a score of 11 to 6.

Each team scored a touchdown in the first half and each touchdown was followed by a goal. Minnesota scored one touchdown in the second half, but failed to kick the goal. Plankers, Johnston, and Pettijohn played sensational for Minnesota, while Hauser, Little Old Man, and Thorpe were the stars for the Indians.[17]

After their defeat at the hands of Minnesota, they played an inspired brand of football, reeling off three straight impressive victories over the University of St. Louis, 17 to 0; over Nebraska University, 31 to 6; and on a "field soft and in spots muddy from recent snows,"[18] over the University of Denver, the Rocky Mountain Conference Champion, 8 to 4. Against Nebraska University, Jim scooped up a loose ball and dashed thirty-eight yards for a score, while his end runs against Denver were the only effective part of the Carlisle offense. Thus in a space of fifteen travel-filled days, the Indians played four games, outscoring their opposition 62 to 21. For the entire season the spread was 212 to 55.

Jim's reputation was growing. In this, his first season as a full-time halfback, he was awarded third team honors on Walter Camp's All-America team.

Vic "Choc" Kelley, Sr. ("Choc" for Choctaw), a member of the 1908 squad, remembered that year:

Jim was a terrific runner, passer, and kicker. He weighed around 190 and had tremendous leg drive. Often you'd see him knock out would-be tacklers simply by running right over the top of them.

He didn't try to overpower you if he didn't have to, for Jim was a snaky ball carrier in a broken field. He gave you the leg and then took it away.

When I came to Carlisle the team already was "made" with a veteran line-up. I didn't have a friend on the club but I was assigned to room with Thorpe and we became close friends. He was a good-natured, easygoing guy.

When you're talking about Big Jim's football ability you can't exaggerate. He was just the greatest, that's all.[19]

The 1909 track and field season was to witness Jim's greatest day against an opposing college. Although he did not defeat the entire Lafayette track team single-handedly, as others have written, he did manage to win six gold medals and one bronze in seven tries.

Harold Anson Bruce, Lafayette's track coach at that time, had to laugh before he set the record straight:

I was called on to talk at a banquet in New York. They asked me to say something about my most impressive experience with track. I told about going to the Central Railroad Station on South First Street in Easton to meet Glenn "Pappy" Warner and the Carlisle team.

At first it was a four-man Carlisle team. Later the story got retold and it was a three-man team and then a two-man club. I'm down to one man—Thorpe.[20]

Six other men accompanied Thorpe: Welch, Tewanima, Goesback, Squirrel, Earth, and Burd. Jim placed third in the 100-yard dash, won by Spiegel with Boyce second, and first in the 120-yard hurdles, 220-yard low hurdles, broad jump, high jump, shot put, and discus; 71–41 was the final score of the meet, Carlisle on top. Bruce concluded:

If Jim were around today, he would be greater than he ever was. He just picked up things and did it. After it was all over, Thorpe couldn't tell you how he did it. Everything came natural. Think of what he could do today with the advancements made in coaching and tactics.[21]

Louis Tewanima won the two-mile race that day in efficient but unspectacular fashion. "Unspectacular" because later on in the season, according to Arthur Martin, "after he missed the train taking the team to a meet in Harrisburg, he ran the eighteen miles, ran his race (two miles) and won."[22] Warner remembered the little Hopi:

One afternoon, Louis Tewanima sidled up to where I stood and managed to let me know that he would like a (track) suit.

"What for" I said. "You're not big enough to do anything." "Me run fast good," he answered. "All Hopis run fast good."

I learned afterward the the favorite Hopi amusement is running twenty miles or so on an afternoon, kicking a ball before them.

Thorpe running for Carlisle track team against Lafayette, 1909

Courtesy Maxine and Robert Lingo

Throwing the javelin for Carlisle, 1912

A skinny little chap, never weighing more than 110 pounds, Tewanima proceeded to clean up everything that America had to offer in ten- and fifteen-mile races. Once I took him over to New York for a ten-mile competition in Madison Square Garden, and after looking at the track, which was ten laps to the mile, he turned to me and said: "Me afraid get mixed up go round and round. You tell me front man and I get him."

Along about the middle of the race I began to catch his eye and point out some runner who led him, and one by one he picked them up, finally finished in a burst of speed that established a new world's record. It came close to proving a costly trip, however, for I put Tewanima and two other Hopi runners in a hotel room and forgot to tell them about the gas. As a consequence, they blew it out. But for an open window there would have been three dead Indians. As it was, they were unconscious when I found them the next morning and it was some time before we could bring them back to normal.[23]

Rounding out the schedule were the Georgetown University Athletic Association Meet, where Jim won gold medals for the 50- and 220-yard hurdles, the high jump, and the shot put; the Johns Hopkins University Meet, gold medals in the shot put and broad jump, and a silver medal in the 100-yard hurdles; and the Harrisburg Track Athletic Committee Meet, gold medals in the 220-yard hurdles, high jump, and 16-pound hammer throw, and a silver medal in the 120-yard hurdles. To conclude the season, Jim gave a repeat performance against Syracuse by again winning five golds in the same events as the previous year.

CHAPTER 7

The Theoretical Superplayer

. . . on two occasions, Thorpe, who kicked wonderfully well for Carlisle, got down the field under his own bootings (50 to 70 yards), capturing the ball each time. Once he kicked a beautiful long spiral almost into the midst of five Pitt players and got down the field in time to grab the pigskin, shake off three or four would-be tacklers and dart 20 yards across the line for a touchdown.

—*Pittsburgh Dispatch*

On June 6, Jim was at the Cumberland Valley depot waiting for the 10:05 train which would take him to his summer job on the "outing system." Other students were there too: Raymond Hitchcock, a neighbor from Shawnee; Joseph Loudbear from Little Eagle, South Dakota; Mary Redthunder from Mt. Pleasant, Michigan; John Bastian from Pacific Beach, Washington; and Stella Bear from Cantonment, Oklahoma.

Just before the train arrived, two old friends approached Jim and began to talk. They said they were not going to work on the "outing system." Jim, unable to forget the conversation, related the story:

A couple of Carlisle ballplayers, named Joseph Libby and Jesse Young Deer, were going to North Carolina that summer to play baseball. I didn't enjoy farming, so I tagged along, just for the trip. Well Libby and Young Deer were fair outfielders and they caught on with the Rocky Mount team. I became short of money, the manager offered me fifteen dollars a week to play third base; I took it. There were a lot of other college boys playing around there too.

I played my first game at Raleigh. After awhile, the manager asked me if I could pitch. I told him I would give it a whirl.[1]

Young Thorpe had never pitched before, but Rocky Mount, the cellar occupant of the league, was hard up for strong-armed hurlers. Jim turned out to the best pitcher on the team, winning nine and losing ten, an average of .474, while the club's final percentage was .315. When he was not pitching he played first base, batting at a .253 clip in forty-four games. It was a creditable performance for Jim's first attempt at organized baseball.

"Frank Merriwell–type" accounts claiming that Jim as a pitcher won "twenty-three of twenty-five games for Rocky Mount"[2] are unnecessary exaggerations.

Thomas McMillan, Sr., remembered:

When the team played at home the players would be met by a crowd of little boys as they came out of the hotel. Each boy sought the privilege of carrying the shoes or glove or bat for one of the ballplayers. This was not exactly hero worship. Carrying a glove or a pair of shoes meant free admission to the game.

I was one of those little boys and Big Jim seemed to favor me as his shoe and glove caddy.

My recollection of the games has dimmed, but I remember Jim perfectly. Black hair, black eyes, high cheekbones in a reddish mahogany face, and physique that gave an impression of strength rather than mere size. His movements were as quick and lithe as those of his ancestors as they tracked wild game in the forests of early America.[3]

At the conclusion of the schedule, Jim packed his bags and set out for Oklahoma. Having no money, he was forced to borrow rides of all sorts, and when they were not available, he walked. Jim's youngest daughter, Grace explained:

Dad was back in Oklahoma visiting relatives and friends the times he wasn't playing summer ball. He didn't need any money because as a member of the clan, the Indian people took him in. He didn't have to worry about food or shelter since most of the clan members were ranchers or farmers, and he helped with the chores. Aunt Mary's, Dad's sister, was one place he worked in return for his room and board. So he just had himself a nice holiday![4]

With the coming of spring, Jim journeyed back to play once more in the Eastern Carolina Association. This time he signed up with the Fayetteville entry. He won ten and lost ten this time, with a batting average of .236 in twenty-nine games. A teammate of Jim's, Pete Boyle, remembered his play:

Thorpe did not burn up the league either as a pitcher or a first baseman, but he was a willing worker and was always valuable on account of his great speed. He could circle the bases like a deer, and his running always made a hit with the crowds.

I had occasion once to test his speed, and he left me nothing but dust. During a benefit, a running race was arranged between Thorpe and myself as one of the features. I kept up with him for about a few yards, but soon I was lost in the rear.[5]

The season had not reached the halfway mark when the club owner approached the squad with the announcement that he would be unable to pay them for the week due. As it turned out, there would be no more paychecks ever, and another minor league went under.

Once more Jim returned home—a discouraged young man this time. It was a dreary day in early November when he made it, and the gloomy weather matched his spirits. He made a half-hearted attempt to adapt to farm life, but it was no use. Soon he began to drift throughout Oklahoma, going from village to village without a purpose in life.

As a result, when he was offered the chance to return to Carlisle, he accepted without hesitation. However, it was not Warner, as countless articles have claimed, who lured Jim back to the Indian school, but his former teammate and athletic tutor, Albert Exendine.

It was late in the summer of 1911 when he had a chance meeting with Jim on the main street of Anadarko, about fifty miles southwest of Oklahoma City. "I bumped into Thorpe on the street," said Albert.

He had been playing baseball down south for a couple of years. I was really surprised at the change in him. He was big as a mule. I felt Carlisle needed him on the team and I talked about his

Thorpe as a pitcher

Courtesy Maxine and Robert Lingo

returning. I phoned "Pop" and told him how Jim had filled out and how he looked to me. "Pop" was a man of action, and it wasn't long until they had a man down here and Jim on the way back to Pennsylvania.

"Pop" further induced Jim, although it wasn't necessary, by promising him an opportunity to qualify for the upcoming Olympic Games of 1912. We convinced him that there were no better facilities for training to be found than those at Carlisle. Of course, Warner sorely wanted Jim's return to the Indian backfield. "Pop" realized this his fat salary checks would not continue if he had another season like 1910 [eight wins and six losses].[6]

The two-year layoff had not blunted Jim's football skills. "He was born a football player," Warner commented seven years later, while coaching at Pittsburgh.

No college player I ever saw had the natural aptitude for football possessed by Jim Thorpe. I never knew a football player who could penetrate a line as Thorpe could, nor did I ever know of a player who could see holes through which to break as could the big Indian. As for speed, none ever carried a pigskin down the field with the dazzling speed of Thorpe. He could go skidding through first and second defense, knock off a tackler, stop short and turn past another, ward off still another, and escape the entire pack; or, finally cornered, could go farther with a tackler than any man I ever knew. He knew everything a football player could be taught and then he could execute the play better than the coach ever dreamed of.[7]

In 1911, he had this to say:

What I like about Thorpe is his close observation of everything going on around him. He has little to say but he is always looking to see what is coming off and sizing up the situation. He is the same way in all sports, always watching for a new motion which will benefit him. Then Thorpe has the marvelous concentrative power which he puts in every move he makes. It is a splendid sight to see him hurl a football thirty yards on a forward pass with merely an abrupt snap of the wrist, direct to the hands of the receiver, or to see him judge and catch a twisting spiral punt on the dead run.[8]

Among Carlisle's opponents for the year were Georgetown, Pittsburgh, Lafayette, Pennsylvania, Harvard, Syracuse, and Brown. These teams, which included the incredible total of twenty-one All-Americans (Mercer, Findeison, Minds, Morris, Jourdet, and Thayer of Penn; Wendell, Fisher, Smith, Storer, and Potter of Harvard; Kelly, Spiegel, Dannehower, and Gross from Lafayette; Sprackling, Ashbaugh, Crowther, and Kulp from Brown; and Probst and Kallett from Syracuse) and twice as many preseason candidates, were unanimously picked by the "experts" to put a halt to the recent publicity that the redskins were on the threshold of building a dynasty under the "Warner System" of "modern" football.

Lebanon Valley College on September 23 and Muhlenberg College four days later provided the opening opposition for Warner's warriors. In these games, which the regulars sat out, the "hot shots" were given the opportunity to show their stuff. And they had a field day. Lebanon toppled 53 to 0 and Muhlenberg was let off a little easier, bowing 32 to 0.

The *Carlisle Evening Sentinel* of November 1, carried the account of the next Indian encounter against neighboring Dickinson:

Dickinson played a fine game against a strong and fast Indian team, Saturday, and it was her first game at that. The Indians won 17 to 0.

The Indians failed to score against the Red and White in the first quarter, and this was most encouraging to the players and their supporters. In Goldstein and Shearer, Dickinson has two men who will prove most valuable in the games to come. The Indians as was expected are a fast aggregation, and Thorpe made several spectacular plays. "Possum" Powell made some outstanding plays. The whole team played with ginger and speed. Some brilliant work was done with the forward pass.[9]

While Jim played the whole of the hard-fought sixty minutes and was the major reason for the Indian victory, in this, their third game of the season, the following description is untrue. Gene Schoor writes: "Glenn Warner sent him into the game against Dickinson, the first clash of the season, for only seventeen minutes. In those seventeen minutes, the Indian scored seventeen points."[10]

Jim scored only one touchdown, but it was one of the most brilliant runs ever witnessed on the Indian Field gridiron. The *New York Times* official game account relates: "Thorpe's 85-yard run for a touchdown was the feature of the contest."[11]

Coach Warner, unworried about the following week's game against Mount St. Mary's College, was looking two weeks ahead to the Georgetown encounter. In a rare display of confidence, he sent his ace quarterback, Gus Welch, to the Georgetown campus, in Washington, D.C., to get a first-hand look at their team.

A revealing testimony to Welch's psychological acumen is demonstrated in his ability to persuade teammate Busch to rise to the occasion. Once Busch

suddenly felt a stiff punch in the face. Welch, the culprit, pointed to the opposing team with a gesture indicating it must have been one of those fellows. Then Busch went wild, blocking, tackling, and running like a mad man. In another game there was the same need for rousing Busch, and this time the wiry quarterback sank his teeth into an exposed leg. Busch reacted as before by playing a good game. Years later, Welch told Busch what had happened. Busch replied, "It was great playing with you but there wasn't one game we played together that some dirty so-and-so didn't hit or bite me."[12]

"Pop" proved to be a good prophet: the Indians swamped the hapless Mount St. Mary eleven, 46 to 5. Jim was at his slippery best as his feet touched pay dirt on runs of 28, 14, and 67 yards during the first half. Warner then decided that Jim had had enough exercise for the afternoon and "rested" his one-man gang.

Gus's scouting paid off when the Indians handily defeated the highly rated Georgetown squad.

The account of the game in the Washington newspaper of October 15, began:

Not since Custer made his last stand against Sitting Bull at the Little Big Horn has a battle between redskins and palefaces been so ferociously fought as that which was waged on Georgetown field yesterday afternoon, when the husky tribe of chiefs from Carlisle savagely forced Georgetown's weak, though gallant, cohorts to bite the dust 28 to 5.[13]

"Carlisle was in front all the way and Warner didn't take the wraps off Thorpe until late in the game. His stiff arm, a fearsome thing that turned tacklers clear around before spilling them, was all he needed to ramble 40 yards for the final score of a 28–5 walkaway,"[14] wrote author, Al Stump. Again it was just not so, but again the facts supported the Thorpe legend, unscathed and untarnished.

First of all, "Carlisle was in front all the way" because it was Jim who had put them there. As recorded in the aforementioned newspaper: "It was just 3:15 o'clock, when Thorpe started the game by kicking to Georgetown." Second, while his stiff-arm was certainly a "fearsome thing," he did not score the final touchdown or any of the touchdowns, for that matter. Stansil "Possum" Powell, the fullback, scored two times using his head as a weapon as he left his feet to blast through the line. James Crane, William Newashe, and Joel Wheelock also tallied scores.

The same journal reads:

For the Indians, Thorpe stood out head and shoulders over the rest of his teammates, the big fellow carrying the ball time and time again for consistent gains. He did the bulk of Carlisle's punting and showed himself a master of the "stiff arm" when, toward the last of the game, he skirted left end for 20 yards, evading Hegarty, his first tackler, by toppling the Georgetown man like a tenpin to the ground.[15]

The Carlisle touchdowns, in chronological order, occurred as follows:

The Indians started their terrible onslaught, and in exactly seven minutes from the beginning of play had rushed the ball down the field to Georgetown's line, where Wheelock, the right halfback, went over for a touchdown. Wheelock dropped the kickout. . . .[16]

Thorpe, opening hostilities in this period [second], gave the spectators a chance to liven up when he made a beautiful open field run of 45 yards, evading all but Costello [who would, in the

future, be Jim's teammate on the Canton Bulldogs] on the Georgetown team. Double passes between Arcasa and Powell kept the
ball in close proximity to the enemy's goal line, and after a short
end run by Roberts, left end, Powell was sent through the line for
a touchdown. Thorpe kicked a perfect goal.

Thorpe made a long end run for ten yards and the ball was on
Georgetown's 5-yard line, from where Powell was sent through
the line for the third touchdown of the day. Thorpe kicked goal
from a difficult angle.

Thorpe struck off tackle for 6 yards, and his teammates got
busy with a series of mysterious double passes, that perfectly
dazzled the enemy, and brought the ball down to the Georgetown
goal line, where it was taken over by Newashe, the big left tackle,
in exactly four minutes after play had been resumed. Thorpe
missed a difficult goal.

Thorpe on a fake kick gained 5 yards, and Crane was then sent
around the end for a clean getaway and a touchdown. Thorpe
kicked goal.[17]

The October 21 battle against the University of Pittsburgh,
according to Walter Camp, convinced football experts that
the Indians and especially "Mr. Thorpe" were a team to be
watched for the remainder of the campaign.[18]

" 'Indians' Trickery Too Much for Pitt. Carlisle Half-Back
Thorpe Stumbling Block Against Locals—Indians a Superior
Team in Every Respect,"[19] blared the headlines in the *Pittsburgh Leader*. In the accompanying article, Henry I. Miller
commented:

Featuring some of the prettiest football ever presented to the
large turnout of fans [12,000] at Forbes Field yesterday, the Carlisle Indian team out-played and out-generaled the University of
Pittsburgh eleven, and won 17–0, although the locals fought every
inch of the way.

To say Thorpe is the whole team would be fifty percent wrong,
but he certainly is the most consistent performer trotted out on
the Forbes gridiron in many a moon. His returning of punts, line-
bucking, fake plays, and other maneuvers getting him great applause.

Thorpe carried the ball two out of every three times for the
visitors, Newashe, Wheelock, Powell, and Arcasa being the other

ground gainers of note. Burd played a strong defensive game.[20]

The *Pittsburgh Dispatch* concurred:

So fast were the Carlisle players that only twice during the many punting duels engaged in were Pittsburgh players able to bring out the ball after it had been booted into their territory. Indeed, on two occasions, Thorpe, who kicked wonderfully well for Carlisle, got down the field under his own bootings, capturing the ball each time. Once he kicked a beautiful long spiral almost into the midst of five Pitt players and got down the field in time to grab the pigskin, shake off three or four would-be tacklers and dart 20 yards across the line for a touchdown. . . .

This person Thorpe was a host in himself. Tall and sinewy, as quick as a flash and as powerful as a turbine engine, he appeared to be impervious to injury. Kicking from 50 to 70 yards every time his shoe crashed against the ball, he seemed possessed of superhuman speed, for wherever the pigskin alighted, there he was, ready either to grab it or to down the Pitt player who secured it. At line-bucking and general all-around work, this Sac and Fox shone resplendent and then some.[21]

Almost as if Camp had given the cue, articles from all over the country were proclaiming:

Jim Thorpe is most versatile athlete known. Carlisle Indian performs in record style in every branch of sports. The 1911 football season has brought into the public eye a young Indian student at the Carlisle School who is the most versatile athlete ever known. Thorpe is at present playing on the Indian football team and is considered one of the best halfbacks in the history of the game.[22]

Easton, Pennsylvania, was the scene of the next Saturday's action, and Lafayette College provided the opposition. The Lafayette goal line, on their home field, had not been crossed since 1908. They believed that a sure victory would be theirs if they could stop Thorpe and they did just that. Jim, with a badly twisted ankle, had to be helped off the field.

There was only one problem. It had taken the Red and White three and a half periods to put "Big Jim" out of commission, and by that time it was too late. Jim had already scored the first touchdown—not the second as has been reported—helped to set up two others, and kicked a thirty-five-yard field goal. And he accomplished all of this in the span of twenty-five minutes, owing to the fact that the time limit of each period was only seven and a half minutes. Since there were no rules to govern this aspect of the game as yet, in some contests the time would be ten minutes, others twelve, but rarely would they last for fifteen.

An Easton correspondent printed the results:

> March Field yesterday afternoon was the scene of the greatest football game played in Easton for many years. The Carlisle Indians defeated Lafayette, 19 to 0.
> When a Lafayette man was able to get through Carlisle's first defense, the sure tacklers in the secondary defense would nab him. When an Indian tackled a runner he brought him to earth immediately. While on the other hand, Lafayette's tackling was not so sure, accounting for the big advances into her territory.
> The entire Carlisle team seemed to be built around Thorpe, the redskins' big halfback. Thorpe was a bad man for the Lafayette tacklers to stop and he seemed to know just what to do at the right time.[23]

"Tough Penn came next and the Indians were at a disadvantage because Thorpe was hobbling about with an injured leg. It cramped his style so much that all he could do was set up two touchdowns, score one himself, intercept Penn passes and charge in so fiercely from the defensive secondary that the Quaker attack never could get unwound."[24]

Despite this story by Arthur Daley, the valiant warrior was unable to give such an admirable account of himself. His ankle was so severely twisted in the Lafayette game that he was ordered to stay off of it for two weeks. True to form, Jim suited up for the game, but "Pop" wisely withheld him from the fray.

The *Philadelphia North American* of November 5, said:

> Each team came on the field minus its star. Penn lacked Mercer [first team All-American fullback], but the Indians were without Thorpe, one of the greatest football players and all-around athletes before the public today.

Both stars were on the sidelines, showing plainly the result of the injuries that kept them idle. Thorpe tried to punt in practice and made an effort to run but the effort plainly cost him so much pain that there was no chance for him to get into the game.[25]

Carlisle, nevertheless, prevailed 16 to 0, with Burd, Powell, Wheelock, Welch, and Arcasa turning in outstanding performances.

The powerful Cantabs, the defending national champions from Harvard, who had conquered the Indians every time but one during the previous thirteen seasons, played host to the redmen on November 11 in Cambridge, Massachusetts. Thirty thousand fans jammed Harvard's stadium to see Carlisle play and Jim Thorpe make more miracles. It made no difference to them that the Crimson had surrendered a mere fourteen points in six previous games. The fact that Jim did not disappoint them is best summed up in his statement: "This game was one of the two greatest I ever played. The other was against West Point the next season."[26] Charley Paddock once wrote that "eleven must have been Jim's lucky number because the Harvard game was played on the eleventh day of the eleventh month of 1911."[27]

Warner tells the story:

Percy Haughton started with his second team, just about as good as the first, by the way, and late in the second half when every Carlisle man was out on his feet, sent in his regulars, all fresh and rampant.

When I hear people say that Indians can't stand the gaff, I always think of that finish against Harvard. Jim Thorpe, particularly, had the heart of a lion. With a heavily bandaged leg and a badly swollen ankle, he kicked four field goals, one from the 48-yard line. Although every movement must have been an agony, not once did he take time out. Because of these injuries, and also because I knew that Harvard expected Jim to carry the ball on every play, I switched the plan of attack, and used him mostly as interference through the entire first half.

It was a bitterly fought game with Haughton throwing in that brand-new team in the last quarter while we were compelled to hold to our original line-up, and as Jim saw the day going against

89

Carlisle football team, 1911. Front row: Thorpe, Arcasa, Jordan; middle row: Roberts, Newashe, Burd, Welch, Busch; back row: Powell, Dietz, Wheelock, Bergie

us, he forgot his wrenched leg and sprained ankle and called for the ball.

And how that Indian did run! After the game one of the Harvard men told me that trying to tackle the big Indian was like trying to stop a steam engine.[28]

"Nothing Can Stop Indians. Led by Mighty Thorpe, Carlisle Outplays Crimson Subs and Regulars, Winning 18 to 15—Dazzling Attack," were the headlines of Paul H. Shannon's article in the *Boston Sunday Post*. He continued, in a most picturesque fashion:

Through a bending, crumbling line of Crimson forwards, around the baffled, disconcerted ends, over the battered forms of the crushed and helpless defenders, a relentless redskin band from Carlisle tore its savage way, and the final score of 18 to 15 in Carlisle's favor tells its sad story of rout and ruin for the Crimson hopes.

In an unequal conflict between the white man's brawn and the red man's cunning, the wiles of the redskin prevailed. Indian strategy developed to its highest pitch when all the speed and the craft of the Carlisle braves working in unison hurled the much-wanted strength and power of the Harvard team to one side and swept away the bitterest opposition. . . .

Harvard had heard of Thorpe and his great resourcefulness and skill. Today the Harvard Eleven, or what remained of the great team that Percy Haughton built up, can tell you more about him. Warned to be on their guard against the bull-like rushes of the speedy Indian back, taught to beware of the unerring accuracy of the Carlisle man's toe, admonitions proved fruitless and the united power of the Harvard team was powerless to stop him.[29]

"Thorpe's Four Field Goals Beat Harvard. Carlisle Indians Superior to Cambridge Team in All Points of Play," were the headlines in the *New York Times*. The account continues:

The Indians scored in every period of the game and in each of the quarters Thorpe made one of his field goals. The first one was kicked from Harvard's 13-yard line and the second from a point 43 yards away from the goal. The third successful kick was made in the third period from the 37-yard mark and the fourth was in the last quarter, when the Harvard veterans were beginning to wear Carlisle down, this kick being made from the 48-yard line, the ball passing over one of the upright posts of the goal. All of the kicks were straight between the posts except the last and all of them would have scored had the kicker been 15 or 20 yards further away from the objective point.

The first half ended with Harvard leading, 9 to 6, but the Indians came back strong in the third period and with a touchdown and goal and another goal from the field by Thorpe, Harvard was left behind 15 to 9, before the regulars came on to the gridiron for the last quarter. In this third period Carlisle made a wonderful showing on its attack, starting from its own 40-yard line and in nine plays rushing the ball behind Harvard posts.

After this the Indians received the Harvard kickoff and rushed steadily down the field to Harvard's 28-yard line, where there was better defensive work by the Harvard men, who had recovered from the effects of a 25-yard end run by Thorpe. But, although stopped 25 yards from Harvard's goal, Thorpe made good again and produced his third goal from the field. In this quarter Harvard once was within 40 yards of the Indians' goal line but never got any nearer.

When the fourth period started, Harvard sent out its regular players, only two players, Freedley at quarter and Jencks at right tackle, staying in the Crimson lineup. The regulars started off at a great pace, but this did not last long, and the Indians soon received a short kick on Harvard's 50-yard line.

The ball was driven up the field until it was past the 40-yard mark, but here the advance was stopped. Then came Thorpe's final effort, his 48-yard placement kick. The three points that came because of this goal were very valuable for the Indians, for soon after the next kickoff, when Carlisle had worked up nearly to the middle of the field, the attack was stopped by Harvard. The Indians kick was beaten down by Storer, the Harvard center, who picked up the ball before Welch could reach it. And then, with the fine interference of Parmenter, Storer was able to get across the goal line.

Harvard worked hard for three points but did not get them. Potter was sent in to play quarterback and a forward pass by him to Smith gained the middle of the field, but the next pass went outside and the Indians had the ball again, holding it for the remainder of the game, except when Harvard once had to kick well back in its own ground. Thorpe, who did such remarkable kicking this afternoon, did it with his leg swathed in bandages.

Even had Harvard had all its regulars in the game today, it is certain that Thorpe's efficiency in kicking goals would not have failed him much. His goals were so clean, and the Harvard men came so far from blocking them, that he would have been dangerous anywhere inside the middle of the field.[30]

After the game, all the stunned Haughton could say was, "I realized that here was the theoretical superplayer in flesh and blood."[31] Jim not only had done all of the kicking but also had been called upon to carry the pigskin three out of every five attempts. Poor "P. D." had every right to be shocked. Only hours before he had incautiously started his second unit (out of three units all told) against the under-manned Indians, whose entire squad numbered sixteen bodies, in an attempt to "sacrifice a game to save a season."[32]

Amid the action of the game, an interesting dialogue occurred between Jim and an official. In Jim's words:

One of the men who bothered me most was the umpire. If you remember, he was clad in a red sweater and golf trousers that looked enough like moleskins to disturb anybody at a critical moment in the play. I am sure that I dodged him at least a dozen times in my open field runs and once or twice I dodged him only to run into the arms of a Harvard player. I asked him to change his sweater several times but he apparently forgot what I had said to him.[33]

In another tale, Stump wrote: "In short, battering charges, he punched 70 yards in nine plays, bowling his way over the goal line."[34] In reality, the original line of scrimmage was 55 yards from the Crimson goal, and of the eight plays it took to score, Jim ran two for 30 yards. And it was Arcasa on the bottom of the pile, after a one-yard plunge, who scored the touchdown.

Back in Pennsylvania, one paper headlined: "Carlisle Goes Crazy. Victory of Team Is Wildly Celebrated by Students." The story continued:

Headed by the famous Carlisle Indian band, the entire battalion of Indian boy students "snake-danced" through the principal streets of the city in weird contrast to the ostensible purpose of their procession, which was that of an escort to the recumbent figure of the Crimson Harvard laid out on a stretcher borne by redskin bearers.[35]

According to Welch it was a "careless" band of young men who ran into Syracuse's Archbold Stadium, a sea of mud the following weekend.[36] They led the nation in scoring with 246 points and were laying claim to the national championship.

For the fifth straight week Coach Warner predicted a slump and the Indians' first defeat. The sports writers laughed and said, "About all that is left for him to fear is that the train that carries the squad to the Salt City may be wrecked and that all his players may lose their eyes, arms, and legs before the game with the Onondaga palefaces."[37]

This time, however, he was right. The Indians were defeated by a solitary point, 12 to 11. All week long the Orangemen had primed themselves by chanting: "Get Thorpe! Get Thorpe! Get Thorpe!" Although they were not able to "Get Thorpe"—he scored both of Carlisle's touchdowns—the spirit they had generated, coupled with a torrential rain, carried them over the "listless" Indians.[38]

The account of the game is as follows:

The speedy Carlisle Indian football team tasted its first defeat of the season today, the big Orange eleven of Syracuse University nosing out the conquerors of Pennsylvania and Harvard by one point. The score was 12 to 11.

The contest, played on a gridiron deep in mud and water, was the hardest fought Syracuse has seen in years. The day was cold and a raw wind made the 11,000 persons in the Archbold Stadium shiver.

Both teams scored in the first period. After losing the ball on downs on the Syracuse five-yard line, Carlisle worked the ball from the center of the field across the line by a series of thrilling open plays. Thorpe, who carried the ball across, failed to kick goal. Kallet recovered a fumble on the Carlisle thirty-yard line, and the ball was carried over in four plays by Fogg. Day kicked goal. Syracuse scored again the second period after a thirty-five-yard run by Thorpe was nullified because of holding. The Indians punted. Castle secured the ball and making his way through the entire Indian team landed it across the line. Day kicked goal.

A remarkable brace by the Indians earned them a touchdown in the last two minutes of play. They had abandoned their crisscross and other trick plays and by a series of short forward passes and smashes at the line landed the ball within a yard of the last chalk mark, only to lose it on downs. Again the Indians marched down the field, and this time they were not to be denied, Thorpe going over for a touchdown.[39]

Jim was inconsolable after the game. He had kept them in the game, but he blamed himself for the defeat because his celebrated toe failed to convert one of the extra points.

Recovering from their letdown before the Syracuse game, they were primed for Johns Hopkins on November 22. Warner had put his charges through a week of torturous training, and they fairly trampled the unsuspecting Hopkins men. On the first two series of downs, Carlisle scored twice, with Jim carrying the "mail" both times, whereupon Warner pulled the starting eleven out and replaced them with such men as Aloysius Sousa, Peter Jordan, Roy Large, Joel Williams, and William Hodge, who performed creditably.

The long campaign finally ended on Andrews Field in Providence against the Bears of Brown University. Brown, with a total of 175 points "for" and 35 "against" on the season were playing on their own gridiron and it was raining. To say that the oddsmakers had established them as the favorite is a gross understatement. The front-page headlines of the *Providence Daily Journal* read, "Indians Rend Bears 12–6 before 12,000. Teams Wage Fierce, Spectacular Battle on Andrews Field." The highlights were recorded as follows:

Carlisle banners wave in triumph over the dismantled Brown ramparts. On a slippery, sloppy field, which was churned to a muddy lather before the first half was ended, Carlisle conquered yesterday with an attack that was almost irresistible and a defense which was like reinforced concrete.

The elevens had been battling on very even terms for about ten minutes of the opening quarter when Thorpe brought the crowd up with a wide sweep of the end and with a burly skirmisher out in front thundered over the chalk marks for the goal 65 yards away. Sprackling was the only Brunonian who stood between him and a touchdown, and the crowd awaited the outcome of the race with bated breath.

On dashed the flying redskins, and the Brown captain, tense as a steel spring, waited for the shock with every muscle quivering. Twenty-five yards into Brown territory the pair sped and then Sprackling, side-stepping the first Indian, left his feet with a panther-like spring, his arms closed around Thorpe's legs like a trap, and the goal was saved.

Carlisle had failed to rush the ball over the goal line, but Thorpe's toe had not been tested. The great Indian back was soon

95

afforded the opportunity to get in his deadly work, however, the chance coming a few minutes after the start of the second period.

Thrown into confusion by the fierce charges, the Indians plowing through the mud with a sureness of foot that was disconcerting and refusing to be downed until buried under an avalanche of tacklers, Brown was driven to the 15-yard line where a brief respite was afforded by a penalty against Carlisle for holding, the team losing 15 yards.

Captain Burd decided to take no further chances at rushing and ordered Welch to try a placement kick. The layers of mud were rubbed off Thorpe's shoe, the teams lined up and swift and true came the pass from center. Thorpe, standing on the 27-yard line, drove the leather over the crossbars, the ball going inside the uprights by a very narrow margin.[40]

Two battering-ram assaults on the line beat Brown back for 15 yards. Before the hill men had rallied to their positions for the second shock, the Indians lined up and without a signal being given, the ball shot back to Welch, who flashed around the right end of Brown's line and began a sensational 62-yard flight for the goal line. The ball was planted directly under the goal posts and Thorpe's toe added the point which sent the Indians out in front with a lead of 9 to 0.[41]

The rest of the game featured a blocked punt by Kulp and a touchdown for Ashbaugh of the Bears, another field goal for Thorpe, this time from the thirty-three-yard line, and an eighty-three-yard punt by Thorpe establishing a new field record. Winning eleven and losing one for the year, the Indians tallied 298 points to 49 for the opposition.

On the train going back to Carlisle, Jim's teammates elected him captain of the 1912 team. Walter Camp selected him as his first team All-America halfback and he was, by near-unanimous consensus, chosen as the "greatest of the season's backs."[42]

George Orton of Penn wrote in 1911:

Carlisle had, in Thorpe, one of the greatest backs that has ever been seen in the history of the game. He excelled in all points. Defensively, he was a tower of strength. Offensively, he was a great factor whether running with the ball himself or interfering for a mate. As a drop kicker and kicker of goals from placement, he

Thorpe as a football player in 1911

Courtesy James C. Heartwell

stood without a peer during the past season. His record of four goals from the field against such a high-class team as Harvard had will be remembered for many years to come.[43]

Christmas, 1911, found Jim, dressed as Santa Claus, passing out toys to the Indian children. When "Santa" was unmasked, he was serenaded, cheered as the "great All-American," and presented with an American flag.[44]

Jim warmed up for the upcoming Olympic Games by establishing this record during the 1912 track season:

Boston Athletic Association: gold medal, 100-yard dash; silver medal, 45-yard hurdles; bronze medal, high jump; bronze medal, shot put.

Pittsburgh Athletic Association: gold medal, shot put (12 pounds); gold medal, 60-yard hurdles; gold medal, high jump; gold medal, 60-yard dash.

Middle Atlantic Association (Amateur Athletic Union): gold medal, shot put (12 pounds); gold medal, shot put (16 pounds); gold medal, 75-yard dash; silver medal, 3 standing jumps.

Carnegie Meet: gold medal, shot put; gold medal, high jump; gold medal, 220-yard hurdles; silver medal, broad jump; silver medal, 120-yard hurdles; bronze medal, 100-yard dash.[45]

CHAPTER 8
The Greatest Athlete

Sir, you are the greatest athlete in the world.

KING GUSTAV V

At nine o'clock on the morning of Friday, June 14, 1912, 164 members of the United States Olympic team boarded the S.S. *Finland,* Red Star Line, in the port of New York City. The American team bound for Stockholm, Sweden, and the fifth Olympiad was comprised of the finalists from the three regional tryout sites of Harvard Stadium, Marshall Field in Chicago, and Stanford University. This highly trained and well-disciplined body of athletes bore little resemblance to previous participating groups. No longer would the United States be represented by small clubs, such as James B. Connolly's Boston Athletic Association, who competed at Athens, Greece, in 1896; the diverse assortment of 55 men at Paris in 1900, many of whom came unannounced and at their own expense; or the athletic clubs of New York and Chicago at St. Louis in 1904. The Olympic Games were now "big-time!"

In the United States, legislators from coast to coast petitioned for the creation of a single governing body which would create and enforce a program of unification. Prerequisite to their plan was a well-known and trustworthy figure to initiate this formidable task.

Such a man was the President of the United States, a leading advocate of physical fitness, Theodore Roosevelt. Thus in 1906, the American Olympic Committee and a unique Olympic fund, which would draw support solely from private contributions, were established.

Gradually gaining momentum, the committee was entrusted with the difficult undertaking of selecting a squad to compete at Athens in 1906[1] and at London in 1908. The 1912 assemblage was unquestionably the finest up to that time and for many years to come.

Once aboard the *Finland,* the team had the rest of the day to unpack and become accustomed to their new surroundings. But for the remaining nine days, beginning at 10:30 every morning, a strict regimen of workouts was the rule. Saturday, June 15, marked the first day of training.

The hard-earned sweat of the athletes gave the ship a gym-like odor. The loud thuds of the high jumpers leaping over makeshift ropes onto piled wrestling mats, the splashes of the swimmers in their canvas tank, the banging of tennis balls against a board devised to simulate an actual court, the loud shots of the riflemen,[2] the groans of the weight lifters from the bow, and the continuous pounding of the runners as they circled the cork-covered deck, all contributed to the auditory effect.

Leading the pack of runners in their monotonous journey was a strapping, broad-shouldered Indian. His sinewy physique was hidden by his bulky track clothing, and his thick shock of coal-black hair was covered with a cap. But the face was unmistakable. Seeing his strong, square jaw set firmly in fierce determination, everyone knew that it was Jim Thorpe.

Grantland Rice in *The Tumult and the Shouting*[3] and Gene Schoor in *The Jim Thorpe Story*[4] said that Thorpe refused to train during the ten-day voyage aboard the liner *Finland.*

Ralph Craig, who won two gold medals for the United States in the 100- and 200-meter dashes in that Olympiad was shocked to hear that people really believed this "backhanded compliment." "It has been more than fifty years since that journey," he said angrily, "but I can certainly remember running laps and doing calisthenics with Jim every day on the ship. In fact," he laughed, "Jim and I nearly overdid it on more than one occasion because we were always challenging one another in the sprints."[5]

Another teammate, Avery Brundage, the former president

Training aboard S.S. *Finland* bound for Olympics, 1912

Courtesy Avery Brundage

of the International Olympic Committee, further debunked Rice's concoction by saying:

Certainly Thorpe trained and never missed 'a session! Even if he, or anyone else for that matter had wanted to loaf, our trainer Mike Murphy, would not have permitted it. Jim's own coach, "Pop" Warner, was hand-picked by Murphy to take great pains to insure that Thorpe and Tewanima (who was to finish second in the 10,000 meter marathon) would be in perfect condition.[6]

One group of athletes, however, were unable to practice their events. These were the gargantuan men who specialized in the shot put, javelin, hammer, and discus. Together the "big three," Ralph W. Rose (gold-medal winner in the shot put, both hands), Patrick J. "Babe" McDonald (gold-medal winner of the shot put, best hand), and Matthew J. McGrath (gold medal winner of the hammer throw), tipped the scales at 796 pounds!

The time was 10:00 A.M., Monday, June 24, as the ship pulled alongside the main pier in Antwerp, Belgium. The athletes were to undergo a three-day final tune-up on terra firma before the final leg of the journey to Stockholm. On Wednesday, at 12 noon, the four-day voyage commenced. During this period, all strenuous training ceased.

As Brundage pointed out: "The trip was of greatest interest, although it was too long to keep a group of high-strung athletes together. Some of the boys, being unaccustomed to the bountiful meals served on shipboard, ate too much with unfortunate effects on their condition."[7]

The most heartbreaking result of this unfavorable aspect of the journey was the case of Abel Kiviat, then the world's record holder and overwhelming favorite in the 1,500-meter race. After Kiviat had been beaten at the tape by A. N. S. Jackson of Great Britain, James E. Sullivan, the American commissioner to the Olympic Games, said: "I realized all along that Jackson was good. Yet not even now will I admit that he is a better man than Kiviat. Kiviat was not in his best form in Sweden. The long voyage disagreed with him. To back up my argument, I wish to call attention to the fact

Start of 1,500-meter Pentathlon in 1912 Olympics. Thorpe is second from left, Brundage is first on right

Courtesy Avery Brundage

that Jackson did not beat Kiviat's record. That is pretty strong proof."[8] Nevertheless, beginning with the very first day of competition, America dominated the field, as no nation had ever been able to do before.

"There is something about it all that is beyond definition, particularly in this country of ours, where athletic meetings are considered 'hurly-burly' affairs," was Sullivan's reaction to the majestic unveiling of the games.[9] An overflow crowd, in excess of 30,000, was packed into the resplendent double-tiered stadium, newly constructed at staggering expense, with the money raised by a public lottery.

When the teams from 28 nations marched through the main gateway, at the end of the horseshoe-shaped stadium, onto the cinder track, a beautiful strain of "A Mighty Fortress Is Our God" was sung by a chorus of 4,400. As each of the groups passed the Royal Box, where His Majesty, King Gustav V; His Royal Highness, Crown Prince Gustav Adolph; and Grand Duke Dimitri of Russia were seated, they removed their hats and placed them over their hearts.

After the parade, the president of the International Olympic Committee spoke first, followed by a presentation discourse given by the Crown Prince to the King. Finally, the hushed crowd burst into a roar as His Majesty formally declared Olympiad V opened. "Then when all is quiet again," continued Sullivan, "the clerk of the course calls, 'all out for the hundred,' and the games are on. If you are interested, you are then under a strain that words can hardly explain."[10]

But since history would record these games as the "Olympics of Jim Thorpe,"[11] the legend was not born until the following day, Sunday, July 7, at one o'clock in the afternoon, when the redman toed the mark for the start of the Pentathlon competition.

The first of the five events was the running broad jump. Previous to Jim's attempt, Ferdinand Bie from Norway had the best mark of the group with a leap of 22 feet 5 and 7/10 inches.

Jim, always unconcerned at the prospect of establishing records, had only one thing on his mind; finish first! Standing

Thorpe in Pentathlon broad jump in 1912 Olympics

Courtesy James C. Heartwell

approximately thirty feet from the take-off board, he confidently fixed his gaze upon the 23-foot marker and began his run. His amazing speed gave him tremendous momentum and, with knees bent at a ninety-degree angle and arms uplifted over his head, he soared to a winning mark of 23 feet, 2 and 7/10 inches.

The loud ovation from the spectators did not ruffle the mighty Swede, Hugo Wieslander, who launched the wooden javelin, in the next event, 162 feet, 7 and 3/20 inches to Jim's 153 feet, 2 and 19/20 inches. Although the Scandinavians had dominated this event ever since its inception in 1906 at the Athens' Olympics, Jim did not relish the taste of defeat.

In what was, unquestionably, the most thrilling race of the entire games, Jim was the first to break the tape in the 200-meter dash. In a blanket finish, he covered the distance in a time of 22 and 9/10 seconds. Donahue and Menaul, two other Americans, were clocked at 23 seconds flat, followed by Canada's Lukeman and Bie with times of 23 and 1/5 and 23 and 1/2 seconds respectively.

Jim was just getting warmed up, and in the next event, the discus, he scaled it nearly three feet farther than his nearest competitor. "One-hundred sixteen feet, eight and 4/10 inches," cried the judge. This time it was Brundage who placed second, while the others were not even close.

The final event was the 1,500-meter race. Because it was almost a mile in length, the highly publicized Scandinavian quality of stamina was expected to prevail. Their only hope for victory rested in the combination of a poor showing by Thorpe and a victory for Bie.

As the gun sounded, Jim got off to a slow start. Having started in the next to the outside lane, he was not in a good position to challenge the front runners. Bie and Brundage had burst into the lead and kept up the fast pace for the first lap. All the while, Jim kept well behind in the pack, waiting to make his move, and midway through the second lap he did just that. By this time Bie was all alone in the lead, but at the start of the third time around, Jim had drawn even with him.

As they entered the final lap, it appeared as if Bie was standing still; the head-to-head duel with Jim had sapped his strength and left him without his favorite weapon, his patented kick. Jim won with yards to spare over two other Americans, Menaul and Donahue. The badly exhausted Bie finished well back, in the sixth position. Jim's time was 4 minutes, 44 and 8/10 seconds.

When the points were tabulated, Jim had tripled the score of runner-up Bie, 7 to 21, figured on a basis of one point for first place, two for second, and so forth. Donahue, 29 points; Lukeman, 29; Menaul, 30; Brundage, 31; and Wieslander, 32, rounded out the top seven.

The experts were dumbfounded, and even the Americans were surprised. This new Olympic event, the Pentathlon, was supposed to be the Scandinavians' forte, or at least the Europeans'. But Jim Thorpe destroyed the odds by turning in a performance that has never been equaled to this day.

Commenting on Jim's performance, Sullivan said: "It answers the allegation that most of our runners are of foreign parentage, for Thorpe is a real American, if there ever was one."[12]

Jim did not stop here, however. On the following Saturday morning, July 13, he was in the stadium participating in the grueling ten-event Decathlon, the second of the two all-around events on the program.

And then something happened that probably added ten years to the age of "Pop" Warner, not to mention a substantial number of gray hairs. It started to rain, and Warner was well aware of what that meant to Jim. Jim thrived on athletic challenge, but could not enjoy competing in miserable weather. Soon the skies opened up to unleash a torrent upon the stadium, sending the spectators scurrying for cover.

The athletes were not as fortunate, however. They were obliged to complete the day's program of events, and three of them were held on this, the first of three days of Decathlon competition. There was the 100-meter dash, the running broad jump, and the shot put. And as the athletes took their marks for the dash, "Pop" could hardly bear to watch.

Sure enough, E. L. R. Mercer, an American sprinter, nipped Jim at the wire in a time of eleven seconds flat. However, Mercer would not prove to be a serious threat, since he was more of a specialist than an all-around competitor and quickly dropped from among the leaders.

Warner was upset but not really worried until the completion of the next event, the running broad jump. Because of the sloppy conditions, the men were having difficulty planting their feet on the take-off board. As a result, there were many faults and one double fault—Jim's. His third jump of 22 feet, 2.3 inches was allowed. All Jim and his coach could do now was to play the waiting game and hold their breath. Eventually the mark was broken by G. Lomberg from Sweden, by 4.4 inches, and Jim was now winless in two starts.

Now, bad weather or not, Jim wanted to close out the day in the leader's position. To accomplish this, he knew that he would have to uncork a mighty heave of the shot. He was able to do this and, at the same time, dispel all doubt in the minds of those who had listened to the already confident foreign supporters. Jim had put the shot 42 feet 5 and 9/20 inches to beat by 2 1/2 feet the distance of his closest rival, Wieslander. At the end of the day Jim had scored a total of 2,544.75 points to 2,299.55 for Lomberg and 2,291.60 for Mercer. In the dressing room Jim laughed about changing out of his wet gear and replacing it with a dry warmup suit before the start of the shot put competition. "Maybe it was the dry uniform that helped me win,"[13] he chided the soaking-wet Warner.

The weather was perfect the next day. The sky was clear, and the flags atop the stadium showed nary a ripple. Despite the previous day's rain, the carefully planned track was dry and in excellent condition. The day's action began with the running high jump competition. Jim's leap of 6 feet, 1.6 inches won another first place for him.

In the 400-meter run, Jim was again beaten by the mercurial Mercer, who turned in a 45.3 by 2.3 seconds. But it was in the 110-meter hurdles that Jim really shone. The best way to describe Jim's time of 15.6 seconds is to compare it with Bob Mathias' mark of 15.7 seconds in the 1948 Olympics in London. Thirty-six years of onslaught, involving improved diets, training procedures, hurdling techniques, and equipment had not been able to break track's longest-standing record.

The final day on the Decathlon calendar scheduled the four remaining trials, the conclusion of the games, and the awarding of medals. Jim's total accumulation of points at this juncture stood at 5,302.87. Mercer had taken over the number two position with 4,752.20 points, and Lomberg dropped to third with 4,664.39. However, Jim's first-day point spread of 245.20 points had more than doubled to a new total of 550.67.

In the discus, pole vault, and javelin, Jim's inexperience was evident, but through his incredible powers of coordination and athletic aptitude, he was able to finish second, third, and third in the respective contests. He was unfamiliar with the sophistication and intricacies of the 1,500-meter race as well, but his showing in this event in the Pentathlon and his abundance of raw power, made him the favorite.

After competing in all of the previous fourteen events, he was expected to show some evidence of fatigue. It was apparent that he did not know the meaning of the word as he bettered his previous time by more than four seconds. The stop watch read, 4 minutes, 40.1 seconds.

"At no time during the competition was I worried or nervous," remarked Jim, "I had trained well and hard and had confidence in my ability. I felt that I would win."[14]

"The wonder and admiration of the onlooking athletes," said Warner, "found expression in what came to be a stock phrase, 'Isn't he a horse!'"[15]

Jim had scored 8,412.955 out of a possible 10,000 points to finish nearly 700 points ahead of Hugo Wieslander, the runner-up who totaled 7,724.495. In order, the other entrants

over 7,000 were Lomberg, G. Holmer from Sweden, Donahue, Mercer, and Wickholm from Finland. This wondrous
record of Jim's was to last twenty years before it was broken
by another American, James Bausch, in 1932. Jim's Herculean feat of sweeping both the Pentathlon and Decathlon
and his score in the former will never be matched; after the
1924 Olympics, held in Paris, the Pentathlon was dropped
from the official program.

The Fifth Olympiad drew to a close that afternoon with
the presentation of honors. "The King gave out the gold
medals," remembered Craig, "and he was a very warm and
human person. As the awards were in numerical order, 100
meter, 200 meter, 400 meter and so on, I was the first man
up. When I returned for the 200 meter, the King said, 'What,
you are back again?'"[16]

Moments later a shy Indian youth of twenty-four stood
before Gustav. The *New York Times* reported the scene:
"When James Thorpe, the Carlisle Indian and finest all-
around athlete in the world, appeared to claim the prizes
for winning the Pentathlon, there was a great burst of cheers,
led by the King. The immense crowd cheered itself hoarse."[17]
Regaining his royal dignity, the King placed the laurel wreath
on Jim's head and presented him with a gold medal and a
life-size bronze bust of the King's likeness, measuring 4 feet
high by 22 inches wide.

Later Jim was recalled to the stand for the Decathlon
ceremony. After the King had again given him the wreath
and medal, he presented him with a magnificent silver chalice, lined with gold and embedded with many precious jew-
els, formed into the shape of a viking ship, 2 feet in length
by 18 inches in height and weighing 30 pounds. This was a
gift from the Czar of Russia. But the King would not allow
Jim to leave before he had clasped his hand in friendship.
"Sir," said Gustav, his voice shaking with emotion, "you are
the greatest athlete in the world!"[18] The Indian response,
a reflection of his noble ancestors, was unpolished but from
the heart. As he extended his hand, his reply was a barely
audible, "Thanks, King."[19]

110

Entrance to Stadium

Interior of Stadium
Parade of Nations

Thorpe at Practice
Running

King of Sweden
Congratulating Thorpe

Thorpe putting shot

Thorpe on the mark

Viking Ship
Presented by the
Emperor of Russia

Bust of the King
of Sweden

Presenting Trophies
to Thorpe

Olympic composite, 1912

Courtesy Cumberland County Historical Society and Hamilton Library Association

Sullivan reported:

The field events at the Olympic games comprised the usual standard events: hammer, shot, discus, pole vault, javelin, high and broad jumps, in which events the American athletes again demonstrated their superiority, but the Swedes had two events on the programme never held heretofore, the Pentathlon and Decathlon. These two events were added to the Olympic Games in Sweden to give the world a chance to see the type of athlete that comes from countries that believe in all-around excellence, the claim having been made that certain nations—especially America—specialized, some in sprinting, some in jumping, throwing the weights, etc.

The work of our men in the two all-around competitions, the Decathlon and the Pentathlon, and the showing of James Thorpe, the winner of them, should forever remove from any doubting minds the impression that Americans specialized for one event. Thorpe's record has not been equalled and will not be equalled for many years. And Thorpe had a reputation in other lines of sport long before he began to attract attention in track and field athletics, for besides being a splendid baseball player, he is a star lacrosse player and has the honor of being selected by the leading authority on football in America, Mr. Walter Camp, as a member of the blue ribbon-though-mythical-team, the "All-American Football Team."[20]

Grantland Rice claimed that Thorpe, after winning the Decathlon, snubbed the King of Sweden, who had invited him to his castle.[21] Author Frank G. Menke in *Sports Tales and Anecdotes* further befuddles the issue by stating that Thorpe didn't even want to bother accepting his gold medal from the King at the stadium.[22]

Jim himself exploded these myths:

Someone started a story that when King Gustav sent for me, I replied I couldn't be bothered to meet a mere King. That story grew until it was related the real reason I would not meet him was that I was too busy doing weight-lifting stunts with stein's of Swedish beer. The story was not true. I have pictures showing King Gustav crowning me with the laurel wreath and presenting me with the trophies and it is no fabrication that he said to me: "Sir, you are the greatest athlete in the world." That was the proudest moment of my life.[23]

Teammate Craig had this to say:

We returned to our quarters aboard the ship after the final ceremonies. There was a man waiting at the gangplank with a message for Jim. It was an invitation from a Russian Admiral requesting Jim's presence on his battleship. Since the hour was late, Jim declined the offer, but has had to pay the price when a reporter striving for sensationalism substituted the Russian Admiral with King Gustav.[24]

After the Olympiad ended, Jim remained in Europe with other members of the team to compete in three exhibitions. When these scheduled events were over, they boarded a ship bound for America.

CHAPTER 9

Gridiron Battles on Equal Terms

Except for him, Carlisle would have been an easy team to beat. On the football field, there was no one like him in the world.

— PRESIDENT DWIGHT D. EISENHOWER

"Hail to Chief Thorpe," "A Carlisle Indian," "Captain of the Football Team of 1912–1913," "The Greatest Coach in the World," and "One of the Greatest Marathon Winners in the World," were some of the banners that greeted Jim, Coach Warner, and Louis Tewanima as they stepped off the 12:30 P.M. Cumberland Valley train in Carlisle. The local journal carried the following statement:

Friday, August 16, 1912, will go down in the history of old Carlisle as the day on which was held the most unique and greatest celebration of its kind ever witnessed in the old town.

Superintendent Friedman was the first to speak: "This is an occasion for congratulation. It is a national occasion. The things we celebrate here and the heroes whom we welcome to Carlisle concern the whole country. All America is proud of their record and achievement. We have here real Americans, known as Indians, but whose forefathers were on the reception committee which welcomed to this soil the famed first settlers who arrived here on the *Mayflower*.

"We welcome you, James Thorpe, to this town and back to your school. You have covered yourself with glory. By your achievement you have inspired your people to live a cleaner, healthier, and more vigorous life. Aside from that, as an American and member of America's Olympic team, you have added prestige to the country and the nation which you represented."[1]

They had bands and different games, and more than 15,000 people turned out to welcome him. They had a speaking stand, upon which several people got up and made various speeches

July 29, 1912.

My dear Sir:

I have much pleasure in congratulating you on account of your noteworthy victory at the Olympic Games in Stockholm.   Your performance is one of which you may well be proud.   You have set a high standard of physical development which is only attained by right living and right thinking, and your victory will serve as an incentive to all to improve those qualities which characterize the best type of American citizen.

It is my earnest wish that the future will bring you success in your chosen field of endeavor.

With heartiest congratulations, I am,

Sincerely yours,

WHTaft

Mr. James Thorpe,
    Carlisle, Pennsylvania.

Letter of congratulation from President Taft, 1912

about all that Thorpe, Warner, and Tewanima had accomplished. Jim was asked to make a speech and so he went up and acknowledged the affair and made a very nice speech. The people really enjoyed seeing and hearing him. After Jim sat down, they asked Tewanima to say a few words, which might have been a mistake to say just "a few words," because when he got up, he looked all around and saw that huge crowd and simply said, "Me too," and promptly sat down. That went on record as being one of the shortest speeches ever made.[2]

The event was touched with sadness by the realization that Jim's mother and father could not share his happiness. Friedman sent them an invitation to be his guests, all expenses paid, at the school. He received a three-word telegram in reply: "Thorpe's parents dead."[3]

The next date on the agenda for the three Olympians, with the rest of the team, was the celebration in New York City. Financed by the contributions of private citizens, the festivities began on the evening of Friday, August 23, with a theater party and ended with a banquet at 10:00 P.M. the next day. Interspersed were a breakfast and a parade.

"Golly! That reception was something!" happily recalled Ralph Craig. "There was a private banquet and a parade in open cars all the way down Fifth Avenue and Broadway to the City Hall. I had been smiling so much that I had a permanent grin on my face. I didn't know if I would ever be able to get it off."[4]

The man in the twenty-second automobile, however, was not smiling. He was happy, to be sure, but his face wore a look of uncertainty and bewilderment. He was not used to all this adulation. He had been overwhelmed at the Stockholm ceremonies, but that had been very brief. This parade was lasting for hours, and it was only the beginning. More rousing welcomes awaited him in Boston and Philadelphia.

Tom Harmon, Heisman Trophy winner and prominent sportscaster, maintained, "If you happen to be a 'name' personality in sports, the people believe that they own you and, most certainly, they were responsible for giving you a great

Thorpe, Carlisle, 1912

portion of the fame and publicity you have. As a result, you have very little personal life."[5]

One more obstacle remained for the marvel of the cinder path to overcome before he returned to the friendly confines of Carlisle for his final year of schooling. This was the A.A.U. All-Around Championship of 1912, to be held at Celtic Park, New York.

The old record was held by Martin Sheridan, who scored 7,385 points in 1909. Jim, hampered by miserable weather conditions and weakened by a severe case of ptomaine poisoning incurred the previous week, totaled 7,476.

After the last event, Sheridan rushed over to Jim and shook his hand saying, "Jim, my boy, you're a great man. I never expect to look upon a finer athlete."[6] He told a reporter from the *New York World,* "Thorpe is the greatest athlete that ever lived. He has me beaten fifty ways. Even when I was in my prime I could not do what he did today."[7]

Jim expressed complete satisfaction at the results of his efforts and for the first and last time in his life admitted that he was tired. He had reason to be. The All-Around was held in one day, while the Decathlon was spread over three! "I have trained hard for this meet and now need a rest, which I will take immediately."[8] His rest would last a total of forty-eight hours.

With the sounds of cheering multitudes still ringing in their ears, Coach Warner and Captain Thorpe began preparation in earnest for the football season almost at hand. Jim's press clippings and congratulatory letters from President William Howard Taft and others would mean nothing to the teams he would shortly meet in competition.

Pete Calac, a teammate of Jim's for nearly two decades at Carlisle and in the professional ranks, remembered that year of glory:

I had never played football before. We had no knowledge of it in California where I was born. Several days after my arrival at Carlisle, I wandered over to the athletic field and watched the boys play the game.

I was always pretty husky for a kid and they took an interest in me. One person in particular, however, took special notice of me and taught me the fundamentals of the game. His name was Jim Thorpe.

Right off the bat he and I became good friends. Oh! He was my idol! Actually, he was the idol of every Indian boy. I had read about him in the papers when he was competing in the Olympics. All the students looked up to him.

118

Oh boy, he was really the drawing card for our team that year and was he in condition! He just ran wild in all the games that we played.

Jim could really run and he was shifty. He had a way of fading, that is, he would fade away from you and then when you went to tackle him, he would come by with that hip of his. He would catch the tacklers alongside of the head somehow and just roll them over and away he would go! He ran with his knees high and if you tackled him head on, boy you were really asking for it! He could knock you out with those knees.

There is no question about it; he was the best. He was good at everything he attempted. He could kick, run, pass, and defensively he could really tackle too. During scrimmages we used to tackle him, or at least try to.

Jim never acted like he was better than any of us, in spite of his great fame. He always tried to be just one of the guys. That 1912 team sure thought a lot of him. We did everything we could to help him break loose and get out in the open. He got the ball on most every play and he received all the punts and did all the kicking. About the only other play we had was for the fullback to run straight up the middle, with Jim handling the other assignments, namely, around the ends, off tackle, and, once in a while, the reverse play.

As for myself, I became a substitute very quickly and eventually got into quite a few games that year. In those days, we used to play the whole game. Since there were not very many substitutions, it was difficult for very many boys to win their letter. I believe only twelve men made it that year. In other words, almost the same team played the entire season.[9]

For the first two games of the season, however, none of the regulars got to see action. Warner wanted to test his bench strength early in the campaign against the only weak opponents on the fourteen-game schedule. If Thorpe had been able to play in these encounters, there is no telling what records he might have set. In any case, the substitutes were so vastly superior to Albright College and Lebanon Valley that it would have been downright unsportsmanlike for Warner to use the first team. The respective scores of the games were 50 to 7 and 45 to 0.

The plucky Dickinson eleven started to take up where they had left off in the first half of their 1911 encounter, and, sure enough, when the whistle blew signalling the end of the first period, the score stood 0 to 0.

But the next two times Jim touched the pigskin, he scored touchdowns. The first was on a 29-yard burst, run straight through the line, while the second was more spectacular. Forced to punt from deep in his own territory, Jim dropped back to call for the snap from center. The usually reliable Bergie sailed it over Jim's head. In vain, he leaped to grab it, and by the time he was able to retrieve it, he was standing in his own end zone, with half of the Dickinson team almost on top of him. Warner had no chance to get angry with Jim for not doing the sensible thing and downing the ball, because Jim was off and running in an instant. With reckless abandon he twisted and plunged the length of the field in a touchdown jaunt covering 110 yards. The rest of the game was all downhill for Dickinson. The final result: 34 to 0.

With only three days' rest before the next game with Villanova, Warner again started the substitutes, and as before, they played the entire game, mauling V. C. 65 to 0. The following Saturday's contest would be an entirely different story as Washington and Jefferson held the Indians to a 0 to 0 tie. Jim's four interceptions and booming punts saved Carlisle from defeat at the hands of this Rose Bowl–bound powerhouse.

Syracuse provided the next opposition, and Dr. Joseph Alexander, later to become a three-time All-American at S.U., witnessed the battle:

My first recollection of Jim Thorpe dates back to when I was a boy in high school in Syracuse. As a result of not having money enough to buy tickets, I used to watch the football games from a hill behind Archbold Stadium. Carlisle's only defeat of 1911 had been at the hands of the Orangemen. So the next year, when Thorpe came back, everybody in the town of Syracuse knew that he wanted to win very badly.

The game ended 33 to 0 in favor of Carlisle with Thorpe scoring three touchdowns and doing all of the kicking. Everyone marveled at the fact that he, on a wet field, was able to do this. I personally saw him start around end one time with the ends and halfbacks coming up to tackle him. But he stopped short, causing them to slide past him, and he went on for a long touchdown run.

He had terrific flexibility and his coordination was absolutely beautiful. He was not powerful in the sense that he had so much strength, it was his coordination that made him strong. His movements were all easy, simple, and flexible, and most important of all, he never played football with any anxiety or fear or anything to hinder his mind from acting on a split second's notice.[10]

Pittsburgh, Pennsylvania, marked the scene of the subsequent gridiron battle for the Indians, and the headline announced, "Thorpe Nearly a Team. Famous Indian Great Star in Indians' Victory at Pittsburgh."

Pittsburgh, Oct. 19—The Carlisle Indians defeated the University of Pittsburgh here today by a score of 45 to 8.

The first period of play had hardly got under way when Arcasa's plugging through the center, with an occasional end run on the part of Welch, worked the ball down to the forty-yard line, where Thorpe secured and carried the ball over for the first touchdown. He easily kicked goal.

The second half was simply a repetition of the first. The Carlisle team had no trouble in scoring in all four periods of play, and held the Pittsburgh boys at bay all the way, with the exception of a few moments of play in the third period, when a costly fumble by Carlisle let Calvin get the ball near the Indian goal, from whence he carried it over. Thorpe was roundly applauded for his flawless work.[11]

A pair of Pittsburgh journalists, Mooar and Guy, wrote:

The Carlisle athletes gave us a football treat that we will not soon forget. The wonderful Thorpe would cooly take the ball from center, wait until his interference would form and then in a matter-of-fact way start on an end run. When a would-be tackler got close, the star would let loose with a burst of his marvelous speed and then sprint toward the goal. . . .

Thorpe's first run for a touchdown was sensational. Getting started on a delayed pass, he went through one side of the Pitt line, warded off tacklers, side-stepped others, and when out in the

121

Carlisle backfield, 1912. Left to right:
Arcasa, Powell, Welch, Thorpe

Courtesy Maxine and Robert Lingo

open, he outran Wagner and had only Connelly in front of him. He kept straight ahead and when Connelly tried to catch him he merely straight-armed him and with one swing of his body was to the side of Connelly and had but a few more yards to run for the touchdown. The crowd gave him a great hand for the feat.

Thorpe's other touchdown came on a 45-yard broken field run. In addition, he did some fine kicking. His punting showed great distance and his field goal negotiated from the 44-yard line was a beauty and would have been good 15 yards farther back.[12]

When the redmen invaded Washington, D.C., soil on October 26, five thousand hostile fans banked the field. In a hard-fought game the Indians triumphed over Georgetown University 34 to 20. Although the play was marked with vicious blocking and tackling, a sight witnessed over and over again was a smiling Jim Thorpe, patting an opposing player on the back, and praising him for good work. J. W. Hart described the scene with this aesthetic testimony:

A more perfect day for football could not have been asked. A glittering October sun shone through a mass of silvery clouds, and just enough breeze floated in from the Potomac Palisades to rustle the brown leaves which were wafted on the field of play.

The streets in that part of Georgetown, within a radius of six blocks from the University gate, were almost impassable. And after the game, it was worth one's life to attempt to get through the line of automobiles.[13]

H. C. Byrd reported from Washington:

Thorpe is a wonderful man to carry a football. He is capable of accomplishing more in gaining ground in a broken field than any of the other backs without assistance.

Always conspicuous, proud, dominant, and defiant, driving, leading, and urging his men, Jim Thorpe, the greatest all-round athlete of modern times, was the greatest factor in his team's success. Never a play, hardly an action in which the powerful figure of the Indian was not to be seen. Time and again he struggled down the field for gains of a few yards with half a dozen men hanging onto him, and then again by sheer speed and agility he would elude tackler after tackler, running with varying success, but seldom failing to advance the ball.

Thorpe is a wizard of the gridiron. His work stands out as conspicuously as if he were the only man on the field. His powers of endurance and ability to cope with various situations are so remarkable as to cause one to wonder at the status of the man. Not only does he excel in almost every requisite of the expert runner with the ball, but he is able to kick from placement and is able to punt much farther than any other man ever seen in this section.[14]

Immediately after the game the team boarded a train for Toronto, Canada. Not only did the west want to view the

123

fabled Indians, but the north as well. The rugby team from the University of Toronto included some of the greatest players in all of Canada, but they bowed before Coach Warner's well-oiled machine. Never did a cog slip as the Indians achieved a 49 to 1 verdict.

The referee's whistle blew and the first international football in history was on. The teams lined up in American style of play.

The Indians received the kick and rushed the ball for the first down. On the next rush Thorpe's signal was called and he received the ball and carried it down the length of the field, dodging, side-stepping, and using the stiff arm, defended by a powerful interference, and placed the pigskin between the goal posts for the first touchdown in an international football game.

The ball was again kicked off to the Indians, and again the champion all-around athlete of the world came forward with the remarkable exhibition of running and dodging for which he is famous and runs the entire length of the field sweeping the "Old Boys" aside and plants the ball again behind the goal for a second touchdown.

Between the second and third quarter, officials of both teams got together and it was agreed to play the remainder of the game under Canadian rules, and with Canadian officials.

The Indians do not seem to be at all bothered by the change in the style of play and are making gains and long runs and kicking considerably.[15]

An editorial comment that appeared in a Toronto newspaper related:

Most of the sharps went away from the stadium with the idea that the superior of Thorpe had not been seen in action in these parts, and possibly never his equal. He had everything, including speed, strength and ability to punt, drop, place, pass, catch, and tackle, besides displaying remarkable coolness and the best of judgment.

The students cheered Thorpe from the start, and were not satisfied until Dutch McPherson, the cheer leader, induced the Carlisle leader to come close. He stood stoically, like a statue, in front of the stand, accepted the cheers, bowed, and smiled, and then loped back to his position at left half, where he continued

Thorpe, Carlisle vs. Toronto, 1912

to catch the punts in the palms of his hands and boot back spirals a good 75 yards.[16]

In an effort not to take their victory for granted, the Indians had track work, fundamentals, and 40-minute scrimmages throughout the week. Although Lehigh was to provide the immediate competition, the Army game was in the back of their minds. After their workout of October 31, the *New York World* reported: "Welch's leg is again in good shape and Arcasa is free from his bruises. Thorpe's punting tonight was as remarkable as any ever seen on Indian Field, frequently covering 70 to 80 yards."[17]

With the headlines, "Thorpe's Playing Vanquishes Lehigh. Speedy Indian Scores 28 Out of 34 Points Made by His Team," the description of the Lehigh encounter declared:

South Bethlehem, Penn., Nov. 2—Lehigh put up a good fight against the fleet-footed Carlisle Indians today but went down to defeat, 34 to 14. It was Thorpe, the world-famous athlete, who virtually defeated Lehigh, for he made 28 of the visitors' points. The Indians had an all-powerful offense which Lehigh could not fathom with any degree of success.

By reason of forward passes, Lehigh scored her touchdowns. On two other occasions Lehigh looked good to score, but the inevitable happened. After receiving the kick-off in the first half, Lehigh went right down the field. The Indians finally seemed to stop Lehigh, when Pazzetti essayed a forward pass. The alert Thorpe gathered the ball and dodged through the entire surprised Lehigh team for a touchdown. Again in the third period Lehigh got the jump on Carlisle, and line plays, coupled with forward passes, brought the ball to Carlisle's five-yard line. Here a Lehigh man fumbled and the ball went to the Indians. . . .[18]

Kyle Crichton remembered that November day of long ago with a gleam in his eye:

Like many another small college that has since subsided to its proper level, we had fine teams at Lehigh in those days. We paid the man an honest monthly salary, housed them comfortably, and sheltered them cautiously from the impact of education. College spirit was never higher, and we had a wonderful time kicking our rivals around.

We took the kick-off against Carlisle and brought the ball right down the field. They stiffened, held us for three downs, and then we produced our miracle play that had won half a dozen games for us. This was a short-pass play in which our All-American quarterback, Pazzetti, took the ball from center, scrambled back and heaved it right over the line. He scrambled, he passed — and Thorpe intercepted — ten yards behind the goal line. Anybody in his right mind would have touched the ball down for a touchback, but not Old Jim. He started weaving his way out of that mass of players. Everybody was jammed into that small compass and it seemed impossible that he could get through, but the next thing anybody knew Jim was on the 20-yard line headed for a touchdown. Pazzetti, our fastest man, took after him. Jim was trotting happily along when he became aware that Pazzetti was at his heels. He turned his head, gave a laugh and kept going. In an instant, he was 20 yards away and Pazzetti seemed nailed to the spot. That little jaunt went 110 yards, and ruined us for the day.

The Indians were the first team I ever saw that disdained the dressing-room rites between halves. In that Lehigh game I was telling you about, they simply wandered off to a side of the field when the half ended and had a hilarious time among themselves until the whistle blew again. Anybody who thinks the Indians are a solemn race is nuts. Do you know how they called signals in that game? They'd line up and then Old Jim would yell, "How about through left tackle this time?" and off they'd go right through that spot. Next time Jim would yell, "Right end, huh?" and away they'd go again. After the first few times, Lehigh realized they weren't kidding and rushed all their defenses to the spot, but it never did any good. They'd pick up three or four or five yards at a clip, and then Jim would break off for a real good gain. And if they got stopped with that monkey business, they'd run sequence plays, three or four quick plays, without a signal. There'd be a wide sweep to the left, line up quick, bang; to the left again. Before Lehigh woke up, the Indians had another 30 yards and were chuckling among themselves.

My brother, Harry, was on that Lehigh team and he maintains that the noblest Redskin of all was Garlow, the Carlisle center. Garlow was a runty little individual who talked all the time in a pleasant, conversational tone, and specialized in commiseration.

127

There was a pile-up on the goal line when Carlisle was going over for a touchdown, and the officials were frantically unraveling legs and torsos to locate the ball. Garlow began talking: "It's a distressing thing to have to break this news to you gentlemen, but I very much fear it is over. We should much prefer that this were happening to somebody else, but the facts are clear and you will very soon see that the little pellet is resting securely beyond the last white line. We regret it, I am sure you regret it, and I hope that nothing happening here will spoil what for us has been a very pleasant afternoon."

The spectators in the stands were amazed to see that in this tragic moment when all loyal Lehigh players should be standing around with bowed head and tortured countenance, they were instead pounding each other on the back and lifting their faces in loud, raucous laughter.

That's why I say the Carlisle Indians were pure amateurs. They played because they enjoyed playing; on a Saturday afternoon when the whole idea bored them, they merely went through the motions. This is the sheerest kind of heresy, and perhaps it is well that Carlisle no longer exists, but when it did, it was certainly fun.[19]

For two weeks the Indians had been pointing toward their meeting with West Point. Gus Welch, the fine quarterback, remembered that "Warner had no trouble getting the boys keyed up for the game. He reminded the boys that it was the fathers and grandfathers of these Army players who fought the Indians. That was enough!"[20]

Pete Calac continued:

He delivered that pep talk just before the game. "Pop" was really excited. He stood at one end of the locker room facing the team who were standing on the benches, and he began to pace back and forth and then up and down the aisle between the men to give them individual instructions.

By golly! I didn't think we had a chance against Army that year. They were very big, much bigger than we were. They thought we would be a pushover but we beat them 27 to 6. Oh boy! They were really after Jim that day but once he got loose, he was gone for big gains all afternoon. Dwight Eisenhower played right halfback that day but he didn't last too long.[21]

Joe Guyon, the team's great tackle and member of the Pro

Football Hall of Fame, added:

"Pop" was anxious to make a good showing against Army, which was boasting one of the finest records in the East. At a meeting before the game, he stressed the importance of a football player who carries out all the details of his assignment. Thorpe and I were detailed to block Army Captain All-American Devore. We high-lowed Mr. Devore so well on one play that Welch ran for a touchdown. On the next kickoff Devore made for me and because he only weighed 240 pounds to my 180, of course another Indian bit the dust.[22]

The *New York Times* headlined the event, "Thorpe's Indians Crush West Point. Brilliancy of Carlisle Redskins' Play Amazes Cadets and Spectators. Show Speed and Accuracy. Thorpe Plows Through Army Line and Cadets Are Unable to Check Him." The particulars followed:

West Point, Nov. 9—Jim Thorpe and his redoubtable band of Carlisle Indian gridiron stars invaded the plains this afternoon to match their prowess against the moleskin gladiators of Uncle Sam's Military Academy, and when the two teams crossed the parade ground in the semi-darkness of late afternoon the Cadets had been shown up as no other West Point team has been in many years. They were buried under the overwhelming score of 27 to 6. . . .

Standing out resplendent in a galaxy of Indian stars was Jim Thorpe, recently crowned the athletic marvel of the age. The big Indian Captain added more lustre to his already brilliant record, and at times the game itself was almost forgotten while the spectators gazed on Thorpe, the individual, to wonder at his prowess. To recount his notable performances in the complete overthrow of the Cadets would leave little space for other notable points of the conflict. He simply ran wild, while the Cadets tried in vain to stop his progress. It was like trying to clutch a shadow. Thorpe went through the West Point line as if it was an open door; his defensive play was on a par with his attack and his every move was that of a past master.

Thorpe tore off runs of 10 yards or more so often that they became common, and an advance of less than that figure seemed a wasted effort. His zigzag running and ability to hurl himself free of tacklers made his running highly spectacular. In the third period

129

Carlisle football team, 1912. Left to right, line: Williams, Calac, Busch, Bergie, Garlow, Guyon, Large; backfield: Arcasa, Powell, Welch, Thorpe

he made a run which, while it failed to bring anything in points [a teammate was declared offsides], will go down in the Army gridiron annals as one of the greatest ever seen on the plains. The Indians had been held for downs on West Point's 3-yard line, and Keyes dropped back behind his own goal line and punted out. The ball went directly to Thorpe, who stood on the Army's 45-yard line, about half way between the two side lines. It was a high kick, and the Cadets were already gathering around the big Indian when he clutched the falling pigskin in his arms. His catch and his start were but one motion. In and out, zig-zagging first to one side and then to the other, while a flying Cadet went hurling through space, Thorpe wormed his way through the entire Army team. Every Cadet in the game had his chance, and every one of them failed. It was not the usual spectacle of the man with the ball out-distancing his opponents by circling them.

It was a dodging game in which Thorpe matched himself against an entire team and proved the master. Lines drawn parallel and fifteen feet apart would include all the ground that Thorpe covered on his triumphant dash through an entire team.

West Point's much-talked-of defense, which had held Yale to four first downs in a full hour of play, was like tissue paper before the Indians. To a corresponding degree the Indian defense, which had been considered so much inferior to their attack, was a wonder.[23]

Ironically, Jim was almost through for the day within minutes after the opening whistle of the second half, when he was tackled with crushing impact. Jim lay on the turf, motionless, when the referee, J. A. Evans, began to enforce the two-minute time limit only to be interrupted by Captain Devore of the Army. "Nell's bells, Mr. Referee. We don't stand on technicalities at West Point. Give him all the time he wants."[24]

This is precisely what Jim did not want to hear, and he quickly rose to his feet. Poor Devore and his teammates would regret those words for the rest of the afternoon.

In the dressing room after the game sportswriters bore witness to something they never would have believed possible if they had not seen it with their own eyes. It was a dejected and thoroughly beaten Leland S. Devore, one of collegiate football's all-time greatest linemen and probably the strongest man competing that year. Concerning Thorpe, the 6 foot 3 inch, 200-pound-plus giant said:

That Indian is the greatest player I have ever stacked up against in my five years experience. He is super-human, that is all. There is no stopping him. Talk about your Ted Coys! Why this Indian is as far ahead of the great Yale back as Coy is ahead of a prep-school player. Thorpe smashes into the line like a pair of Coys. There is nothing he can't do. He kicks superbly, worms his way through a field like a combination of grey-hound, jackrabbit, and eel. He is as cunning and strategic as a fox. He follows interference like the hangers-on follow an army. You may have your Lefty Flynns, Brickleys, Bakers, and Coys, but Thorpe for mine every time.[25]

"I will never forget," concluded Welch,

Walter Camp rode the train back to New York after the game. The boys had a lot of fun talking over the game with him. Camp said we had a strong team and that Thorpe was a great runner, but he said, "your quarterback," I was quarterback, "calls his plays too fast; he doesn't study the defense." Thorpe said, "Mr. Camp, how can he study the defense when there isn't any defense?"

Five times during the game we went into punt formation on fourth down and ran the ball instead of kicking—all went for good gains.

Mr. Camp said, "At Yale we don't play that kind of ball—your quarterback should have used Thorpe's kicking ability." Big Bear spoke up and said, "Mr. Camp, we didn't want Thorpe to punt, we wanted touchdowns."[26]

A tough Army halfback by the name of Eisenhower had played a spectacular game. Without him, the Cadets surely would have been beaten by a much higher margin, but this had been "Big Jim's" day. In an outburst of enthusiasm, writers were not content to adhere to the truth. For as football historian Colonel Weyand observed, "Great as was Thorpe, pitiful attempts have been made to 'gild the lily.' "[27] Arthur Daley has written the following story so many times it is almost fact:

One West Pointer was so severely injured trying to tackle Thorpe that his football career came to an end. Fortunately, though, he was to go on to bigger and better things. He was Dwight D. Eisenhower, the starting right halfback that day.[28]

Gene Schoor goes Daley one better by testifying that Eisenhower was only a substitute and upon entering the game helped knock Thorpe unconscious.[29] The former President became irate at the mention of these stories and he brought his rocking chair to a sudden stop and declared:

I was not hurt at all in the Carlisle game! As a matter of fact I was thoroughly enjoying the challenge that Jim was presenting. Except for him, Carlisle would have been an easy team to beat. On the football field, there was no one like him in the world. Against us, he dominated all of the action. On the particular play in question, my pal in the backfield, a man named Charles Bennedict, decided that we could stop him. So we came at him fairly fast with heads lowered, but he stopped short and we collided. Apparently, when we got up, we staggered a little bit and the Coach, Captain Ernest Graves, was signalling to call us out.

Ike leaned forward in his chair and peered over his glasses as he concluded:

The both of us ran to the sidelines and begged him to let us remain in the game but he said to take a rest and then return in the next quarter. You see, in those days, you could not reenter a game in the same quarter. By the next quarter, however, Carlisle was so far in front he told us we might as well go to the showers.[30]

Daley's coverage of the West Point encounter did not stop with the Eisenhower fabrication:

Once three West Pointers hit him simultaneously. He gave them a free ride over the goal line. He threw six straight passes to Arcasa for another score.

In the second half Thorpe caught an Army kick on the 10-yard line and went through the cadets like a salmon through minnows. He went 90 yards. But there was a penalty against Carlisle. West Point kicked again. Thorpe caught the ball on the 5-yard line. He went 95 yards.[31]

Dwight D. Eisenhower punting for West Point, 1912

Courtesy Dwight D. Eisenhower Library

Grantland Rice added: "After faking a kick, Thorpe ran 90 yards and the Indians broke open the game and won 27–6."[32]

Jim's first return covered 45 yards and was indeed nullified, but Keyes of Army kicked the second punt away from Jim to Welch. And while Jim set up most of the touchdowns, Alex Arcasa with three and Joe Bergie with one, did the scoring from point-blank range. Finally, the Carlisle Indians only threw four completed passes all day, obviously disproving the "six straight passes."

The Indians lacked inspiration for their next encounter. Even hearing the Carlisle yell: "Minnewa Ka, Kah Wah We! Minnewa Ka, Kah Wah We! Minnewa, Kah Wah We! Carlisle! Carlisle! Carlisle!" from the student body, making their annual trip to Philadelphia for the Penn game, didn't help.[33]

The West Point game had sapped their psychological strength and left their razor-sharp competitive edge unrecognizably dulled. The hapless Pennsylvania eleven had been beaten four times in nine games, by Swarthmore, Brown, Lafayette, and Penn State. This weakest of recent Penn teams could not possibly pose any semblance of a threat. But it did.

Pennsylvania, since last Saturday holder of the proud title of "the team that came back," rode to glory this afternoon when it took the heroic, unbeaten Carlisle Indian football team and hurled it to defeat by a score of 34 to 26, before 30,000 spectators at Franklin Field.

If the first half, which Penn won by 20 to 13, was sensational, the final session beggars description. The Indians got a touchdown in the third period and were within one of their rivals.

Then, on a trick play, as the Penn team settled into the line-up after the kick-off, Thorpe got away and carried the ball to Penn's 15-yard line, where a double pass shot it over and gave the Redskins the lead.

But Penn braced. In the fourth period, after trying the trick without result, Minds got a forward pass off to Jourdet, who scored, Minds kicking the goal. Then, Mercer went around the right end for a touchdown, and Minds kicked the goal.

This, however, does not tell the full tale, as Penn outplayed the Indians in every department of the game. The Indians' second score, for instance, was the result of a 75-yard run by the redoubtable Thorpe.[34]

Walter H. Lingo, eyewitness to the game, wrote:

Thorpe's unconquerable spirit, even in the face of odds, was never better demonstrated than during the game with Penn when the marvelous Carlisle machine had crumpled. Big Powell and Arcasa, Thorpe's fellow backs, were out of the game, one for the infringement of rules, and the other with an injury. Thorpe kept fighting on. He was fatigued to a degree that in most men would mean submission, yet he would gather all of himself together each time and hurl it at that rival phalanx.[35]

Ironically, this defeat occurred exactly one year after the Syracuse debacle of 1911. Both losses had ruined undefeated seasons, and both followed monumental upsets.

At Springfield, Massachusetts, against the highly touted Springfield Y.M.C.A. College, the team was able to rebound with a hard-earned victory.

"Thorpe Scores All Carlisle's Points. World's Champion Athlete Electrifies Springfield Crowd by Winning for Indians," trumpeted the headlines.

Springfield, Mass., Nov. 23—Jim Thorpe, world's champion all-around athlete, was the particular star in the Carlisle Indians' victory, 30 to 24, over the Y.M.C.A. College today. Thorpe made four touchdowns and kicked three goals from the field and one from placement.

Half a dozen players were battered. Welch, the Indians' quarterback, though scarcely able to stand after being laid out in the third period, tearfully protested against being retired, but was finally prevailed upon by Glenn Warner to give way to Arcasa. There was a cheer for the game quarterback which shook both grandstands. There was frequent applause, too, for Thorpe, who played one of his best games, in spite of the pain incident to an injured back and a lame arm.

The third period was Thorpe's inning. The Indian sprinted 57 yards before being tackled, the star run of the game. He showed wonderful work in a broken field. A forward pass netted three yards. Bergie got the signals mixed, and the ball went to no one. Thorpe recovered for a loss of ten yards. Thorpe made ten yards around right end, and then punted over the goal line. Finally Thorpe plunged through the Y.M.C.A. line for a touchdown, scattering the opposing players as though they were mere chips. With graceful ease and unerring accuracy he kicked the goal. At the close of the third period the score stood: Carlisle, 27; Y.M.C.A., 14.

The Y.M.C.A. made a desperate effort to pull out a victory in the fourth period, and did succeed in keeping Carlisle on the defensive. The Springfield men added a touchdown, a goal from field, and a goal from placement to their score. Carlisle's scoring was limited to a beautiful kick for a goal from the 40-yard line by Thorpe.[36]

Brown, fresh from its 30 to 7 thumping of Pennsylvania's "giant killers," was lying in wait for the Indians, but Jim, closing out his Carlisle career, wanted to give an exhibition that no one would forget, and his teammates wanted to win it "for him."[37] The report stated:

The Carlisle Indians overwhelmed the Brown University team on Andrews Field by a score of 32 to 0 today.

Thorpe was the stellar performer of the game, and figured directly in all the scoring, making three of the five touchdowns and kicking two goals. It was Thorpe's long runs that repeatedly put the Indians within striking distance of Brown's goal.

A driving snowstorm swept across the field during the entire game, making conditions uncomfortable for the 8,000 spectators.

There was no score in the first period, though Thorpe got away with two runs of 20 and 30 yards each. In the second period the Indians scored twice, the first time directly after a 33-yard run by Thorpe, and the second time after a 50-yard run by the same player.

Carlisle scored again in the third period, marching from their own 15-yard line over the Brown goal line. In the final period the Indians made a whirlwind finish with two more touchdowns, the first coming after Thorpe had received Crowther's punt on his own 40-yard line and dashed 50 yards to Brown's 10-yard line, and the second near the close of the period, following gains by Thorpe, Wheelock, and Bergie, aided by a forward pass which netted 22 yards.[38]

Carlisle Indians, 1912. Left to right, bottom row: Vetternack, Large, Arcasa; middle row: Calac, Bergie, Wheelock, Powell, Guyon, Busch; top row: Williams, Welch, Thorpe, Warner, Hill, Garlow

"The greatest football player, ever!" said the Carlisle-Brown referee, Michael Thompson.[39]

"Thorpe, Carlisle, showed again the greatest individual prowess of any back on the gridiron," wrote Walter Camp, as he nominated Jim for first-team All-American the second consecutive year.[40]

"So summing everything up, Jim Thorpe appears to have possessed about every quality necessary to make a player close to perfection," read the *New York Herald*.[41]

"The world's greatest athlete, the best football player that ever trod the gridiron, and a peerless leader," the *Carlisle Arrow* of December 20, 1912, acclaimed Jim.[42]

Out of fourteen games, the team of 1912 had won twelve, lost one, and tied one. They outscored their opponents 504 to 114. Jim accounted for 198 points and 25 of the total 66 touchdowns. The team was so good (it led the nation in scoring) that Calac and Guyon, who later shone brilliantly as backfield men at Carlisle and in the pros, were relegated to the line.

Amid all this adulation, Marianne Moore sheds some light on the private nature of "James":

He was liked by all, rather than venerated or idolized. He was off-hand, modest, casual about everything in the way of fame or eminence achieved. This modesty, with top performance, was characteristic of him, and no back talk.

I used to watch him practice football; he had a kind of ease in his gait that is hard to describe. Equilibrium with no strictures, but crouched in the lineup for football, he was the epitome of concentration; wary, with an effect of plenty in reserve.

I never saw him irascible, sour, or primed for vengeance.[43]

Jim was the toast of the football world as well as the realm of track and field, and athletic trainers and newspaper reporters clustered around him in an unprecedented effort to explain his incredible feats. And so, a panel of experts, physicians, mathematicians, and the like, using only the most accurate of measuring devices, arrived at the following measurements:

Height	71.2 inches		Right foot	10.8	"
Sitting	37.5	"	Left foot	10.6	"
Knee from top of fibula	18.7	"	Head	22.1	"
Right shoulder to elbow	14.5	"	Neck	15.9	"
Left shoulder to elbow	14.5	"	Chest, normal	39.7	"
Right elbow to tip	19.2	"	Chest, inflated	41.3	"
Left elbow to tip	19.3	"	Waist	32.3	"
Arm reach	72.5	"	Hips	38.2	"

Biceps, right arm	13.2	"	Right calf	14.9	"
Biceps, left arm	13.1	"	Left calf	14.8	"
Right arm	12.1	"	Right instep	10.2	"
Left arm	11.6	"	Left instep	10.1	"
Right elbow	11.0	"	Head	6.4	"
Left elbow	10.5	"	Neck	4.6	"
Right forearm	11.6	"	Shoulders	18.0	"
Left forearm	11.2	"	Chest	11.8	"
Right wrist	7.0	"	Nipples	9.2	"
Left wrist	6.8	"	Waist	11.4	"
Right thigh	21.5	"	Hips	13.8	"
Left thigh	22.4	"	Chest	8.9	"
Right knee	13.7	"	Abdomen	10.1	"[44]
Left knee	14.2	"			

CHAPTER 10

Wise in the Ways of the World

I have always liked sport and only played or run races for the fun of the things and never to earn money. I received offers amounting to thousands of dollars since my victories last summer, but I have turned them all down because I did not care to make money from my athletic skill. I am very sorry, Mr. Sullivan, to have it all spoiled in this way and I hope the Amateur Athletic Union and the people will not be too hard in judging me.

—JIM THORPE

At the age of twenty-four, Jim had permanently emblazoned his name upon the pages of the sporting world's ledger of champions. No athlete had ever surpassed his genius for versatility. Besides being the mightiest all-around football and track and field competitor in history, he was the captain of the Carlisle basketball team, playing all positions. He was a member of the school's lacrosse team, and its acknowledged superior tennis and handball performer. He could bowl in the 200's and shoot golf in the 70's, although he seldom played. He was a fine swimmer and a standout in billiards. Baseball, gymnastics, rowing, hockey, and figure skating round out the known list of sports in which he excelled.

Because of his early environment, he was well versed in marksmanship, hunting, fishing, and general forest lore. As if to prove the point, Jim was even a good dancer. A byline in the January 31, 1913, issue of *The Arrow* stated: "For the Two-Step the winners were Clemce La Traille and James Thorpe."[1] "He was able to do everything that anyone else could," said Eisenhower, "but he could do it better."[2] The

141

year of 1913 had just begun, and he was at the very pinnacle of success, an international celebrity, when a bombshell exploded, plunging him into the depths of humiliation.

"Olympic Prizes Lost; Thorpe No Amateur" were the front-page headlines of the *New York Times* on Tuesday, January 28, 1913.[3] Five days earlier the initial story had broken in the *Worcester* (Massachusetts) *Telegram.*

There are many versions of the circumstances surrounding Jim's exposure, but in reality, Charley Clancy, Jim's manager at Fayetteville, was inadvertently responsible. Although he made a sincere effort to deny Jim's guilt, it was too late.

A Pawtucket reporter, in quest of a hot-stove league story, was interviewing Clancy in the latter's office. As the conversation progressed, the newspaper man, whose name has been left conspicuously anonymous, became interested in a large photograph hanging over Clancy's desk. It depicted several players who had returned from a hunting trip. One of them, astride a mule, looked very familiar. "Why that's . . . that's Jim Thorpe, the Olympic star!" the man stammered. "What's he doing in that picture?" Clancy, momentarily at a loss for words, had given himself, or rather Thorpe, away.[4]

Ernie Shore, former New York Yankee pitching great (perfect game: June 23, 1917) and friend of Clancy's, had this to say:

Charley was the highest type of a gentleman and the conversation in question was a friendly one. If he had known how it would turn out, he wouldn't have told for the world. I talked to him after it had happened and he felt awfully bad.[5]

In Henry Clune's words:

The material rewards of his greatest triumph, a few medals and a couple of statuettes, were taken from him when a snide little man in the newspaper business weaseled out the story that Thorpe, as a teenage kid, had taken a few coppers and a bag of peanuts for playing a game of baseball with a cross-roads team in the Ozarks, or someplace, and the Olympic purists fouled him out. One might wonder whatever became of the reporter who dug up THAT story.[6]

Thorpe as a basketball player, Carlisle, 1912

Courtesy Cumberland County Historical Society and Hamilton Library Association

The aforementioned Sullivan once proclaimed Jim "unquestionably the greatest athlete who ever lived. None of the strong men of history could have competed with him successfully. They had great strength we may infer, but they lacked his speed, his agility, his skill. A wonder, a marvel, is the only way to describe him."[7] Now he, along with Gustavus T. Kirby, the president of the Amateur Athletic Union, and Judge Bartow S. Weeks, asked for a statement from Jim.

In a straightforward confession Jim wrote:

Carlisle, Pa., Jan. 26, 1913

James E. Sullivan

Dear Sir:

When the interview with Mr. Clancy stating that I had played baseball on the Winston-Salem team was shown to me I told Mr. Warner that it was not true and in fact I did not play on that team. But so much has been said in the papers since then that I went to the school authorities this morning and told them just what there was in the stories.

I played baseball at Rocky Mount and at Fayetteville, N. C., in the summer of 1909 and 1910 under my own name. On the same teams I played with were several college men from the north who were earning money by ball playing during their vacations and who were regarded as amateurs at home. I did not play for the money there was in it because my property brings me in enough money to live on, but because I liked to play ball. I was not wise in the ways of the world and did not realize this was wrong, and that it would make me a professional in track sports, although I learned from the other players that it would be better for me not to let anyone know that I was playing and for that reason I never told anyone at the school about it until today.

In the fall of 1911 I applied for readmission to this school and came back to continue my studies and take part in the school sports and of course I wanted to get on the Olympic team and take the trip to Stockholm. I had Mr. Warner send in my application for registering in the A.A.U., after I had answered the questions and signed it and I received my card allowing me to compete on the winter meets and other track sports. I never realized until now what a big mistake I made by keeping it a secret about my ball

144

playing and I am sorry I did so. I hope I would be partly excused because of the fact that I was simply an Indian school boy and did not know all about such things. In fact, I did not know that I was doing wrong because I was doing what I knew several other college men had done, except that they did not use their own names.

I have always liked sports and only played or run races for the fun of the things and never to earn money. I have received offers amounting to thousands of dollars since my victories last summer, but I have turned them all down because I did not care to make money from my athletic skill. I am very sorry, Mr. Sullivan, to have it all spoiled in this way and I hope the Amateur Athletic Union and the people will not be too hard in judging me.

Yours truly,

James Thorpe[8]

Also brought to their attention was the fact that, three weeks before, Jim had refused to sign Pittsburgh or Washington baseball contracts in preference to the retention of his amateur standing. The A.A.U. responded by issuing the following statement:

The Team Selection Committee of the American Olympic Committee selected James Thorpe as one of the members of the American Olympic team, and did so without the least suspicion as to there having been any act of professionalism on Thorpe's part.

Thorpe's standing as an amateur had never been questioned, nor was any protest ever made against him nor any statement ever made as to his even having practiced with professionals, let alone having played with or as one of them.

The widest possible publicity was given of the team selected by the American Olympic Committee, and it seems strange that men having knowledge of Thorpe's professional conduct did not at such time, for the honor of their country come forward and place in the hands of the American Committee such information as they had. No such information was given as to Thorpe being other than the amateur which he was supposed to be.

Thorpe's act of professionalism was in a sport over which the Amateur Athletic Union has no direct control; it was a member of a baseball team in a minor league and in games which were not reported in the important papers of the country. That he played

145

under his own name would give no direct notice to anyone concerned, as there are many of his name. The reason why he himself did not give notice of his acts is explained by him on the ground of ignorance.

The American Olympic Committee and the Amateur Athletic Union feel that while Thorpe is deserving of the severest condemnation for concealing the fact that he had professionalized himself by receiving money for playing baseball, they also feel that those who knew of his professional acts are deserving of still greater censure for their silence.

The American Olympic Committee and the Amateur Athletic Union tender to the Swedish Olympic Committee, and through the International Olympic Committee, to the nations of the world, their apology for having entered Thorpe and having permitted him to compete at the Olympic Games of 1912.

The Amateur Athletic Union regrets that it permitted Thorpe to compete in amateur contests during the past several years, and will do everything in its power to secure the return of prizes and readjustment of points won by him, and will immediately eliminate his records from the books.[9]

Weislander and Bie were awarded the Decathlon and Pentathlon victories, respectively, and contrary to the beautiful legend, they did, indeed, accept Thorpe's treasures. They did not send them back unopened, nor did Weislander insist: "Not for me. I did not win the Decathlon. The greatest athlete in the world is Jim Thorpe."[10]

In all fairness to the two winners by default, however, it must be understood that they were always quite agreeable to returning the prizes to Jim if the dictum was ever reversed. On December 3, 1951, the sixty-one-year-old Weislander was quoted as saying, "The Americans speak of me as the 'stubborn Swede' making me feel like the villain although I never meant any harm. I promised to donate the medal to the sports museum. If the sports museum directors decide to return it to Thorpe, for whom I am genuinely sorry, then it is up to them."[11]

Sheridan, whose All-Around record had been smashed by Thorpe the previous September, was the first to rise to his defense: "I don't want that record back and I would give most anything to see Jim cleared. He is the greatest athlete that ever lived."[12]

H. C. Byrd challenged the decision:

The case of Thorpe brings up the question as to whether or not the fact that a man has received money for participation in one branch of sport makes him a professional in all. Just what connection there is between baseball and track athletics is hard to understand.

Granted that Thorpe played professional baseball, why should he be declared a professional in track athletics and football or any other sport in which he desired to indulge? To get at the real ethics of the matter, is Thorpe really a professional in track athletics? He has never been paid for competition on the track; he has refused offers for his appearance at meets, and has never allowed himself to go beyond the pale to the least extent in any manner of track competition. That being the case, is he really a professional runner?

College men are being given out-and-out scholarships for their ability in athletics, others are helped to obtain places so that they can work their way through school, and according to the A.A.U. rulings every man thus aided is a professional. It is known that there are thousands who are competing under A.A.U. sanction who come under the above, and yet they go unmolested. Whether these conditions are right or wrong is not a question to be discussed here, but as long as they are known to exist there might have been some leniency shown a man who did something that was not a greater infringement on the rulings of the amateur body.[13]

Was America's greatest athlete being done an injustice? Damon Runyan, the country's leading sports authority, penned:

Jim Thorpe, greatest all-around athlete that this or any other country has ever known—Jim Thorpe, the wonderful Indian football, basketball and lacrosse player, broad and high jumper, hurdler and sprinter—laurelled by a king and acclaimed by millions—has finally admitted his sins against the laws of amateurism.

One small indiscretion of his athletic youth has come forward at this late hour, after he won all the glories that could be gained in his chosen field and he finds himself branded as a "professional"—the most heinous offense that may be committed among amateurs.

147

It seems a little thing enough that this great Carlisle star did. All the material honors that Thorpe gained in the Olympic games of 1912—the trophies and what not—have been stripped from the Indian holder, and they will be returned to the donors. None of his marvelous records will stand. They will be wiped out completely as if they never had existed, although it is rather doubtful if this summary method will remove them from the memory of the people who follow athletic events.[14]

An editorial in the *Philadelphia Times* showed no mercy for the A.A.U. when it printed the following:

The Amateur Athletic Union should feel proud over its accomplishment in "purifying" athletics by disgracing Thorpe and kicking up a muss that will be heralded the world over as a disgrace to this country.

All aspiring athletes will do well to ponder this action of the American Athletic Union and not play croquet, ping-pong, tiddly winks, or button-button-who's-got-the-button for compensation. It puts them in the ranks of professionals and absolutely disqualifies them from being able to run, jump, hurdle, throw the discus, pole vault, or wrestle.

What will it [A.A.U.] do with the college athletes that are given their tuition free, and made the recipient of special favors "on the side," in order that their services on the football field and in track events may be utilized? All colleges and universities are not guilty of so doing. But many of them are and it is generally known and taken for granted as being justifiable.

A great number of instances might be cited where the "stars" of collegiate sports were strangers to classrooms and were retained by the educational institutions for the sole purpose of advertising the institution with which they were identified by their athletic prowess. There is every reason to believe that the Amateur Athletic Union knew of many such instances, but winked at them. . . .

If their move against Thorpe was not animated by sinister and personal motives, the Amateur Athletic Union will have a busy time cleaning up the ranks of collegiate athletics in order to make all amateurs as thoroughly amateurish as the Amateur Athletic Union insists Thorpe should have been in order to keep the honors he so clearly won.[15]

The most venomous bombardment was printed in the *Buffalo Enquirer:*

Jim Thorpe, amateur or no amateur, is the greatest athlete today in the world. They can take away his tin medals and his pieces of pottery and they can hold him up to the scorn of a few "pure athletes," but the honest world, the thinking world, the great majority of men and women will always consider him the athlete par excellence of the past fifty years in this country.

A.A.U. officials think nothing of taking money for their services as managers of athletic meets at the various world's expositions, still these men at the head of this A.A.U., who accept thousands of dollars, are so "pure" that they cannot be approached. To talk of that bunch as "money getters" would be lese majeste, but the fact is becoming more evident every day that the people of this country refuse to accept the judgment of this clique as to the athletic standing of a man.

In Thorpe's case he played ball one summer for a few months. It was three years ago when he was attending a preparatory school. Other college men did the same thing. Instead of hanging around all summer grafting pin money from their hard working parents they went out and worked for their living playing baseball, earning a living that way, which is as fair a way as if they had been digging ditches or working on a farm pitching hay.[16]

Reactions from abroad were surprisingly sympathetic toward Thorpe. Many Americans had believed that others would take this opportunity to indulge in some mudslinging.

"Excommunication is too severe a punishment for Thorpe," declared the *London Pall Mall Gazette*.[17] "Great Britain thinks none the worse of the Indian for his baseball crime," concurred the *London Daily News*.[18] Scandinavian publications, in unanimous agreement, went their British counterparts one better, however, by telling Jim to retain whatever he so desired.[19]

An editorial in the *Toronto Mail and Empire* was most eloquent, "Canadians Stand Firm with Our Jim Thorpe. Canada Has Declared for Jim Thorpe."

The amateur world reels under the blow, and falls upon the rest of the world to stagger with it. The rest of the world, however, will decline to see any great difference between a man running a race and receiving twenty or fifty dollars for his efforts, and a man running a race and receiving a gold watch worth twenty or fifty dollars.

Yet one is a professional and the other is an amateur. In fact, the rest of the world has some sense of humor, and is inclined to regard the distinction between amateurism and professionalism as the modern counterpart of the distinction between Tweedledum and Tweedledee.

Jim Thorpe may surrender his prizes, but if amateurism is what its prophets try to make us believe, the high-spirited athletes who finished second to him will decline to take the prizes that another and a better man fairly won.[20]

Miss Moore, speaking on behalf of the teachers and student body, stated simply: "Everyone felt it should not be held against him, since any violation was accidental rather than intentional."[21]

The Pittsburgh Steelers' Art Rooney, a professional football pioneer, offered this insight:

Like most athletes of those times, I played semi-pro football and baseball while still attending college. It was, as you point out, a common practice, and I believe most athletes thought there was nothing wrong in so doing. There was a much stonger puritanical approach to all sports then, than there is today.[22]

Jack Cusack, Jim's manager with the Canton Bulldogs, further disclosed:

Jim explained to me that after returning from the Olympics, being unmarried at that time, he turned the medals over to "Pop" Warner for safe keeping.

When the charge of professionalism was made, Warner advised that they be returned. Jim regretted the action later and told me if he had it to do over, he would have kept them. In my opinion, he was ill-advised by "Pop" Warner. Many college players in my time played pro football but under assumed names, which Jim did not do.[23]

"Yes, 'Pop' Warner knew he was playing summer baseball," concluded Grace Thorpe.

I've heard Mother say that "Pop" knew what it was all about and that it was wrong, according to the rules and regulations, for Dad to compete in the Olympics. Dad didn't comprehend this.[24]

Finally, Avery Brundage, the perennial whipping boy held most responsible for the loss of Jim's awards, voiced his opinion:

I believe ignorance is no excuse but I had nothing to do with the ruling that Jim Thorpe had to return his medals. As a matter of fact, I was a competitor at that time and the idea of my having taken his medals away is ridiculous.

They are now in the Olympic Museum in Lausanne, Switzerland. The gold medals were given to the athletes who originally won second place.

Jim was, I must say, a wonderful competitor because he excelled under pressure. You must admire him when you consider that he was an outstanding football player and later a famous professional baseball player as well as a track and field athlete.[25]

With all the testimonials considered, it is difficult to imagine that Warner, who helped develop the youngster into a man of national renown in the world of football and amateur athletics, was not sufficiently curious to keep tabs on his prize pupil. Considering the countless hours spent together and the confidence existing between them, could Thorpe have left Carlisle for two full years and Warner not have known where he had been?

As early as 1909, toward the end of the Rocky Mount schedule, Jim McAleer of the Boston Red Sox was negotiating for Jim's contract. And back at Carlisle, "I never made any secret about it," said Jim.

I often told the boys, with the coaches listening, about things that happened while I was at Rocky Mount. They wanted me to play football at Carlisle and compete in track and field in 1911 and I was agreeable.[26]

Nor should the A.A.U. authorities escape part of the blame. Jim generated attendance gains wherever he played ball. Numerous articles appeared in local papers praising the

151

ability of the Indian, and yet the A.A.U., with its swollen bureaucratic ranks, would have everyone believe they never heard of it, "as there are many of his name."

As early as the autumn of 1911, when the search was beginning in earnest for the Olympic squad, Jim's professionalism was being whispered in athletic circles.[27] Nonetheless, America needed a Decathlon and Pentathlon representative of the caliber of the retiring Martin Sheridan, and Thorpe was their man, rumors or no rumors.

Warner, Sullivan's friend and Thorpe's coach, traveled on the steamship bound for Sweden. Each evening for two weeks, Warner, Sullivan, and the other coaches met in the conference room to prepare the strategy for the upcoming games. There was certainly ample time for Sullivan to have questioned Warner about Thorpe or for Warner to have volunteered the information.

Immediately after the Olympics Thorpe's photograph had appeared in the newspapers of the proud towns where he had once played, because their former dweller was now an international celebrity,[28] and Sullivan, as has been mentioned, was quoted as praising Thorpe for being a "splendid baseball player."

At best, Jim held only a nebulous conception of the meaning of amateurism, but those individuals under whose jurisdiction he was permitted to compete at Stockholm knew full well what they were doing.

The vast majority of cognizant sportsmen, both at home and abroad, had exonerated Thorpe, but the damage was done. Warner, Sullivan, and the entire A.A.U. structure, were never interrogated.

For the time being, the unsophisticated and truly unspoiled redman, who failed to use the *nom de guerre* ruse, was more bewildered than hurt. Five days would pass before he would break his silence. "I must have time to consider my future plans," he stated simply.[29]

CHAPTER 11

Unbounded Good Nature and Unlimited Courage

Jim missed a signal while running the bases and it cost a run. McGraw was furious and called Jim a "dumb Indian." This was the only thing that Jim would not tolerate and he took out after McGraw and chased him all over the Polo Grounds. It took half the team to stop him. When Jim was dismissed, McGraw used the excuse of his inability to hit a curve ball and the writers have echoed his statement ever since.

—AL SCHACHT

Harry Edwards, a Philadelphia fight promoter, said that Jim could "put all the black and white 'hopes' to flight" and offered him fifty thousand dollars to become a professional boxer.[1] R. Edgren, writing for the *New York World,* agreed:

Wouldn't some searcher for a "hope" like to get Jim Thorpe? Imagine what Jim would do if he were turned loose among the heavyweights!

Six feet tall and heavy in proportion, Thorpe has the height and reach of a champion. He is amazingly strong. He could fight a hundred rounds without breaking down, if necessary. This is shown by his phenomenal endurance in athletics, which enabled him to win both the Pentathlon and the Decathlon at Stockholm. Moreover Thorpe can take any amount of battering.

And here we have the most important fighting characteristic he possesses. Everyone knows that there's no sport in the world better than boxing for developing self-control. That's because self-control is absolutely necessary to the boxer. Without it he has no more chance to win than a nerve-shaken sharpshooter has to hit the bull's eye.

Look at the photograph of Thorpe's face. You can see, unhidden by the massive chin and neck and the high cheek bones and keen

153

Jim Thorpe, 1917

Courtesy James C. Heartwell

eyes, unbounded good nature combined with unlimited courage
and determination and aggressiveness.

As for the "headwork" that a boxer needs, Thorpe has shown
plenty of it in football. He's keen enough to be selected as captain
of Carlisle's team. Captaining any big football team is a thing that
requires a good head. Thorpe's individual play as well as the way
he runs his team shows that he has an active brain.

I've seen many a good man go out for the heavyweight title and
a few good men land it. But there wasn't a Thorpe in the lot. Sullivan had the physique. Corbett had the head, but physically he
wasn't to be compared with Thorpe. Fitzsimmons was the Indian's
equal in stoical courage and in craft, but certainly not his equal
in strength and endurance. Jeffries was a bigger man than Thorpe,
stronger, but no more enduring. He was just as determined and
stoical in the face of punishment, but less aggressive, less swift
in attack. Tommy Burns had everything but the height and weight.[2]

From the world of entertainment came more offers. Vaude-
ville managers, theatrical agents, and motion picture moguls
all tried to outbid one another. One thousand dollars a week
to perform feats of strength on the stage was his for the asking.[3]

Jim, however, was a man of rare courage. He spurned the
boxing and show business opportunities in favor of a more
difficult endeavor.[4]

The date was February 1, 1913, and the setting was the
main office of the New York Giants Baseball Club. Jim,
under the watchful eye of manager John J. McGraw, had
just affixed his signature to a three-year contract stipulating
a salary of six thousand dollars per year. Although this was
one of the largest sums ever paid to an untried prospect,
it was only a fraction of the amount offered Jim by the vaude-
ville manager.

He had weighed equal offers from a total of six major
league clubs: Pittsburgh, Cincinnati, and New York of the
National League and Chicago, St. Louis, and New York of
the American circuit. The Giants were the number one team
in baseball and would present the toughest lineup to penetrate. They had Mathewson, Snodgrass, Merkle, Tesreau,

Meyers, Marquard, Wiltse, Wilson, Becker, Burns, Dyer, Harrison, Lobert, Crandall, Schauer, and Robertson to name just a few. But Jim wanted to go with the best.

As he was leaving, Jim was approached by members of the press and the following conversation developed: "I am glad to go with the Giants, but I would rather have remained an amateur athlete," and adding sadly, "but that is all over now."[5] He looked very serious for a moment when his lost Olympic trophies were mentioned. "There is nothing more to do or to say about that. The quicker that is dropped, the more I will be pleased."[6]

Although some persons have expressed an opposing viewpoint, Jim was never exposed to organized baseball at the Indian school. There surely was no team at that time.[7] Furthermore, once he became involved in the many other sports at the school, he did not even get a chance to play baseball for fun. Jim's experience was limited to his boyhood days in Oklahoma and to the portions of two summers spent at Rocky Mount and Fayetteville.

This fact, however, did not faze McGraw. "If he can only hit in batting practice, the fans that will pay to see him will more than make up for his salary," McGraw told a friend.[8]

This was the first premeditated exploitation of the great Carlisle Indian, and it was only the beginning. A contemporary editorial read as follows:

One might have thought that baseball was a sufficient drawing card in itself, but Manager McGraw's reported decision to sign Jim Thorpe, the famous Indian athlete, for the New York Nationals without knowing anything about his ability as a player, arouses the suspicion that it is "anything to get the money" in baseball, same as in pretty much everything else. Thorpe, on account of his international prominence, growing out of his winning several championships in the Olympic contests and the sensation resulting when he was stripped of the medals as a professional, would indeed be a drawing card for some, even if he only strolled back and forth in front of the grandstand.[9]

There was friction, between Thorpe and McGraw at the very beginning of their relationship. They were as different

With the New York Giants, 1917

as any two men could be. "Muggsy," the toughest and most successful manager in all of baseball, had inherited the fiery spirit of the Irish. Jim, on the other hand, was a very peaceful individual. Even while making a spectacular play in the field he gave the appearance of nonchalance.

Al Schacht, the famous "Clown Prince of Baseball," was a pitcher for the Giants during that period. He was able to give a rare insight into this misunderstood era of Jim's career:

This is my fifty-seventh year in baseball, but my experiences with Jim Thorpe gave me some of my biggest thrills. I first met him in 1915. He had been sent down to the Harrisburg club in the

157

International League for some seasoning, and the secretary said to me: "Big Jim Thorpe is joining us now, and I want you to room with him."

He was always very modest but at the same time the thought of his medals hurt him. I clearly remember asking him only twice, if he thought he would ever get them back and he wouldn't answer me. He wouldn't even say "yes" or "no." Jim was not the kind of a fellow who would care about the medals. It was his pride that was damaged. He was just a big good-natured fellow who wouldn't hurt anybody, even though he had come up under tough conditions.[10]

Once, however, Jim did confide in someone and release the sorrow that was walled up inside him. Chief Meyers, a full-blood Mission Indian from California and a star catcher for the Giants, when he was Jim's roommate, told the story:

Jim was very proud of the great things he'd done. A very proud man. Not conceited, he was never that. But proud.

I remember, very late one night, Jim came in and woke me up. I remember it like it was only last night. He was crying, and tears were rolling down his cheeks.

"You know, Chief," he said, "the King of Sweden gave me those trophies, he gave them to me. But they took them away from me. They're mine, Chief, I won them fair and square." It broke his heart, and he never really recovered.[11]

Continued Schacht:

Jim was a fantastic guy. He had a terriffic personal appeal to people and was just like a big overgrown kid, in the same mold as Babe Ruth.

McGraw had just the opposite type of personality, and the two clashed time and time again. He was a very strict manager. But don't get me wrong, he was a great guy and great to work for.

McGraw always wanted to think for the members of his team. He would take all of the responsibilities. He ran the ball game. You could make all the errors in the world, but if you pulled a bum play or if he thought you weren't hustling, he would call you everything. He would get on you and tear you apart, no matter how important you were. He was all order and was the boss at all times.

With the New York Giants, 1917

Courtesy James C. Heartwell

Of course, he was the last word in New York as far as the ball club was concerned.

I want to dispel the story that Jim was released from the club for drinking. Although McGraw drank quite a bit himself, he never allowed it to interfere with the performance of his ballplayers.

Jim's drinking, as well as the rest of the team's, has been greatly exaggerated. The players in those days didn't drink any more than they do now.

You see, if we were two ballplayers and were to walk into a place, go up to the bar and order a beer, just one beer, people would notice us there. And if I happened to drop a fly ball the next day, they would say I was drunk.

Now as soon as Jim Thorpe came to the Giants, the pressure was on him. It would have been unbearable for anyone else. Here he was, the greatest athlete of all times. He had to be. Maybe some guys can shot put or do a few things better than he can, but for all-around ability as a trackman or as a football player, no one else excelled in so many different departments.

But when it came to baseball, he had virtually no experience and was faced with the very best of pitching as soon as he started. You just can't do that! He was a football player, first, and an athlete in everything else, except baseball. He was originally signed only because his name was Jim Thorpe but, after that first year, he stayed in the big leagues on his own.

In my opinion, for a fellow that never played much baseball before, he was a hell of a ballplayer. He could hit the ball as far as anybody and he was one of the fastest men I ever saw running the bases. He played the outfield, mostly right field, and he was good at that, too. He had a great arm.[12]

Schacht paused, stood up from the sofa and walked over to the window. When he turned to continue, his jovial demeanor had disappeared:

Many people have said that he was a disgrace as a baseball player. This is not true. They also say that he was curve-balled out of the major leagues. This is not true either. He had difficulty with it in the beginning. What do they expect? He had never even seen one before and all of a sudden he was up against the greatest.[13]

Unfortunately, Robert Leckie, who wrote the following reason for Jim's dismissal from the Giants, is the author most

Zanesville Greys baseball team, 1925. Left to right, seated: Warren Miller, Bill Purtell, Dutch Meissner, Fred Hasselmann, Bill "Whitey" Wietelman (batboy), Guy Sagle, Dizzy Nutter, Paul Nutter; standing: Charles Ketchum, Fred Carmichael, Ben Dyer, Jim Thorpe, Johnny Walker, Harry Silverman, Turk Reilley, Bill Wietelman, Sr.

Courtesy Jim and Dave Campbell

frequently quoted, "He turned from football to professional baseball, playing for the New York Giants. But he could not hit a curve."[14]

Soon after the opening of the 1913 season, Jim was farmed out to Milwaukee, and after the schedule had been completed he was married to his sweetheart from Carlisle, Iva Miller. Although she had attended the Indian school, she was a white girl. Charlotte Thorpe Adler revealed the truth:

My mother's sister, Grace Miller, acted as her guardian when their parents died. At the time of their death, Grace was teaching at Carlisle. So, in order to take care of her, she falsified the enrollment of my mother at the school. Glamorized stories relate that my father failed to discover that she was not an Indian until after he had proposed to her or after their marriage but this is not accurate. He knew long before that and, in fact, almost lost her hand to Gus Welch, who had proposed to her earlier.[15]

She proved to be a comfort and inspiration during the next trouble-filled decade of Jim's life. Their honeymoon was spent on a world tour of Great Britain, Egypt, Italy, France, and Japan. Jim had been recalled to the Giants to participate in their famous exhibition journey with the Chicago White Sox. One of their foreign hosts was the British sportsman, and merchant, Sir Thomas Lipton, who upon meeting Jim uttered the prophetic statement: "Young man, I have studied your remarkable and unusual physique carefully, and I am of the opinion you will still be making your mark in athletics ten years from now."[16]

After returning to America aboard the ill-fated *Lusitania,* Jim began to prepare for spring training, and it was not long after camp opened in Marlin Springs, Texas, that he clubbed three homers in one game. Years later, he remembered that experience: "One day, I hit three home runs into three different states. We were playing an exhibition game in Texarkana, which is right up there in a corner formed by Texas, Arkansas, and Oklahoma. I hit one over the right field fence into Oklahoma, one over the left field fence into Arkansas and one over the center field fence, which was in Texas."[17]

162

Marriage of Iva Miller and Jim Thorpe, 1913

Jim's success in baseball, however, was short-lived. A good-natured fellow at heart, he was even more jovial on the field, where he was most comfortable. His nickname at Carlisle had been "Libbling," meaning "horsing around,"[18] and this characteristic rubbed the serious-minded McGraw the wrong way. In his own words, Jim explained the occurrence that precipitated his downfall:

We were shagging flies in the outfield before a game, and Jeff Tesreau, who was a pretty good pitcher, began scuffling around with me. Finally I pinned him with an arm lock. The next day McGraw wanted him to pitch and Jeff said he couldn't because he had a sore arm but Jeff wouldn't squawk, so McGraw said,

163

"You don't have to tell me. I saw you wrestling with that big Indian yesterday. I'll have no more of that on this ball club." He called me in and threatened to fine me if I roughhoused any of the other players, and I said that was all right with me, because I didn't want to roughhouse with them anyway, but they were always challenging me.[19]

Never on good terms with McGraw, Jim now played even less than before. In 1917 he was loaned out to Cincinnati. But a more serious and personal misfortune was at hand.

The happy union with Iva had been blessed with a son, James, Jr., who was now three years old. Jim's world revolved around his family and he adored the boy, but again the ominous hand of death was to disrupt his life. His little son, stricken with infantile paralysis, succumbed to that dread disease.

"It was a great tragedy," said Grace, "I know. I lost my son when he was sixteen and I don't believe there's anything worse that can happen to a parent. It hurts worse than after a child is grown. It was a terrible and traumatic shock.[20]

Said Schacht:

I will never forget seeing Jim together with his little boy. It was during the spring training of 1917 and they were there with Mrs. Thorpe, who was a very beautiful woman. After practice, they would all be out on the front lawn, in front of the hotel, and the kid would climb up one of Jim's arms and down the other and would grin that great big wide grin just like his old man and the two of them would laugh. After his death, Jim was never the same.[21]

No longer could Jim be depended upon to show up for practice for the antagonistic McGraw. The "Little Napoleon" was firm when he should have been understanding. And while his attitude of iron discipline toward Jim surely was inaugurated in the best interests of the club, it later developed into a conflict of personalities.

The fuse was set to go off at any instant, and when it did, it touched off an explosion that, for all intents, ended Jim's major-league career. According to Schacht:

164

Jim Thorpe and son, 1917

Courtesy Beth and Homer Ray

Jim missed a signal while running the bases and it cost a run. McGraw was furious and called Jim a "dumb Indian." This was the only thing that Jim would not tolerate and he took out after McGraw and chased him all over the Polo Grounds. It took half the team to stop him. When Jim was dismissed, McGraw used the excuse of his inability to hit a curve ball and the writers have echoed his statement ever since.[22]

His batting averages were: during the 1919 season with Boston, .327; 1920 with Akron, .360; 1921 with Toledo, .358, including three home runs in one game; and 1922 with Portland, .308. "He was on these ball clubs," said Schacht, "because of his ability, not because his name was Jim Thorpe."[23] Jim added: "I hit .327 my last year in the National League; I must have hit a few curves."[24]

One might argue that Akron, Toledo, and Portland, all triple-A teams, were members of an inferior league. "There was not much difference in those days," concluded Schacht. "In 1917, for example, Providence had four pitchers, Babe Ruth, Herb Pennock, Carl Mays, and Ernie Shaw, who were great stars. The next year, they were stars in the big leagues. In other words, they were great in the International League."[25]

Jim concluded his baseball career moving from one town to the next, but, right up to the end, hitting the ball with authority and consistency and fielding his position brilliantly day in and day out. His last official game was with Akron in 1928. He was forty years old.

CHAPTER 12

Professional Football in Swaddling Clothes

On the field, Jim was a fierce competitor, absolutely fearless. Off the field, he was a lovable fellow, big-hearted and with a good sense of humor.

—JACK CUSACK

Jim's tenure with the Giants had been a frustrating one. His contract signing had made the headlines and caused a tremendous amount of publicity. For brief stints he would play regularly and hit over .300, but these periods were infrequent.

Relegated to the bench, he grew sullen and morose. Day after day he was forced to watch his teammates make baseball history. What a difference one year had made! In 1912 he had been the all-conquering athlete who was the recipient of the applause of the Royal House of Sweden and of countless thousands the world over.

When Jim was offered a position with the Canton Bulldogs of the reorganized sport of professional football, he jumped at the opportunity. Jack Cusack, the visionary manager of the Bulldogs, was the man responsible for Jim's entrance into professional football. This is his own story, in detail, of the Bulldogs, *circa* 1915–20, and of the man called Thorpe. This account, incidentally, is by far the most ordered and factual one in existence and clearly refutes Grantland Rice's contention that Jim's pro days "started nearly eight years after he finished at Carlisle"[1] and that he was by then past his prime.

Unfortunately, records and statistics were not kept during this time, and these were Jim's greatest years.

The year 1915 brought the beginning of the big-time era in professional football, and happily it brought Massillon back into play. A group of Massillon businessmen, headed by Jack Whalen and Jack Donahue, invited me to a meeting to discuss details, and they

With the Canton Bulldogs, 1915

Courtesy Pro Football Hall of Fame

were now willing to agree with the principles I held out for the year before. Their decision to field a team brought back the old rivalry that all of us needed so badly and furnished the drawing power that meant good gates.

Then, just in time for Canton's first game with the newly revived Massillon Tigers, I hit the jackpot by signing the famous Jim Thorpe, the Sac and Fox Indian from Oklahoma who was rated then (and still is today) as the greatest footballer and all-around athlete that the world of sports has ever seen! The signing marked the start of a warm friendship between us that lasted until Jim died.

Some of my business "advisers" frankly predicted that I was leading the Bulldogs into bankruptcy by paying Jim the enormous sum of $250 a game, but the deal paid off even beyond my greatest expectations. Jim was an attraction as well as a player, and whereas our paid attendance averaged around 1,200 before we took him on, we filled the Massillon and Canton parks for the next two games—6,000 for the first and 8,000 for the second. All the fans wanted to see the big Indian in action.

On the field, Jim was a fierce competitor, absolutely fearless. Off the field, he was a lovable fellow, big-hearted and with a good sense of humor.

Most of the Massillon lineup played under assumed names which still remain unknown to me, but if you will take a look at the Massillon roster you will find at least one player who was using his correct name. The Rockne listed there is the famous Knute, who already was putting Notre Dame on the map and who was destined to go down in football history as that university's greatest great among its players and coaches. Rockne, as left end, and his Notre Dame teammate, Quarterback Dorais, made a tricky and famous combination on passes.

In order for the reader of this narrative to have the full import of the first 1915 Canton-Massillon game, I quote from the writeup of Warren Cross, a highly respected sports scribe for the *Canton Repository,* who recently retired after half a century of reporting:

"Only the slippery surface of the field kept the Indian [Thorpe], ideal in build and a finished football man, from scoring at least one touchdown. In the second period he broke through the Massillon defense and headed for the goal, with only Dorais in his path. In attempting to get by the Massillon luminary he lost his footing and slipped, going out of bounds, on the eight-yard line. On another occasion, after skirting Massillon's left end, he slipped with almost a clear field in front of him. He was the only Canton man feared by the Massillon defense. He showed the 6,000 yelling fans the reason for this fear.

"Fisher (Greasy Neale), the unknown halfback from the East, and Carp Julian were the only other Canton men able to accomplish anything. For Massillon, in addition to Dorais, there stood out Fullback Hanley and Ed Kagy, Captain. The first scoring came in the first quarter when Dorais of Massillon dropped the ball over from the twenty-eight-yard line.

"Early in the second quarter, a pass from Dorais to Kagy took the ball to the Canton two-yard line. Canton held for three downs. On the fourth attempt, Hanley plunged through. Fleming booted the goal. Score: Massillon 10, Canton 0.

"After the next kickoff and the exchange of punts that followed, Canton made its best showing. Gardner intercepted a pass on Canton's 41-yard line. Thorpe grabbed a short pass over the line for nine yards and then shot outside of Massillon's left tackle for the longest run of the game. He covered 40 yards before he slipped and went out of bounds on the 8-yard line. Massillon's line held, Canton making only four yards in three attempts. On the fourth down Julian shot a pass over center, the ball was batted down by a Massillon forward and into the arms of Guard Drumm. He pushed through and over the goal line, but the touchdown was not allowed. Umpire Durfee ruling that a Canton man had touched the ball before it was batted down by the Massillon lineman. Protest was unavailing, although it appeared to be a legal touchdown for Canton. Not until late in the third quarter could Massillon score again. Then Dorais scored a dropkick from the 42-yard line. An intercepted pass by Massillon paved the way for the last scoring, another Dorais dropkick from the 45-yard line.

"After a lapse of nine years barren of the intense rivalry that has always been the outstanding feature of the athletic relations between the two cities, the same old Massillon Jinx still holds its mystic power over Canton. Massillon and the Jinx conquered, 16 to 0."

In preparation for our second game with Massillon, to be played at Canton on November 29, I further bolstered the Bulldogs with the addition of Robert Butler, Walter Camp's All-American tackle from the University of Wisconsin; Abel, another Camp All-American tackle from Colgate; and Charlie Smith, a fine tackle from the

Michigan Aggies. Jim Thorpe was now serving as the Canton Captain.

Our Canton park would hold as many as 8,000 people but on this November afternoon we had an overflow crowd of spectators.

The contest was a hard-fought, nerve-knotting game with both teams about equally matched on line play. We were able to make but two first downs on line play, while Massillon was held to one. We made several forward pass attempts without completing one, while Massillon completed four. Jim Thorpe succeeded in making a dropkick from the 18-yard line and later followed up with a placement kick from the 45, giving Canton a 6–0 advantage. Massillon was held scoreless in the first three quarters, but in the final quarter the visitors opened their stock of passes and the situation began to look bad for Canton.

At this juncture I saw that something was wrong with Abel, our new tackle. Our opponents were making far too much yardage through his position, and when Captain Thorpe made no move to replace him I took it upon myself to do so—in keeping with an agreement I had with Thorpe that it would be my right to substitute from the bench if I felt it to be necessary. I found that Abel was ill with a heavy cold, and I replaced him with Charlie Smith.

Then, with only a few minutes left to play, the fireworks really started. Briggs, right end for Massillon, caught a forward pass on our 15-yard line and raced across our goal line right into the midst of the "Standing Room Only" customers. Briggs fumbled—or at least he was said to have fumbled—and the ball popped out of the crowd right into the hands of Charlie Smith, the Canton substitute who had been following in hot pursuit. Referee Conners, mindful of the ground rules made before the game, ruled the play a touchback, but Briggs had something to say about that.

"I didn't fumble!" protested the Massillon end. "That ball was kicked out of my hands by a policeman—a uniformed policeman!"

That was ridiculous on the face of it. Briggs was either lying or seeing things that didn't happen to be there—for most everybody knew that Canton had no uniformed policemen in those days. But Briggs was unable to accept this solid fact.

"It was a policeman!" he insisted. "I saw the brass buttons on his coat."

The spectators could stand the strain and tension no longer. With only three minutes left to play, the fans—of both Massillon and

171

Canton persuasion—broke down the fences surrounding the playing area and swarmed across the field by the thousands, the Massillon fans protesting the referee's decision, the Canton citizens defending it. The officials strove manfully to clear the field and resume play but found the task impossible and called the game.

It wasn't all over yet, however. The Massillon team and its loyal supporters demanded that the game officials settle the matter conclusively by making a statement on the referee's decision, and at last they agreed to do so—on the condition that the statement be sealed and given to Manager Langford of the Courtland Hotel, to be opened and read by him at thirty minutes after midnight. This arrangement was made in order to give the officials plenty of time to get out of town and escape any wrath that might descend upon them from either side. Tension remained high throughout the evening, and the hotel lobby was filled with the bedlam of argument until Manager Langford read the statement at 12:30 A.M. It backed Referee Conners' touchback decision, saying that it was proper under the ground rules, and the Canton Bulldogs and Massillon tied for the championship.

The "Mystery of the Phantom Policeman" who had caused Briggs of Massillon so much unhappiness was solved about ten years later, long after I had left professional football and had gone to live in Oklahoma. While on a visit back to Canton I had occasion to ride a streetcar, on which I was greeted by an old friend, the brass-buttoned conductor. We began reminiscing about the old football days, and the conductor told me what had happened during that crucial final-quarter play back in 1915. Briggs, when he plunged across the goal line into the end zone spectators, fell at the feet of the conductor, who promptly kicked the ball from Briggs' hands into the arms of Canton's Charlie Smith.

"Why on earth did you do a thing like that?" I asked.

"Well," he said, "It was like this—I had thirty dollars bet on that game and, at my salary, I couldn't afford to lose that much money."

And that's how the Canton Bulldogs tied for the 1915 championship—on Jim Thorpe's two field kicks, with assists from a streetcar conductor and a lucky catch by Charlie Smith.

Canton's banner year came up in 1916. With the intense rivalry between Canton and Massillon, I knew we had to have the best players available regardless of cost, and I question that any team to this day can boast of as many All-American players as were fielded by Canton or Massillon in the 1916 season. On the Canton team I often had a reserve of four or five All-Americans warming the bench.

We believed in heavyweights who were fast on their feet, and the Canton line, at one time, averaged 213 pounds, with the overall squad averaging about 200. That was the sort of player material that made the 1916 Bulldogs one of the greatest teams ever assembled—one that I would match against any team in professional football today, if they played under the rules and with the same ball in vogue at that time.

The season—from which the Bulldogs were to emerge with only seven points scored against them in ten games—was opened on October 2 with the Altoona Indians, and we defeated them 23–0. One of the most brilliant Canton stars in this contest was newly acquired Georgetown graduate, Halfback Costello, a Camp All-American.

Costello was again the big noise on October 9, when Canton won a 7–0 victory over Pitcairn, a fine Pennsylvania team composed mostly of college stars, including several from Carlisle. We made no substitutions in this game, playing the full sixty minutes with our starting lineup.

Canton took on additional strength before the October 16 meeting with the Buffalo All-Stars. We obtained the services of Ernie Soucy of Harvard to replace Dr. Hube Wagner, who had quit the game to give more time to his medical practice. Soucy, one of Camp's All-American ends, was outstanding on both defense and offense, and he was to contribute greatly to our success during the remainder of the season. And Jim Thorpe, who had missed the first two games of the season because he had been out playing baseball, returned in time to take over as captain in the game with Buffalo's All-Stars, a team of college players which included two Carlisle stalwarts, Tall Chief and Mt. Pleasant.

The Canton steamroller had no trouble in flattening Buffalo. The backfield combination of Thorpe, Costello, and Julian, together with a stellar performance by Soucy, netted eleven touchdowns and eleven field goals. The game ended 77–0.

The sports writer who covered the game for the *Repository* was jubilant:

"Those pessimistic fans who have been declaring that Canton will have no chance against Massillon this fall must now take in their horns. They will have to admit that Jack Cusack has gathered a bunch of football talent which gives the Red and White a chance

173

against any team in existence or that will be in existence. . . .

"Cusack struck gold when he corralled this Soucy. Canton has seen a lot of stars during the last ten years but a more brilliant end than Soucy has never flashed across the local horizon. . . . No need to say that Thorpe is a star. Every grid fan knows that. From the first time Canton got the ball—the Indian snatching a Buffalo punt and going down the field for the first touchdown—until he retired at the end of the second quarter, Big Jim held the center of the stage. His presence in their midst gave the Canton men vim and vigor. . . ."

We had still another All-American in our lineup when we took on the New York All-Stars on October 23. He was Buck, of Wisconsin University, a 254-pound tackle who knocked down every New York attempt to advance through his portion of the line. Again the principal ball carriers were Thorpe, Costello, and Julian, and only once did the self-styled "champions of New York State" make a first down before they went down, battered and mauled, under a humiliating 67–0 defeat.

Our next opponent, on October 30, was the burly Columbus Panhandles, long rated as the toughest team in Ohio, but even this formidable aggregation found the Canton defense too strong. At times, Captain Ted Nesser, one of five brothers who played for Columbus through the entire battle, managed to pierce Canton's first defense line, but he never got past Fullback Carp Julian. It was in this game that Captain Ted's redoubtable brother, Frank, met a superior in punting when he competed with Canton's Thorpe. The Indian got all of his kicks away in beautiful style and on one occasion lifted the ball down the field for eighty-five yards, booting from his own 15-yard line over the Panhandle goal. It was a rough-and-tumble game filled with penalties, but the Bulldogs, playing it carefully, gave the Panhandles their first defeat of the season, 12–0.

In preparation for the forthcoming games with Massillon, the two games we wanted most to win, I added five more All-Americans to our roster—Wilkinson of Syracuse, King of Harvard, Doc Spears and Ghee of Dartmouth, and Garlow of Carlisle, the latter recommended by "Pop" Warner, who so often gave me good advice in the selection of new players.

At Canton on November 6 we played the Cleveland Indians, now managed by our former Akron rival, Peggy Parratt. It was another great day for Jim Thorpe, who carried the ball more than half of the time, did most of the kicking and passing, and thrilled the crowd of 7,000 fans with a 71-yard dash down the field after catching a punt. While Parratt's team was made up of college stars, they did not make a first down during the game, and Canton won a 27–0 victory.

So far, so good! The Bulldogs had wrapped up six of the season's ten games, and not one of the six opposing teams had scored a single point against us! But in the return game with Cleveland, played one week later at the American League baseball park there, something did occur to slightly tarnish that shutout record.

For some reason, the Bulldogs were off their stride at the start and were outplayed by the Indians in the first quarter, but never once did Cleveland get into Canton territory. In the second, the Bulldogs settled down and Thorpe managed a run around left end for the first touchdown. With the count now 7–0, Canton was forced on the defensive in the third period. When Costello attempted to punt from his own 12-yard line, the kick was blocked and the ball bounced back of the Canton goal line, where Lobert fell on it for a Cleveland touchdown. Throughout most of the final quarter it looked like a 7–7 standoff but, with only five minutes to play, Soucy tackled Derby so hard after he had taken a punt that a fumble resulted. Canton recovered, and on the fourth down Jim Thorpe sprinted around the Cleveland right end for the touchdown that gave the Bulldogs a 14–7 victory.

The next game, with the Youngstown Patricians on November 20, was another close one, with the only scoring in the last few minutes. Canton was unable to throw its full strength into the fray. Soucy and Buck had gone to Minneapolis and had not returned in time to play; and Costello had to be replaced in the first quarter because of a foot injury. Thorpe, who had injured an ankle in the last Cleveland game, took to the field against the advice of his doctor, but had to drop out at the end of the first quarter. The Patricians, who had blanked all previous opponents during the season, put up a valiant battle, holding Canton scoreless for three full periods and most of the fourth; and then, with only three minutes to play, Canton's Ghee and Wilkinson manipulated a pass that enabled Wilkinson to make the only touchdown of the day. Wilkinson failed on the try for goal, and the Bulldogs trotted off the field with a 6–0 win.

And now we had reached the high point of the 1916 season—the two closing games between the Canton Bulldogs and the Massillon Tigers for the professional football championship of the world.

175

The first game was played at Massillon on November 27, and not even the high wind that whipped across the muddy playing field was able to cool the football fever that gripped the 10,000 or more spectators who jammed the stands. The players for both the Bulldogs and the Tigers were, with a few exceptions, men who had been Walter Camp All-American selections.

The Tigers outplayed us from the start that Sunday afternoon. The Bulldogs, although led by Thorpe, never penetrated inside of the Tiger 30-yard line—but Thorpe, Sefton, Kellison, and Buck proved themselves to be bears in stopping the Tiger offensives. The slippery footing robbed both teams of speed, and throughout the game neither goal was seriously threatened. It all ended in a scoreless tie.

The return game at Canton, on the following Sunday, drew another gate of around 10,000 fans. Rains had fallen the day before on League Park, and the dirt infield portion of the baseball diamond, a part of the football playing area, was ankle deep with mud in some places. Threatening clouds hovered over the park as the teams took the field, and the Bulldogs had a new star in the lineup—Fullback Pete Calac, a hard-hitting Carlisle Indian and running mate of Thorpe, whom I had just obtained from West Virginia Wesleyan.

Canton ran all over Massillon that afternoon. At no time in the game did the Tigers prove dangerous, and never once did they set foot inside the Canton 31-yard line. The Bulldog quarterback, Milton Ghee, directed strategy skillfully, and time after time the two big Indians, Thorpe and Calac, ripped the Tiger defense to shreds with their powerful drives. "Fat" Waldsmith, the Bulldog center—who had never attained All-American rank, but was a great star for all that—took a lot of fight out of the Tigers early in the first period when he scooped up a fumble and dashed fifteen yards for a touchdown.

In the second period, after Canton had battered through the Tiger line for fifty-one yards, Calac bucked through for the second touchdown; but, like Waldsmith in the first, he failed at goal. Near the end of the contest Thorpe rammed through the Tiger line for the last touchdown, but on the kick Doc Spears missed the uprights by six inches.

It was all over; and the Bulldogs, with a 24–0 victory, were the undisputed champions of the world!

Canton played the entire game without making a single substitution. Warming the bench were several All-Americans—like Wilkinson, Costello, and Neale—but we saw no reason for making changes while we already had a winning combination on the field.

Besides winning the coveted championship, there was another thing in which the 1916 Bulldogs took great pride—although the Cleveland Indians had scored against us by reason of that blocked punt they recovered behind our goal line, the Canton goal line itself was not crossed during the season.

The 1917 season brought problems with which professional football could not cope for long. The United States had entered World War I, and besides the drafting of manpower which made the building of teams difficult, attendance at games fell off drastically in ever-increasing numbers as more and more men were called to the colors. Before we got around to our traditional arch-enemy, Massillon, we had no difficulty in defeating the following:

Pitcairn, Pa.	12–7	Youngstown, Ohio	3–0
Altoona, Pa.	80–0	Akron, Ohio	14–0
Columbus, Ohio	54–0	Youngstown, Ohio	13–0
Syracuse, N.Y.	41–0		

Massillon, still smarting from the 1916 defeat, was going all-out to take Canton's measure, and in the hope of doing so had engaged Charlie Brickley, the great Harvard drop-kicker and an All-American on Camp's selections, to pilot the Tigers. Meanwhile, I had made some important additions to our own squad—Gus Welch, an All-American from Carlisle; Matthews, an All-American from the University of Pennsylvania; and Williman from Ohio State. We opened the first game at Massillon, on November 26.

A striking example of the Bulldog power was given the 6,000 fans right at the start. Opening up on their own 23-yard line, Big Jim Thorpe and his eager helpers marched the ball down the field for seventy-seven yards without hesitating. It took just four minutes to travel the distance and send Thorpe across for a touchdown. Russell kicked the extra point.

Before the game, Brickley had boasted that his own kicking would win the contest for Massillon but his Harvard-educated toe garnered only three points, with a drop-kick in the second period. In the fourth quarter, after a fast Canton drive of sixty yards, Dunn went over for another touchdown, with Welch kicking the goal. And that was it—a 14–3 victory for the Bulldogs.

Jim Thorpe (Canton Bulldogs) and Charlie Brickley
(Massillon Tigers), 1917

Courtesy Beth and Homer Ray

The second with our old rivals was played December 3 on our
home grounds, and I think Massillon was just as surprised as we
were when the Bulldogs, until then considered the unbeatable
champions of pro football, were forced to bow down before the
Tigers, 6–0, in one of the most bitterly fought battles we ever
played in League Park.

178

It was a battle of Goliaths in which the leading roles were taken by the rival left halfbacks—Canton's great war chief Jim Thorpe and Massillon's rough-and-tough Stanley Cofall, a topnotch kicker of Notre Dame origin. In fact, the contest developed into a personal duel between them, and for the first time in memory the Canton players saw Thorpe lose his temper and his famous smile—because Cofall engaged in some rough work that Jim considered uncalled for. The Indian was injured in the second quarter but he stuck it out for the remainder of the game, carrying the ball more than any other man, doing more than his share on the defensive, and hoping for a chance to even up things with Cofall.

During most of the game the Bulldogs were on the short end of the so-called "breaks," which cause so many upsets in football, and it was bitter medicine for the Sac and Fox tribesman when the only breaks of the game went to Stan Cofall. The Tiger halfback succeeded in booting two field goals over the bar—the first from 34 yards, the second from 31—and that's how Massillon took the 6–0 victory.

In the meantime, I had been engaged in the oil business in Oklahoma, and in the spring of 1919 I received a letter from Ralph Hay of Canton stating that he would like to carry on with the team if I was not returning. Ralph was a very good friend of both Thorpe and myself, was acquainted with most of our 1916 and 1917 players, and therefore was in position to organize a team from that nucleus.

In 1921 . . . Jim Thorpe had transferred his interests to Cleveland's Indians, and the old warhorse asked me to come to the Ohio metropolis and look after his financial affairs. His contract called for a guaranteed amount for each game or a percentage of the gate, whichever was greater, and he felt that there were times when he was not getting his full due.

When I arrived, the management for the Indians showed some resentment over my presence. As the representative of the players, I insisted on checking the tickets wherever Cleveland played and for this purpose I always took sufficient help to man the gates, along with an ample supply of gunny sacks. I counted all of the tickets into the sacks, then checked the roll figures, and this simple method of audit paid off for the players. On two different occasions I found discrepancies running from $900 to $1,000, and complimentary tickets totaling 800 to 900, far in excess of the number that should have been allowed. In both instances, after strong and

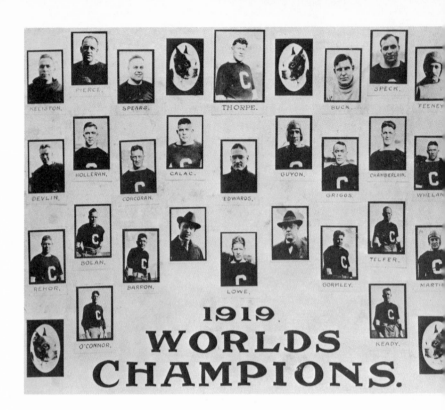

World Champion Canton Bulldogs, 1919

vivid argument, I succeeded in collecting our share of the deficiencies. . . .

After the regular season ended, Cleveland booked a December 3 exhibition game at the New York Polo Grounds with an All-Star team that Charlie Brickley had assembled. The net returns after the baseball management deducted the percentage for use of the park amounted to only $3,750, which was $250 short of the guarantee, but we accepted, and a check for that amount was written by the baseball management and made payable to the Cleveland treasurer.

180

We were staying at the old Imperial Hotel, Thorpe and I occupying a room together. It had been understood that the players would be paid at the hotel—a procedure that had been followed during the season—but around seven o'clock a bellhop came to our room with a statement covering our hotel expenses, and I became suspicious. I made inquiry at the desk and discovered that the Cleveland treasurer, just as I suspected, had checked out—which meant to me that he was running out with the check, without paying the players.

Thorpe and I went to the Pennsylvania Station and, as good fortune would have it, found the treasurer and his lawyer awaiting a train which was scheduled to leave in half an hour. I demanded that he return to the hotel and pay the players, but he refused, saying he would mail them checks from Cleveland—which meant they would receive expenses only. Getting nowhere, and with time running out, I sought out two detectives stationed in the lobby and explained the situation, whereupon they decided (for a certain sum) to help us. They talked to the treasurer and his lawyer, but the Clevelanders insisted again that they would mail the checks.

When the train was announced and the gates opened for boarding the two men reached for their grips, but at that juncture the detectives grabbed them and we all went down to a precinct station by taxicab. The two frustrated birds of passage were not long in deciding that they did not care for the atmosphere of the police station and agreed to return with Thorpe and me to the hotel. There, with several big gridsters giving me silent support, I succeeded in convincing the treasurer that the time for settling accounts was at hand. I gave him a statement for the payroll and expenses of the players, and in return he endorsed the $3,750 check over to me, and we paid him the difference in cash.

After this adventure in football finance, I took over the Cleveland team and booked two more exhibition games—one on December 10 with the Richmond [Va.] Athletic Club and the other with the Washington [D.C.] All-Stars. We took a rather pleasing dividend out of these two ventures, and then disbanded. And that was my last active connection with professional football.

Many of the stories written about the great Jim Thorpe were pure fabrication.

One current in those days was that Thorpe bet $2,200 on one of our games with Massillon. This was pure fiction, because to my certain knowledge Jim never carried more than $200 during an

Canton Bulldogs, 1919. Left to right: Cecil Griggs, Pete Calac,
Jim Thorpe, Joe Guyon, Guy Chamberlain

Courtesy Pro Football Hall of Fame

entire season. At his own request, I kept all of his earnings until the end of each season and then gave him a check for the full amount, which he banked when he went back to Oklahoma. There was not one iota of truth, either, in that preposterous story that Thorpe made a standing offer to pay $1,000 to any team that could keep him from gaining ten yards in four downs. He simply wasn't the type to do a foolish thing like that.

There are those in professional football today who refuse to recognize the birth date of the game as having occured at any time and place in the years previous to 1920. They use the argument that the teams fielded in the first two decades of the century were not strictly "pro" because they recruited so many "amateur" college players and coaches who were eager to pick up a few dollars on the side by working for teams other than dear old alma mater. They contend that the professional organizations did not become "pro" in fact until that time in the Twenties when they made it a rule not to hire college stars until after they had graduated.

But there are old-timers around (including myself) who can look back on the exciting years of the 1910's and feel high satisfaction in having had a hand in dressing professional football in its swaddling clothes. Consider such giants of the game as Big Jim Thorpe, Doc Spears, Milton Ghee, Carp Julian, Bill Gardner, Pete Calac, Dr. Hube Wagner, Robert Butler, Howard "Cub" Buck, Greasy Neale, Fred Sefton, P. C. Crisp, Bill Garlow, Costello, and Soucy; if they were not real "professionals"—well, what were they?[2]

CHAPTER 13

Just Remember You're a Thorpe

Pity the poor Indian? Not Jim Thorpe! There is a certain stripe of writer who takes maudlin delight in weeping over once-great athletes who have fallen on supposedly darker days. They worked themselves into a tearful frenzy over Jack Dempsey's farcical "comeback" against a parade of unglamorous wrestlers. The land was filled with their weeping when Babe Ruth turned momentarily to "undignified" public appearances to make an honest buck.

—EDDIE ALLEN

On the sweltering afternoon of September 17, 1920, representatives from eleven professional football teams gathered in the showroom of Ralph Hay's automobile agency in Canton, Ohio. According to Chicago Bears owner George Halas, "He didn't have enough chairs to go around, so while we were sitting on the running boards of his cars, we formed the American Professional Football Association"[1] (later renamed the National Football League). The meeting lasted all of ten minutes. The eleven teams that signed up were Akron, Canton, Chicago (Cardinals), Cleveland, Dayton, Decatur Staleys (Chicago Bears), Hammond, Massillon, Muncie, Rochester, and Rock Island.

They wanted to appear sound and stable to the public, so they reported that each club had paid a one-hundred-dollar membership fee, which was not true. But more important, they announced their league officers. A. F. Ranney, sponsor of the Akron entry, was elected the secretary-treasurer; Stanley Cofall, coach of Massillon, was the vice-president; but the name that the owners wanted on the league's masthead as president was "Jim Thorpe."

Leo Lyons, then of the Rochester Jeffersons and currently

Thorpe with Ralph Hay, Canton Bulldogs manager, 1920

Courtesy Pro Football Hall of Fame

pro football's honorary historian, contends that the forerunner of the National Football League actually was started in July, 1919, instead of the generally accepted date of September, 1920. He states:

> We met in Hay's automobile showroom on McKinley Avenue. The representatives and their teams were Jim Thorpe and Ralph Hay, Canton Bulldogs; Frank Neid, Akron Pros; Joe Carr, Columbus Panhandles; Carl Stork, Dayton Triangles; and I was with the Jeffs.
>
> Each team put up twenty-five dollars for the league franchise and Thorpe was elected the unsalaried president of the American Football Association.[2]

In either case, professional football was becoming a big-time sport. The year 1920 also marked the popularization of a novel idea—the charity game, or, to be more specific, "the forerunner of the present East-West game."[3] Sponsored by Ohio State University to raise funds for the underprivileged of Columbus, the event, which matched former college stars against O.S.U. alumni greats, attracted

> a pageant of heroes. Among those present were Jim Thorpe, famous Sac and Fox warrior. An evidence of the splendid spirit which brought athletes from all parts of the country came to light in one incident. When Thorpe was asked following the game as to his expense account, the famous Indian replied that he would accept no money. "I came here to aid a worthy cause and my expenses were too small to mention. I was particularly glad to come and next year if I am in this part of the country, I will return for your game."[4]

After the financially turbulent year with Cleveland (1921), Jim played briefly with Canton once more and then with the Toledo Maroons. Art Rooney described his encounter with Jim:

> My memory is strong of one game I remember playing against Thorpe. The reason:
>
> My attempted field goal was blocked and he picked it up and ran for a touchdown. The score was Canton Bulldogs, 6; Hope Harveys, 0. The Harveys were a top semi-pro team in the district, manned by some of the best names from the schools in our area. Pittsburgh

186

was and is great football country and then it had some tremendous teams—Pitt, Carnegie Tech, Washington & Jefferson, and Geneva, just to name a few. Our semi-pro teams signed the top players from these schools.[5]

Remembering that touchdown run, Carp Julian, one of Jim's great Canton backfield mates, remarked:

You'd dive at him and hit him and after a time, when you came to, you'd wonder if the roof had fallen in. He'd run down the field and in his wake you'd see a string of prostrate football players. He seemed to run with his knees up to his chin, and no one wanted any of that. If you went for him from the side, he'd bump you into next week with the swerve of a hip. He was like an oak tree doing a hundred yards in 10 seconds.[6]

Carp's thoughts went back to his personal favorite Thorpe feat:

Late in his career, he encountered an opposing tackle who played dirty and ignored Jim's slow motion warnings to stop it. The next time he tried a dirty trick, Jim stopped dead, put the ball down and looked at the tackle. The tackle dived for the ball. He picked it up. That put the shoe on the other foot. Jim tackled him so hard it shook the earth. "You must not do that to Jim," Thorpe admonished. But the tackle never heard. He was out cold.[7]

Steve Owen, former coach of the New York Football Giants, recalled that Jim brought him his first "contract" with pro football:

By contact I mean contact. Thorpe played with the Toledo Maroons, one of the colorful early teams of the game, in 1922. Old Jim played wingback at right half and I played left tackle. The day before in Tulsa, I had been overawed by the great man. I used my hands very gently on Mr. Thorpe and took my time going in. Jim didn't pay much attention to me and didn't try to block very hard.

The next day I figured Thorpe was getting old and didn't care, so I decided to hike in there real fast and ignore old Jim. I lined up and took off. First thing I knew I was on my back on the ground, with the wind knocked out of me. Thorpe had hit me, and the ball carrier had gained about fifteen yards through my position. The Indian had showed me a real professional mousetrap.

187

Thorpe
with New York
Football Giants,
c. 1925

Courtesy James C.
Heartwell

Thorpe hauled me to my feet and advised: "Son, never take your eyes off the wingback, because he can hit you from the blindside something awful."[8]

Before the year was over, Jim undertook a new venture, the formation of an all-Indian team. Walter Lingo, owner of the Oorang Airedale Kennels in La Rue, Ohio, agreed to sponsor the team, and "Jim Thorpe's Oorang Indians" became a team.

Indians came from all corners of the country to try out. Most of the great ones, however, were Carlisle graduates. The starting lineup had Ed Nason and Little Twig, ends; Bill Newashe and Long Time Sleep, tackles; Busch and Hill, guards; Saint Germaine, center; Red Fox (MacLemore), quarterback; Thorpe and Guyon, halfbacks; and Calac, fullback. Thorpe, Calac, Busch, and Guyon had been captains at Carlisle.

Most of the players were older than Jim, since Carlisle had closed down in 1917, thereby shutting off the flow of trained talent from there. Therefore, it was agreed to play just the one season. As things turned out, the team quickly became professional football's number-one draw.

In an infinite number of articles, Jim has been described as being disdainful toward training and just plain lazy. "Jim was not lazy," Patricia Thorpe related. "He was relaxed. How a man can play professional baseball during the spring and summer, professional football during the fall and winter and go coon hunting the rest of the year, and be called lazy is beyond comprehension."[9]

The Indians played one more year (1923), and Jim was an ancient thirty-five. The "experts" were beginning to write his obituary, but they were six years off. He had kept himself in perfect condition, and as Lingo, elaborating on Patricia's observations, wrote that same year:

He is an ardent sportsman and his activities keep him in the open at all times and call for a great deal of strenuous exercise. One of the secrets of his great lasting powers is the fact that he never quits training. Playing baseball in the summer, football in the fall and the intervening months in hunting, his body is in the pink of physical condition at all times.

190

Thorpe with team backers Archie Bowley and
James D. Bruner, Sr., 1924

Courtesy Pro Football Hall of Fame

Jim Thorpe is not only a great athlete, but he looks the part. He is six feet tall and his weight of two hundred pounds does not include a single ounce of fat or surplus flesh. His muscular development is beautifully smooth. He combines in his perfect type the best attributes of the sprinter and strong man. In point of disposition no man is possessed of more qualities that endear him to his friends; he is never quarrelsome, but when aroused shows an aggressive spirit that neither obstacles nor pain can conquer. He is the real fighting type of man when occasion demands, but at all other times is both gentle and kind. He is modest, laconic, and stoical. His greatest virtue is his love of honesty and his hatred of untruthfulness or deception.[10]

The following year Lingo said:

He still has his speed, action, quick eye, and coordination of mind and body. Recent medical examination and physical tests have disclosed the fact that this phenomenal man Thorpe has lost but little of the vitality, strength, action, and speed of his youth. His remarkable physique and constitution unimpaired by the workings of Father Time still baffles all theories of the medical world.[11]

After playing for the Rock Island Independents (1924), New York Giants and Rock Island (1925), St. Petersburg (1926), Canton (1927), Portsmouth (1928), and Hammond and Chicago (Cardinals, 1929), he had reached the end of the line. He was forty-one years old when he hung up his cleats for the last time.

Toward the end of his career, Jim paid a visit to "Pop" Warner, who was then coaching at Pitt. Ross Porter, the personable general manager and editor of the *Shawnee News Star,* remembered:

One afternoon, during a football scrimmage, we looked up and saw this fellow wearing a dark suit come through the gates. He walked with a swagger. We asked "Pop" who he was, to which he replied: "Boys, he's the best damn football player who ever lived! I want you to meet Jim Thorpe." With this we reared back with excitement.

Then "Pop" said: "Jim, just for old time's sake, show these boys how you can drop-kick. Here we are on the 50-yard line; take your coat off and go ahead and kick one." Jim said that he didn't have his

192

football shoes on but "Pop" insisted. So Jim drop-kicked the ball straight through the uprights 50 yards away.

Several years later, I met him again in Shawnee while I was doing some sports broadcasting and he would do the commentary.

One evening, when I was no longer announcing, my son, Ross, Jr., who was eight at the time, and I were sitting in the stands watching a game and Jim came up to sit with us. I introduced them and explained to my young son who Jim was and to this very day, Ross, who is sports coordinator for KNBC in Los Angeles, remembers his meeting with Jim Thorpe as his greatest sports thrill.[12]

Seldom in the annals of athletics has a man survived so long in such a demanding sport. He had withstood nineteen years of brutal bodily contact in organized collegiate and professional football. It is regrettable that Jim was far past his peak as a player when professional football was extended out of the general confines of its original hotbed, the state of Ohio.

When the depression came, Jim was hard put to earn a living. Just as Black Hawk had discovered nearly a century before, he realized that fame was fleeting.

Iva had presented him with three beautiful daughters, Gail, Charlotte, and Grace. Although he dearly loved the girls, he had secretly longed for another son. But by this time, irreparable damage had been done to the good marriage. "After my brother, Jim, Jr., died," wrote Charlotte, "Dad and Mother began the estrangement that eventually ended in their divorce."[13] Iva had been able to give encouragement through the difficult years following the Olympic exposé, but she was not able to reach him this time.

On October 23, 1925, two years after his separation from Iva, he married Freeda Kirkpatrick, a Galion, Ohio, girl. Four sons, Carl Phillip, William, Richard, and John, were born to this couple, and the domestic side of Jim's life appeared to be secure.

In the meantime, he experienced the struggle for survival. There was no obstacle in the world of sports that he had not been able to overcome, but of the dollar-oriented society he had little understanding.

Thrust into the maelstrom of modern earning and spending, Jim, the uninitiated Indian, was lost. After his request to the A.A.U. for reinstatement as an amateur was denied, he went to Hollywood, where he sold the motion-picture rights to his life story, a valuable piece of property, to MGM for the sum of fifteen hundred dollars—a pittance. The proposed film, *Red Son of Carlisle,* was never made.

Shortly after his arrival in California, sportswriter Art Cohn met with him and penned the following article:

There he was—a powerful giant, 210 pounds of All-Time All-American—watching the shuffling feet of several worn and weary couples as they fought themselves through the dance marathon. For Jim Thorpe, you know, is referee of this latest madness!

Thorpe, although close to or at the forty-fifth milestone, has kept in exceptional condition. He played professional football only a year ago, and had had a notion to go into training again this season. The old competitive urge is still his and if it is nothing more than to officiate a marathon dance, he wants to be in on the show.

For the most part, he sits alone in a sequestered corner of the big tent. Perhaps thinking of the days that were—when he booted four field goals against Harvard, when he won highest laurels at the 1912 Olympics, when Walter Camp made him All-American—and when he was stripped of his honors. Pleasant memories and bitter ones. He is like a restless pilgrim, never remaining long in any one place.[14]

It was now January, 1930, and Jim signed up as the master of ceremonies with Charlie C. ("Cash and Carry") Pyle's "Bunion Derby," an international cross-country marathon race. When the show went bankrupt, Jim was forced to sue Pyle for his fifty-dollar paycheck. In February, Jim was employed as a painter for a Los Angeles oil firm. "No one knew me," he commented, "and I was lost in the oblivion of paint buckets and brushes while I painted filling stations and trucks."[15]

That job ended in October and he went to Universal Studios, where he succeeded in landing a bit part, playing Chief Black Crow. MGM hired him for a baseball film and later came a football picture with his old coach, "Pop" Warner.

194

With the depression increasing in intensity day by day, Jim began work as a laborer on the excavation for the new Los Angeles County Hospital. Earning fifty cents an hour, he said: "It's a long trail and a hard one, but I'm still carrying the ball."[16]

The 1932 Olympics were held in Los Angeles, and the greatest Olympian of them all was too poor to afford the luxury of a ticket. When the story reached the press, letters poured in from all over the country offering Jim a seat for the games.

Charles Curtis, the Vice-President of the United States and the man who would officially proclaim the games open said: "Jim Thorpe will sit with me."[17] Curtis was an American Indian.

The capacity crowd of 105,000 gave Jim a standing ovation when he took his seat, but the show of affection was all too brief. *Jim Thorpe's History of the Olympics,* written by T. F. Collison, that year, did not sell many copies, and Jim went back to minor roles in western "B" films. In August of the following year, he was working for Warner–First National in *Telegraph Trail.*

On December 6, 1934, Jim spoke before the student body of Poly High School. His concluding remark was: "Athletics give you a fighting spirit to battle your problems of life, and they build sportsmanship."[18] Jim was certainly a living example of that. Speaking engagements were more frequent now, but since he never had the heart to ask the schools or clubs who were "honoring" him for money, he had to work even harder to pay for all of these new traveling expenses.

Said Slim Harrison, owner of the Bank Cafe in San Pedro,

I had the pleasure and honor of knowing Jim Thorpe and associating with him for the last twenty years of his life. In my opinion, the only fault he had was that his heart was too big for him. He never failed to accommodate a friend. Any money-raising charitable event that came along, if a request went to Jim to put in an appearance, he was never too busy. He would devote his time to that and he enjoyed it.[19]

As the motion-picture industry began to rise from the depths of the depression, Jim was able to work more frequently. At the same time, his roles began to increase in significance. He was also able to recruit other Indians for movie work. During the spring of 1935 he was playing a major part opposite Helen Gahagen in *She*. The following year he had another "good role," according to columnist Edith Gwynn, in the Errol Flynn picture called *The Green Light*.[20] Later he worked for R.K.O. in *You Can't Take It With You*.

By the end of 1937 Jim had returned to his native state of Oklahoma to become active in current issues involving Indians. He urged his own tribe, the Sac and Fox, to vote to abolish the United States Bureau of Indian Affairs and repeal the legislation granting the federal government control of Indian property. He said:

The Indian should be permitted to grow out of his tribal bonds into representative American citizenship. He should not be forced into communistic cooperatives fostered under the Thomas-Rogers Act. Instead, the 6,000 now employed in political jobs administering Indian affairs should be dismissed and the Indians should begin management of their own business.

Governmental paternalism has failed in all aspects, even in the alphabetical agencies of the New Deal. The administrators, all the way from John Collier, commissioner of Indian Affairs, to agents and reservation superintendents, have built up a perpetual guardianship. The Indian should be permitted to shed his inferiority complex and live like a normal American citizen.[21]

In place of the Thomas-Rogers Act, he requested the passage of the Wheeler Bill which would not only repeal the former but also provide for a corporation, composed of 460 tribe members, which would "do what the Indian bureau has failed to do—instruct the Indian to exercise his citizenship."[22] However, Jim lost another battle, by a House vote of 202 to 120, and, in his opinion, the Indian was returned "to the blanket."[23]

The year 1938 found Jim in Idaho working for MGM on

Jim Thorpe holding his Indian outfit, 1935

Courtesy Pro Football Hall of Fame

Northwest Passage. According to Frank Scully and Norman Sper:

Some college athletes were in the picture and they were jumping around between takes, placing bets on their skill in the standing broad jump. They got up to ten feet.

Bill Frawley [who later played the "Fred Mertz" role in "I Love Lucy"], an actor, learned from the director that the stage Indian was Jim Thorpe. Frawley decided to cook up a surprise. He told the crowd that he had an old man of 50 who he thought could beat the college athletes. Bets climbed until Frawley had to cover a pool of $100 before the books closed.

Jim took off his feathers, left on the moccasins. He flexed his leg muscles three times and jumped—10 feet 8 inches. That's only six inches behind the world's record.[24]

When the picture was completed, Jim returned to his small, ivy-covered cottage at 3904 One Hundred and Fourth Street in Inglewood, California. But his name was destined to be brought out of oblivion once more when Knute Rockne, Grantland Rice, and Fielding Harris "Hurry Up" Yost, the great Michigan coach, published their respective "all-time All-Americans." Thorpe, Grange, Gipp, and Pfann were Rockne's backfield choices. Thorpe, Grange, Strong, and Nevers were Rice's. Yost's were Thorpe, Eckersall, Heston, and Oliphant. Although his backfield mates had differed in each instance, one name remained constant, Thorpe. Only one "all-time" team failed to carry Jim's name that year, and that was the one which Jim picked himself. Modestly omitting his own name from the list, he selected Mahan, Eckersall, Grange, and Coy; with Mahan listed as his personal favorite. Georgia's Charlie Trippi was his number one player of the modern era.

The resultant publicity brought reporters to his door. Allan Dale wrote: The finest all-around athlete the world has known said, "Come in."

A quarter of a century has passed Jim by since his glorious presentation to King Gustav of Sweden, and the march of time has done things to the rugged redskin who was a veritable Red Grange,

Joe DiMaggio, Jesse Owens, and Glenn Cunningham molded in one human frame.

At 52 he's lecturing for a living. Extra work in the movies helps feed four Jim Thorpes in miniature. Four husky, fast-growing boys.

Phillip, 13; Billie, 11; and Dickie, 7 (Jim thought Dick was 6 until his pretty wife rushed in from the kitchen to correct his mathematics), all attend Jefferson School in Lennox.

Jackie, 2 going on 3, fiddles around at home.

Each youth has the famous Jim Thorpe physique, in the bud. Wide-shouldered, slim-hipped, lithe, fast of foot, they'll be perfect athletic specimens if they grow up that way. And they probably will.[25]

Wallace X. Rawles reported: "There is a wife, a sparkling-eyed beauty, and four little papooses."

"I call 'em the 'four little horsemen' in honor of the players on one of Knute Rockne's great football teams at Notre Dame," said Thorpe. "Knute was a great friend of mine.

"I saw him personally put into practice the motto with which he was to take in later years, his Notre Dame teams to the pinnacle of football. That motto, expressed shortly before his death in an airplane accident over Kansas, was: 'Only one side can win. There isn't room at the top for everyone. Don't be overambitious. Merely do the best you can.'

"I've quoted those words of Rockne to my four sons a hundred times. I want their lives, their acts, to be bound by those sage remarks."[26]

The W. Colston Leigh Bureau, a small booking organization, and later the Circus Saints and Sinners in New York got in touch with Jim and sent him on a country-wide lecture tour. Dressed in an Indian costume, he gave a talk consisting of four subjects: an analysis of the current sports season, the story of his career, an inspirational talk on the significance of sports in modern life, and a commentary on Indian culture and traditions. He appeared before hundreds of school assemblies, traveling thousands of miles with two of his hunting dogs in the back seat of his old jalopy. He was clearly out of his element, but he had to earn a living, and

Jim Thorpe's family. Left to right: Jack, Grace, William, Gail, Carl, Charlotte, and Richard

Courtesy Beth and Homer Ray

so he struggled on. He was in demand once more and had four scheduled lectures each week.

One of his stops on the circuit was Basom, New York, where he was able to visit with old Indian friends. One of them, Mrs. Harrison Ground, Carlisle Class of 1912, smiled broadly when reminded of the day:

> He gave a wonderful speech. A tremendous crowd turned out to see him; those that had attended school with him along with the children who had heard so much about him. And he loved to see and talk to all of them.
>
> Was he ever jolly! He had small eyes and when he smiled you couldn't see them at all.
>
> I was at Carlisle for nine years—it was really just like home to me. I got to know Jim quite well and always thought a lot of him.[27]

From California, he received news that would send him into further misery. On April 4, 1941, Freeda, his wife of fifteen years, was suing for divorce. Embedded deeply in his Indian heritage was the tendency to spend long periods of time away from home. Furthermore, there was not a great emphasis on a close day-to-day family life. Grace Thorpe agreed:

> Dad used to take off for two or three weeks. She wouldn't know where he was. Nothing. He did the same thing with my mother. It goes back to the old days when the men used to do that. They would go off and hunt buffalo. That was just the Indian way of doing it. White women don't understand.[28]

Jim was guilty of negligence by the law, but he was unable to fully comprehend it, and his heart was broken again. The next four years were to be the darkest ones of his entire life. "I cannot decide," he said, "whether I was well named or not. Many a time the path has gleamed bright for me, but just as often it has been dark and bitter indeed."[29] But the speaking engagements continued, and his personal appearances were more in demand than ever. Before the letter from Freeda, there had been, to name just a few, lectures in Annapolis, October 5, 1940; Baltimore, October 6–8; Troy,

With "Major Oorang" airedale, 1927

Courtesy Maxine and Robert Lingo

New York, October 23; Rochester, New York, November 26; Phillipsburg, Pennsylvania, December 13; Newark, New Jersey, February 9, 1941; Springfield, Massachusetts, March 14; and Waterbury, Connecticut, March 16. At times, he was averaging three lectures a day.

Jim was becoming a good speaker by now. He was getting a great deal of practice and was touching on subjects that he sincerely believed in. The following is a reconstruction of the typical format of a Jim Thorpe lecture.

Yielding to the demands of the audience, he would begin the program by relating the highlights of his career. And when asked about his own technique for downing Mercer, Pazzetti, or Steffen, he would laugh with a wink, and say:

I was just big and strong and tough and still am. I hated to retire from the game. I was never out of training. When the football season began, I was in as good a shape as at the end of it. Many players stop exercising in the summer, then come out and work off their fat and harden up their muscles and prepare for the game in a few weeks. Almost all of the injuries on the gridiron come early in the season, before the men are hardened.

Kicking has become a lost art. In my day, we had any number of backs who could boot field goals. To be good you've got to keep your eyes on the ball all the time. Get your direction first and then when you are ready to kick, never look up. Nine times out of ten the ball will go exactly where you desired.

In order to punt the spiral with accuracy, the ball should be held as far away from the body as possible, directly in front of the kicking foot, with one hand on each side of it and the outer point of the ball slightly lower than the end nearest the body, at the same time taking a short step with the other foot, drop the ball so that it falls without turning and meet it with the instep of the kicking foot about two and one-half feet from the ground. The foot should be extended and the leg should swing mostly from the hip and but little at the knee. The punt should be followed through with the leg as far as possible with the body bent backward so as to get the full weight into the kick.

An important fact to remember in catching punts is to watch the ball every instant and be in the proper position to receive it by seeing the direction toward which its lower end is pointing while descending. When the spiral descends with its forward end nearest the ground, the ball will carry much further than it will when it descends with its back end inclined downward.

The punt having been caught, the best plan is to shoot straight ahead. Dodging back and forth looks pretty, and eluding several tacklers may create a little enthusiasm among the spectators who know little about the game, but the opposing forces are gathering all the time, and such tactics usually result in no gain or a loss.

But there is something else on my mind. I came from the Sac and Fox tribe in Oklahoma, and I have never forgotten that I am an Indian. No Indian can forget it.

Indians, you know, are misnamed. We aren't Indians. We are Red Men and we settled this country long before the white people ever came to these shores. Why then should we be deprived of citizenship until we can qualify through a written examination? None of you here is a government ward. You are citizens because that heritage has been passed on to you. But Red Men are wards of the government.

There were 30,000 Indian volunteers in the last war. They fought for this country. Many gave their lives for its people and its resources. In return, the Indians should be granted full citizenship, with all the rights and privileges that go with it. Eighty-five per cent of them are literate and qualified for the privilege.

Years ago, the Indians were made wards of the government. Yet their reservations are taken away from them if the government wants the land.

I have four sons who want to be loyal American citizens. So that's what I'm working for, that and better athletic training for all American youth.

I would like to ask every one of you here to work for the improvement of Indian conditions. They can be bettered with your help. Perhaps some day another Abraham Lincoln will come along to free the Red Men of this country.[30]

This lecture was heard by Ray Witter, former Syracuse, Alfred, and Rochester Jefferson football star. Said Ray:

Jim was speaking at Fredonia State Teachers College in the fall of 1941, just before Pearl Harbor. His appearance was very greatly in his favor because he was big and well built. He had a good voice,

Jim Thorpe, lecturer, 1941

Courtesy Pro Football Hall of Fame

a good usage of the English language and was friendly in his attitude.

We had a very pleasant visit going over our old pro football games and the days of auld lang syne. I never forgot my football years and always look forward to seeing the boys with whom I played. Some of them of course, have gone to their glory by now.

The first time we played the Canton Bulldogs, we were awfully curious to see what the famous Thorpe looked like; and let me tell you, he looked tough!

I was playing offensive and defensive end that day and right away, he came toward my position. He was running an end sweep. I was able to drive him out of bounds and as we fell, my knee went into a water bucket and was twisted rather badly.

At any rate, they beat our club because we didn't have the offense they did by any means. That man Thorpe was powerful! Practically every time he ran with the ball, he made a gain of 5, 10, or 20 yards and on the other occasions he went over for a touchdown. And I'll say this much, he was just as great defensively as offensively.

Yes, the old knee still bothers me on occasion. I guess I've had water on the knee ever since that day. And that visit was the last time I ever saw Jim because, four months later, I left for World War II.[31]

With the war in progress, Jimmy Corcoran tried to find out what was on the Indian's mind!

"I want to get into this war somehow, but they tell me in Washington that there isn't any room for old guys like me. I believe I could help the boys in the Army, the Marines, and Navy a lot— y'know, just by going around from camp to camp and saying a little something. Maybe they'd get a kick out of listening to some little things I had to say."

He wasn't a hulk—but just a tremendous figure of manhood. He asked:

"If Gene Tunney can get into the service, why can't I?"

Then he mused:

"Well, I guess it's because I'm older."

Jim went through calisthenics. He bounced up and down on his knees a few times. He asked:

"Do you think that I'm in good shape?"

206

Jim Thorpe, unquestionably the greatest athlete of all time, certainly was. He picked up a chair and handled it like a boy would juggle a toy.

"Wonder why age makes so much difference in this war. We'll all have to be in there and doing something. I still can shoot straight."[32]

And there was a Marine unit that could have used him. Before their landing in the Guam invasion, the boys aboard an LST took a poll to determine the world's greatest athlete. Jim McCulley of the *New York Daily News* tells the story:

Though the Indian's athletic heyday took place long before most of these marines were born, they had no doubts regarding his prowess. One put it this way: "If Jim was half as good as my Dad said he was, he would be able to broad jump from our LST over the reef to Guam. He'd pick up a bushel of hand grenades and throw them like a football 80 or 90 yards. If any pillboxes barred his path, he would vault over them. And whatever Japanese he could find, he would dropkick into the ocean."[33]

Harry Bennett, Henry Ford I's right-hand man, heard of Jim's desire to do war work and brought him to Ford's River Rouge plant in Dearborn, Michigan. Working with plant security, Jim was in good company. Since Bennett had an affinity toward athletes, the entire staff was comprised of boxers, baseball players, and, at one time, the entire University of Michigan football team, including head coach Harry Kipke.

Jim was grateful for the opportunity to remain in one spot for awhile. During the previous year, he had covered sixty-seven thousand miles on his lecture tour! He began work on March 20, 1942, and was apparently in good health, but eleven months later he suffered his first heart attack.

Again, as during the 1932 Olympics, he was besieged with letters. One came from the Oklahoma legislature appraising him of their resolution introduced by two Indian representatives, that the A.A.U. be petitioned to reinstate his Olympic records. The Union took no action.

But most of the letters were from young boys and girls, children who knew about him only through their fathers' reminiscences. His favorite, and one that he kept until his death, was printed by Braven Dyer. It reads as follows:

"Dear Mr. Thorpe:

I was eating supper tonight when over the radio Bill Stern said something about America's greatest athlete. I knew right away he was talking about you. He said this athlete was sick. Then he said it was you.

He said you had a heart attack. I went right to my desk and started writing you this letter. Mr. Thorpe, he said that Knute Rockne once said that you couldn't be stopped, but that now you were almost stopped. You can't die, Mr. Thorpe! You will always live in my memory.

I have never seen you perform, but I have heard so much about you that I have begun to like you very much. I am only a boy of 15, but I like sports, and I like to play them. As one sports lover to another, please, Mr. Thorpe get well.

If you get well sports will mean more to me and millions of other American boys like me to know that a true sportsman can pull through anything, that they have guts enough to face death in the face and defeat death.

So, Mr. Thorpe, *please, please* get well soon.

> Yours truly,
> Ben Templeton
> Raleigh, N.C.

P.S. I know that you have never heard of me and don't know me, but I know you are the greatest sportsman that ever lived."[34]

Jim's great heart did not give up. He gradually recovered and decided to take a vacation in Oklahoma. He formally resigned on November 29, 1943, with a "first-class work record."[35]

He wrote to Lon Scott, in Tulsa, in an effort to gain admittance for his four sons to the Indian schools. According to Scott,

Executives of the Indian Agency at Shawnee made arrangements quickly and I advised Jim to bring the boys down. Some Detroit Sports Writers put up travel expenses and one afternoon an old Ford coupe showed up with Jim and his four handsome lads packed in like sardines. We quickly put Phil and Bill in the Indian school at Chilocco and the two little ones at Pawnee. A couple of years later I became Phil's guardian so he could enter the U.S. Navy and soon after that the other boys returned to their mother in California.[36]

In the interim, another "eternal" All-American team was announced, this time by Clark Shaughnessy. He chose Thorpe, Clark, Grange, and Gipp for his backfield. "Jim Thorpe," he said, "played football at Carlisle like a man playing among boys."[37]

On June 2, 1945, Jim married Patricia Gladys Askew, a native of Louisville, Kentucky. She had been an admirer of his since his professional football days. Jim's life, from this time forward, began to proceed on an altogether different timetable. Patricia, a sincere and forceful businesswoman, credited Dorothy Kilgallen with suggesting that Jim place adequate fees on his engagements. After this, the charge was $500 plus expenses.

It was now late in World War II, and the dream of actively defending his country had all but vanished when he was unexpectedly accepted for duty by the Merchant Marines. He was immediately assigned to the U.S.S. *Southwest Victory,* which embarked for the battle fronts of India carrying ammunition to the American and British troops stationed there. He served anonymously as the ship's carpenter.

When they landed in Calcutta, however, Jim was asked to appear before the G.I.'s. He readily obliged. The official Armed Forces newspaper, *Special Service,* of August 4, printed the story:

Upon reaching downtown Calcutta, "Big Jim" was greeted by Brig. General Robert R. Neyland, Commanding General of Base Section. Tales of olden times when Thorpe, then with Carlisle, played against General Neyland, who performed with West Point, were once more renewed during their chat. Another gridder to meet Thorpe was a former member of the Chicago Bear's eleven, Capt. Chester Chesney, Athletic officer at Base Section Special Service Office.

Visiting G.I. installations on a tour of the area included wards in the 142nd General Hospital, Base Section Special Service Office athletic installations, Rest Camp No. 1, Seamen's Club, ARC Burra Club and at Monsoon Square Garden, where he made a personal appearance and address at the opening of the India Burma Theater Invitational Volleyball Tournament. Also on Tuesday evening he graciously made a guest appearance on the Special Service Office Sports Parade heard over Station VU2ZU.[38]

Jim was "back in the game," and he was happier than he had been in two decades. "We had some rough weather and some rough times," said Jim, "but we had teamwork. Co-operation is important in everything you do and that is what made us winners.

"We also had some fun. In Calcutta, a lot of those Army fellows, like Bob Neyland, that I knew when they were at West Point, looked me up. The Captain of our ship couldn't figure it out. He was not able to understand why brigadier generals and people like that would be glad to see someone who was as far down in the ship as I was."[39]

Jim returned to America, to the port of Jersey City, on September 7, 1945, and was greeted by Mayor Frank Hague. From there is was more appearances, in places such as La Mesa, California, Rock Island, Illinois, and Canton. This time he had a constant companion, Patricia. By doubling as wife and manager, she was able to ensure that Jim would reap at least some of the rewards befitting a personality of his stature.

In March, 1946, Jim attended the St. Joseph's Sports Banquet in Buffalo. He was presented the key to the city by Mayor Bernard J. Dowd and was made an honorary lieutenant by Police Commissioner McMahon. As Jim was leaving, the elevator operator, noticing his badge, asked if he was a captain. "No," he answered, with a straight face. "I'm a member of the FBI, that is, full-blooded Indian."[40]

Jim's speech reiterated his philosophy regarding physical fitness. This time, as a result of his military service, he was able to present a valuable insight into that system. He strongly urged:

America must become health- and sports-minded. It is a national disgrace that during the war, only one out of every ten men examined was well enough to serve in the armed forces! The main reasons were faulty eyesight, unhealthy teeth, weak hearts, and poor feet.

We should have a boys' and girls' Olympics each year at some centrally located site. Sports will improve health and keep the children out of trouble. If they start young, and I'm talking about the girls, too, they will grow up to be healthy men and women and make a healthier nation. Our entire family, including my brothers, George and Eddie, sisters Mary and Adeline, and half-brother Frank and half-sister Minnie, all could ride and shoot. Our mother and father taught us.[41]

Although efforts by Mrs. Thorpe, the International Rotaries, and sportswriters across the country, including Jim Burchard, Bill Corum, Henry Clune, Al Stump, Grantland Rice, Dan Parker, Bill Stern, Arthur Daley, Maxwell Stiles, and Frank Graham, Jr., met with failure in the attempt to regain his trophies, Jim was in Chicago on January 29, 1947, helping to spur a drive to bring the 1952 Olympics to Chicago's Soldier's Field.

At the request of the Bloomington, Illinois, Kiwanis Club, Jim, on the evening of April 28, acted as "Historian of Athletics." He charmed everyone with a "twinkle in his eyes" and added a surprise when he told about his heretofore unknown basketball prowess, the highlight of his "career" being a two-point victory over the Quakers of Pennsylvania.[42] By July, Jim and Patricia were in South Carolina, where Jim was appearing at the Beachcombers Club on Charleston's Folly Beach and earning $500 a week.

In February, 1948, Jim wrote a letter to Attorney General Tom Clark expressing his concern about the juvenile delinquency problem and a possible solution or counter-measure. Jim spoke to columnist Vincent K. Flaherty about it:

His idea is of the nature of a national junior olympics which would take in the entire country and capture the interest of kids from, say 12 to 17 or 18.

Jim reasons that the project could be pushed into every little town and big city in the country. It could be coordinated with athletic programs in the nation's grammar schools. Jim thinks of it in terms of it being the talk of kids in every neighborhood everywhere. And properly promoted and exploited, such a program could easily reach into every American home.[43]

211

In an effort to personally make his idea into reality, Jim began work a month later as a member of the recreation staff of the Chicago Park District. He appeared at every field house in the city, promoting the Junior Olympics and teaching youngsters the fundamentals of track.

During Thorpe's employment in Chicago, Jim Burchard of the *New York Telegram* asked on July 21, if he would like his Olympic awards restored. He quickly answered in the affirmative and the following discussion transpired:

Sure! I played baseball in 1909 and 1910 in the Carolina League but I had no idea I was a pro. I got $60 a month for expenses and that's all. I wouldn't even have tried for the Olympic team had I thought I was a pro. If Warner had backed me up, I wouldn't have had to send back the trophies in the first place.

He [Brundage] could get those things back for me but so far, he just played shut-mouth. To give him a break, however, I think he's followed his convictions.[44]

The Olympic Committee did not respond, and another effort to regain the awards failed. Jim did hear from Prescott Sullivan of the *San Francisco Examiner* inviting him to the Golden Gate city to be honored, along with "Pop" Warner and Ernie Nevers, in a whirlwind weekend of testimonials.

Jim not only attended but put on a field-goal kicking exhibition between halves of the 49er-Colts game. Dressed in a football uniform, the sixty-year-old, showed "just enough to lend credulity to the oft-repeated assertion of many an old timer than Injin Jim was, in his day, the greatest of them all."[45]

Two evenings before, Jim ran into Jack McDonald, sports editor for the *San Francisco Call-Bulletin* at the Palace Hotel. The following is a result of that get-together:

Now crowding 61 Indian summers, his abundant hair is still coal black without even a tinge of gray and his arms and legs (he let us feel of 'em) are still remarkably hard.

Only two weeks ago he appeared in an old timer's baseball game at Wrigley Field in Chicago and belted a 384-foot home run off Urban Faber, the former Chicago White Sox spitballer.[46]

With Chicago Park District youngsters, 1948

Courtesy James C. Heartwell

Jim's next task was to prepare the Israel National Soccer Team for their international match against the United States Olympic Soccer Team at the Polo Grounds in New York on Sunday, September 26. This surprise commission was brought about at the insistence of the president of the Israel Football Foundation, Haim Glovinsky, who told reporters:

> I deem it an honor to appoint America's greatest athlete to train our team. Our country, when its troubles are over, will accent sports. We feel certain that Thorpe will bring our soccer team to the peak of condition for the game, and the people of Israel are happy to have Jim Thorpe as the trainer for their team.[47]

He spryly gave another drop-kicking exhibition between halves of the game and in ten tries from the 50-yard line, he sent the pigskin over the bar three times. He then punted twice from midfield, in opposite directions, achieving a distance of 70 yards on the first and 75 with the other.

Later that year, back in Los Angeles for the National Sports Award Dinner, Jim had the opportunity to meet the seventeen-year-old Decathlon champion, Bob Mathias. *Los Angeles Times* sportswriter, Jack Geyer, described what happened:

> I intercepted Thorpe on the way to his table and asked him if he'd mind posing for a picture with Mathias. "I'd like to meet that boy," Jim said, so we started for Bob's table. Bob saw Thorpe coming, got up and ran toward him with his hand outstretched, "I'm glad to know you, Mr. Thorpe. I've heard so much about you," Bob said. "I've heard a lot about you too," Jim answered. Then they shook hands and just beamed at each other for several seconds without saying anything.[48]

In August, 1949, Warner Brothers made the announcement for which Jim had been waiting a long time; work would begin on his movie biography. Although he no longer owned the rights, he was hired as a technical adviser for the film.

Another goal, for which he went on record in 1937, was his desire to see his Sac and Fox tribe secure remuneration

Drop kicking exhibition, Polo Grounds, 1948

Courtesy James C. Heartwell

for their original land holdings. Earl Eby of the *Philadelphia Evening Bulletin,* conducted the interview:

Jim Thorpe, the fabulous Carlisle Indian, is in town and his mind is not on athletics.

"I've never mentioned this to any other reporter," Jim said, "because most of them have always been interested in my athletic career. This claim, however, has been on my mind for years.

"Here's the story: In 1814, the government purchased 70,000 acres from my tribe, which was part of the land used in the famous 'Land Rush.' That money was deposited in a St. Louis bank for the Indians. The compound interest on that land now amounts to $456,760,000."

Thorpe reached into his pocket and pulled out sheaves of paper with figures on them to prove his point. He also showed letters from influential men in Washington, who are working with him.

"The land that was purchased from us has since yielded millions and millions of dollars in oil. Too bad we didn't hold on to it."

Thorpe, who weighed 183 when in his prime, is now 203. His eyes are bright, his appetite good, and his mind quick.[49]

Jim's effort on behalf of the Indians made headlines, to be sure, but they were overshadowed by those that soon followed, "Jim Thorpe Named as Greatest Gridder of Past Half Century."

New York, Jan. 24—Jim Thorpe, whom his Indian mother named Bright Path, is the greatest U.S. football player of this century in the opinion of [391] sportswriters and broadcasters who participated in the Associated Press' poll.[50]

Sports writer, Harold Claassen, printed the entire results:

Player	College	Votes
James Thorpe	Carlisle	170
Harold (Red) Grange	Illinois	138
Bronko Nagurski	Minnesota	38
Ernie Nevers	Stanford	7
Sammy Baugh	Texas Christian	7
Don Hutson	Alabama	6
George Gipp	Notre Dame	4
Charles Trippi	Georgia	3

Two votes each: Sid Luckman, Columbia; Steve Van Buren, Louisiana State; Willie Heston, Michigan; and Chick Harley, Ohio State.

One vote each: Bill Henry, Washington and Jefferson; Bennie Oosterbaan, Michigan; Nile Kinnick, Iowa; Glenn Dobbs, Tulsa; Glenn Davis, Army; Clyde Turner, Hardin Simmons; Doak Walker, Southern Methodist; Frank Albert, Stanford; Felix (Doc) Blanchard, Army; and Charles Brickley, Harvard.[51]

A little over two weeks later, the results of an even more prestigious poll were announced. On February 11 the headlines announced, "Jim Thorpe Selected as Best Male Athlete of Half Century. Babe Ruth Nabs Second Spot in 50-year Survey," and Gayle Talbot wrote:

Jim Thorpe, that almost legendary figure of the sports world, had additional laurels heaped upon his leathern brow today when the nation's sports experts named him the greatest male athlete of the half century.

Previously voted the No. 1 football player of the past 50 years, the wonderful Sac and Fox became the only double winner in the Associated Press poll when 252 out of 393 sports writers and radio broadcasters accorded him the ultimate honor.

The ballot:

Name	Points
1.—Jim Thorpe (252)	875
2.—Babe Ruth (86)	539
3.—Jack Dempsey (19)	246
4.—Ty Cobb (11)	148
5.—Bobby Jones (2)	88
6.—Joe Louis (5)	73
7.—Red Grange (3)	57
8.—Jesse Owens (0)	54
9.—Lou Gehrig (4)	34
10.—Bronko Nagurski (1)	26
11.—Jackie Robinson (2)	24
12.—Bob Mathias (0)	13
13.—Walter Johnson (1)	12
14.—Glenn Davis (0)	11
15.—Bill Tilden (0)	9

16.—Glenn Cunningham (0)	8
17.—Glenn Morris (0)	8
18.—Cornelius Warmerdam (1)	7

Others: Joe DiMaggio, Charlie Trippi, John Kelly, Paavo Nurmi, Ernie Nevers, George Gipp, Stan Musial, J. Howard Berry, Gene Tunney, Johnny Weissmuller, Clarence Herschberger, Duke Kahanamoku, Paul Robeson, John Wooden, Les Patrick, Mickey Cochrane, Dr. Dave Freeman, Ben Hogan, Bennie Oosterbaan, Rogers Hornsby, Frank Gotch, Sammy Baugh, Willie Hoppe, Ernest Torrance, Byron Nelson, Sidney Franklin, Rube Waddell, Clarence Demar, Torgel Tokle, Carl Hubbell, Ted Williams, Honus Wagner, Barney Berlinger, Henry Armstrong, Joe Fulks, Christy Mathewson, Sam Snead, and Otto Graham.[52]

In rapid-fire succession, word came of another honor, election to the Helms Hall Professional Football Hall of Fame (he was already a member of their College Football Hall of Fame).[53]

Caught up in the world-wide trend to pick the outstanding athletes of the century, sportswriters on the staff of *El Universal,* the daily Caracas, Venezuela, newspaper published the results of their own fascinating poll of South Americans:

	Puntos
1.—Jim Thorpe (Atletismo)	410
2.—Babe Ruth (Beisbol)	399
3.—Jesse Owens (Atletismo)	221
4.—Jack Dempsey (Boxeo)	200
5.—Joe Louis (Boxeo)	187
6.—Bill Tilden (Tennis)	159
7.—Johnny Weissmuller (Natacion)	130
8.—Bobby Jones (Golf)	95
9.—Juan M. Fangio (Automovilismo)	95
10.—Fausto Coppi (Ciclismo)	86
11.—Ty Cobb (Beisbol)	81
12.—Ray "Sugar" Robinson (Boxeo)	72
13.—Alfredo Di Stefano (Futbol)	65
14.—Manuel Rodriguez "Manolete" (Toros)	51
15.—Jackie Robinson (Beisbol)	47
16.—Paavo Nurmi (Atletismo)	45
17.—Babe Zaharias (Golf)	39

18. —	Juan Belmonte (Toros)	32
19. —	Adolfo Pedernera (Futbol)	28
19. —	Bob Mathias (Atletismo)	28
21. —	Alejandro Alekhine (Ajedrez)	25
22. —	Emil Zatopek (Atletismo)	24
22. —	Jose Raul Capablanca (Ajedrez)	24
24. —	Eddie Arcaro (Hipismo)	22
25. —	Ireneo Leguisamo (Hipismo)	21
26. —	Lou Gehrig (Beisbol)	16
26. —	Ricardo Zamora (Futbol)	16
28. —	Roger Bannister (Atletismo)	15
28. —	Henry Armstrong (Boxeo)	15
30. —	Valery Brumel (Atletismo)	13
30. —	Pancho Gonzalez (Tennis)	13
32. —	Suzanne Lenglen (Tennis)	12
32. —	Willie Hoppe (Billar)	12
32. —	Red Grange (Rugby)	12
32. —	Joselito (Toros)	12
36. —	Leroy Satchel Paige (Beisbol)	10
36. —	Christy Mathewson (Beisbol)	10
36. —	Donald Budge (Tennis)	10
36. —	Walter Johnson (Beisbol)	10
40. —	Armin Hary (Atletismo)	9
40. —	Gene Tunney (Boxeo)	9
40. —	Goss Duke (Automovilismo)	9
40. —	Ted Williams (Beisbol)	9
40. —	Rafer Johnson (Atletismo)	9
45. —	Stanley Mathews (Futbol)	8
45. —	Donald Campbell (Automovilismo)	8
45. —	Charles Lindbergh (Aviacion)	8
45. —	Jack Johnson (Boxeo)	8
45. —	Tazio Nuvolari (Automovilismo)	8
45. —	Jimmy Foxx (Beisbol)	8
45. —	Benny Leonard (Boxeo)	8
52. —	Joshua Gibson (Beisbol)	7
52. —	Ben Hogan (Golf)	7
52. —	Lefty Grove (Beisbol)	7
55. —	Goose Tatum (Basket Ball)	6
55. —	Earl Sande (Hipismo)	6
55. —	Alain Gerbault (Rugby)	6
55. —	Bill Spivey (Basket Ball)	6

55.—Cy Young (Beisbol)	6
55.—Erdoza Menor (Jai Alai)	6
55.—Carl Hubbell (Beisbol)	6
62.—Bob Fitzsimmons (Boxeo)	5
62.—Pele (Futbol)	5
62.—Helen Wills (Tennis)	5
65.—Gertrude Ederle (Natacion)	4
65.—Johnny Longden (Hipismo)	4
65.—Jim Londos (Lucha)	4
65.—Alberto Albertondo (Natacion)	4
65.—Pancho Segura Cano (Tennis)	4
65.—Humberto Mariles (Ecuestres)	4
65.—Joe DiMaggio (Beisbol)	4
72.—Ranhild Hvegerz (Beisbol)	3
72.—Aldo Nadi (Esgrima)	3
72.—Kid Chocolate (Boxeo)	3
72.—Max Schmelling (Boxeo)	3
72.—Stanley Ketchel (Boxeo)	3
72.—Harry Greb (Boxeo)	3
78.—George Mikan (Basket Ball)	2
78.—Bill Russell (Basket Ball)	2
78.—Sonja Henie (Patin)	2
78.—Edmund Hillary (Rugby)	2
82.—Althea Gibson (Tennis)	1
82.—Roger Maris (Beisbol)	1
82.—Nat Holman (Basket Ball)	1
82.—Rodney (Rugby)	1
82.—Miguel Najdorf (Ajedrez)	1
82.—El Gallo (Toros)	1
82.—Gene Sarazen (Golf)	1[54]

As a result of all this recognition, requests for his appearance at dinners and testimonials came from every state in the union and many foreign countries.

Jim's first stopover was Pennsylvania where he rode the "shuttle" between Carlisle and Harrisburg for a week of festivities. At the Harrisburg Sportswriters Association banquet:

When the genial giant was introduced, the assembly rose and shook the ballroom for five full minutes with their tribute to the finest athlete the country has ever known.

Dedication of tablet monument at Carlisle, 1951. Left to right:
Carl Phillip (Thorpe's son), Jim Thorpe, actress Phyllis Thaxter,
who played Jim's wife in the movie, *Jim Thorpe—All American*,
Governor Fine of Pennsylvania, and General Trudeau
(commandant of Carlisle Barracks)

Thorpe spoke briefly . . . condemning the policies whereby
deserving athletes are denied privileges of scholarship and tuition
under threat of losing their amateur standing.[55]

At Carlisle, the tributes were so moving that more often
than not his eyes were filled with tears.

On January 29 he was given a leather and velvet case containing a golden key to the city of Philadelphia, and the next night he was in Canton to receive a check for $1,000 and a wristwatch bearing the inscription: "Jim Thorpe, Canton Bulldogs. From your many friends in Canton, the cradle of professional football."[56]

The featured speaker, Branch Rickey, then general manager of the Pittsburgh Pirates, brought up the subject of the restoration of Jim's medals. Four congressmen in attendance, one of whom sat on the Indian Affairs Subcommittee, said they would get behind the movement.

True to their word, within a week the subcommittee voted unanimously to try to have the medals restored. "Restoration would right the wrong done to Thorpe and would give recognition to him and to the American Indians," said Rep. Bow, Republican, Ohio. Rep. Morris, Democrat, Oklahoma, added, "It was ridiculous and absurd for the medals to be taken ruthlessly on a technicality." As before, however, "No comment" was the posture of the Olympic board.[57]

Throughout that summer Jim and Patricia traveled the pro wrestling circuit with Jim's protégé, Sunny War Cloud:

War Cloud is 24 years old and hails from California, where he grew up on the reservations of the Sac and Fox tribes. His discovery by Thorpe happened rather accidentally. While in Montana, Thorpe, who never lost touch with his people, witnessed a wrestling tournament staged by various Indian tribes and became so impressed by War Cloud, who incidentally won the tournament, that he signed him right then and there.

Ever since that day, the two have become inseparable and both are profiting handsomely from each other's experience. The climax of the schedule was "Jim Thorpe Night" at Madison Square Garden.[58]

In August, 1951, Warner Brothers released the film *Jim Thorpe—All-American.* This event was particularly timely because Jim had just been inducted into the National College Football Hall of Fame in New York City.

On August 23, 1951, the film *Jim Thorpe—All-American*

was "Twin World" premiered in Carlisle and Oklahoma City. Jim, eldest son Carl Phillip, Phyllis Thaxter, who played Jim's movie wife, Governor Fine of Pennsylvania, LaRue Martin, Indian representative from the Governor of Oklahoma and "Bo" McMillin, Philadelphia Eagles coach, were among those in attendance at the Carlisle showing. In addition, a beautiful tablet monument which read, "In Recognition Of The Athletic Achievements Of JIM THORPE Student Of The Carlisle Indian School, Olympic Champion at Stockholm In 1912 And In 1950 Voted the Greatest Athlete And Football Player Of The First Half Of The 20th Century,"[59] was unveiled at the courthouse.

The movie was an immediate box office smash and the subject of innumerable articles. According to one, "Thorpe Film Tells Honest Story."

Starring Burt Lancaster as Thorpe and with Charles Bickford looking remarkably like a younger "Pop" Warner than we know today, the film brings to the screen highlights in the saga of Chief Bright Path, a man whose path has at times shined the brightest of all the world's athletes, but which at times has been overcast by shadows of doubt and indecision . . . shadows, too, of charges of professionalism, loss of Olympic Games medals and the bitter tragedy that comes with the death of a first son.[60]

So what does Thorpe get from all this, from the 50-cent pieces—give or take a couple of nickles—that are tossed through the box office as Mike the high school phenom takes Nellie from next door down to the Bijou to see a real football player operate? The same as you and I, bub. Nothing.[61]

And how does Jim feel about the present-day victims of the overemphasis of sports—the lost battalion of Cadets just dismissed from West Point?

"Those boys have my sympathy but I blame the over-emphasis and commercialism of college athletics for their downfall. Actually they are the innocent victims of the excesses of our collegiate sports system. Our colleges are being surrounded by commercialism in athletics. It is this over-emphasis that has caused the downfall of the athlete and the non-athlete involved in the West Point cribbing case."[62]

While he was heading an all-Indian song and dance troupe,

Jim Thorpe, 1952

Courtesy Pro Football Hall of Fame

"The Jim Thorpe Show," in Philadelphia that November, Jim noticed an infection on his lower lip. After several days it had failed to heal and he stopped by Lankenau Hospital. It was cancer, but he had come in time for the doctors to remove the tumor with no aftereffects.

To help pay his bills and to get him back "on his feet so he can resume his work as soon as possible,"[63] fans, young and old, Indian and white, responded to the "Fair Play for Thorpe Committee" with contributions totaling over $4,500 and a renewed cry for the return of his medals.

One serviceman, stationed in North Korea, wrote, "I never saw Jim Thorpe, but I've read a lot about him. We don't have any dollar bills out here, but enclosed is my lucky 50-cent piece which I've carried for years. Hope it brings Jim the luck it has brought me."[64]

A naturalized French woman said in her letter, "This is why I love America,"[65] and even a hitchhiker, whom Jim had given a lift, sent ten dollars. "Old Jim," the man with the "heart as big as all outdoors,"[66] who had "spent money on his own people or who just gave it away,"[67] was being paid back.

The "good feeling"[68] he experienced was short-lived. In less than ten months he lay in Henderson, Nevada's, Rose De Lima Hospital after suffering his second heart attack. The doctors were incredulous when he arose from his bed one night after less than seventy-two hours of hospitalization and walked out of the building under his own power. Jim had been brought in unconscious, placed in an oxygen tent, and listed in serious condition.

Jim's third attack occurred on March 28, 1953. Dr. Rachel Jenkins was summoned to his trailer in Lomita, California. According to Dr. Jenkins: "It was mid-afternoon on a Saturday, and he had just showered and was in the process of eating when he collapsed. He was lying on a bed when I arrived. I administered an intra-cardiac injection of adrenalin but the heart attack was massive."[69]

His great heart had faltered for the last time and he was gone. All the front-page obituaries in the principal dailies notwithstanding, his boyhood school's publication, Haskell's *Indian Leader,* said it best: "The Great Spirit has taken Jim Thorpe's life. Will He ever replace him?"[70]

Jim's widow remembered:

He was so easy going, so trusting. He was always concerned about people in distress. One of his friends needed $105 to pay his wife's hospital bill. Jim gave him the $100 he had and borrowed the extra $5. I discovered later that the friend didn't even have a wife. I guess you could say Jim had two-way pockets.

But did we ever starve? No indeed! I had to fight to keep the weight off him and would even run him around the block to slim him down.

It has been written that Jim died destitute living in a second-rate trailer. We had lived in trailers for years because Jim liked to live in something small for good movement.

He was content to get up at sunrise and take just a string, hook, sinker, and worms and go fishing. He might nap, but whenever there was the slightest nibble, he'd awaken. He wouldn't care if the fish weren't big or even if he didn't catch any; that just wasn't important.

You wouldn't think a man could be so perfect. He didn't have a mean bone in his body.[71]

Said Grace:

Dad was a strong individualist. I think more people should be that way instead of being so structured. We no longer have many free thinkers or people who can create. Who's got the time? We're so busy pushing all this red tape around. I call it white tape.

I find it absolutely refreshing that many of our Indian people are not going to get themselves tied down.

As far as a steady coaching job, Dad was kind of cantankerous and he'd be expected to show up and he wouldn't. He was his own man and people couldn't understand it. That is probably what made him a good athlete—the power, the strength, the guts—the same thing that doesn't work out within the system.

In other words, he wouldn't let them regiment him. I can't blame him for that. I kind of like it and respect him for it. I won't let the system regiment me either. So I guess I come by that very naturally. It didn't mean he didn't train. He'd train very hard.[72]

Charlotte concluded:

When I saw my father it was a joyous moment and one that sufficed until the next meeting. There was always the feeling of need and love between us that seemed to erase the interim. I'm sure my two sisters will agree.

I remember his laugh and his great grin, the most beautiful and widest I've ever seen. He was a quiet man, not a keen conversationalist.

He had an enormous amount of personal integrity and never uttered a bad word about anyone. Nor did he swear. He didn't think badly so how could he talk badly about anyone? The four-letter words were foreign to his lips.

His posture was always erect and his manner mild. He exuded manliness and warmth.

"Just remember you're a Thorpe," I can remember him saying many times. I was proud of him and proud to be with him. I loved him very much.[73]

It was once written that Jim "never kept a clipping."[74] Suffice it to say, without his massive scrapbook, compiled for nearly half a century, this biography would not have been possible.

One article that he treasured because it placed the final, and most misunderstood, years of his life into proper perspective, was written by a Charlotte, North Carolina, columnist, Eddie Allen:

Pity the poor Indian? Not Jim Thorpe! There is a certain stripe of writer who takes maudlin delight in weeping over once-great athletes who have fallen on supposedly darker days. They worked themselves into a tearful frenzy over Jack Dempsey's farcical "comeback" against a parade of unglamorous wrestlers. The land was filled with their weeping when Babe Ruth turned momentarily to "undignified" public appearances to make an honest buck.

So shed a few tears if you must for the "poor Indian" who is forced to capitalize on his feats of other years and become a night-club spectacle for a living. But leave me out when you do. One glance is enough to convince me that Thorpe is not a descendant of the Red Men who were rooked out of Manhattan island for $25 in Dutch money. There is still about him an aura of greatness, and nothing would please me better than to see the Charlotte Quarterback Club bring Thorpe here for one of their early meetings—if they can afford it.[75]

CHAPTER 14

Reinstatement

I live, believe me, in great hope. I think something good yet is going to come of our plans. We are making more progress now than we ever did before. Jim Thorpe brought these two towns together and gave us our first positive movement in a hundred years.

—JOE BOYLE,
Jim Thorpe Times-News

Through the kindness of Bill Schroeder, of the Helms Athletic Foundation, and Dave Malloy, a local funeral director, the burial arrangements were completed. Relatives and friends numbering more than four hundred recited the rosary for Jim, a Roman Catholic. Another 3,000 mourners filed past the open casket to view the body, clad in a soft chamois Indian jacket of tan, with the massive hands holding a rosary and a Carlisle bible.

A multitude of tributes were sent to the widow, including a telegram from President Eisenhower and a floral gift from the Norwegian Sports Association. Many states drafted resolutions honoring the fallen warrior, and the California Senate moved to adjourn.

Initially it seemed that Jim would be enshrined in Shawnee. Ross Porter tells the sequence of events:

When Jim died, his brother, Frank, came to see me and said, "I would like to bring Jim back to Shawnee. I've spoken with Mrs. Thorpe and she has agreed. This is where he always wanted to be buried but we don't have enough money." I had no idea what it would cost but we immediately formed a committee and set out to raise some funds.

Eventually we raised about $2,500 and brought him, his widow and children here. We wanted to build a memorial in the park area between the baseball park and football field. During the campaign,

228

I presented the request to the board of education that the name of the stadium be renamed, Jim Thorpe Stadium.

I told Mrs. Thorpe we would do everything possible to make it work. I took the matter up with Senator Walker and Representatives Levergood and Stevens and asked them for $25,000 to begin preparing architects' plans and specifications. Then Governor Murray called and asked me to serve on the Jim Thorpe Commission. I assured him that I would if he agreed not to veto the proposed bill.

"Oh, why would I veto it, Ross? I'm part Indian myself. Oh no! If this thing goes through, don't worry about it!" was his answer. Sure enough, it went through, and within forty-eight hours it was on Murray's desk, and he double-crossed us and vetoed the bill.

While all this was taking place, Tom Steed called from Washington to see how things were going. I said that I was busy on the Commission and asked him to contact President Eisenhower for an endorsement. I had spent an afternoon with the President at the Oklahoma City Golf and Country Club, when he was the president of Columbia University, and I thought he might remember me. Besides he had played against Jim at West Point. Ike was glad to do it and even sent a personal telegram, including in it a beautiful tribute to Jim.

But because of the veto, Mrs. Thorpe negotiated with representatives from Mauch Chunk, Pennsylvania, and that is where Jim is buried today.[1]

Cradled by the Lehigh Valley on the lower stratum of the eastern Pennsylvania anthracite coal region lie the remains of the man universally recognized as the finest all-around athlete of the first half of this century.

Joseph Boyle, the dynamic editor of the local newspaper and the individual most responsible for the community's rebirth, recalled the day in 1953 which proved to be the turning point in the fortunes of the town:

I was standing in the National Bank talking to Gerry Jackson, the cashier, when this woman came in. She went up to Hal Bitterline and said, "Where's Joe Boyle?" So Hal sent her over to me and she introduced herself as Mrs. Jim Thorpe.

She had been visiting in Philadelphia when she heard of this unique nickel-a-week plan which we were then developing with the

229

idea of bringing industry to our town. Under this program each resident would contribute five cents a week to the fund. She was impressed by a small town, trying to do a big thing with a little thing—a nickel.

Before leaving, Mrs. Thorpe proposed the idea that if we would consent to change our name to "Jim Thorpe," she would bring Jim's body here, and then the National Fraternal Order of Eagles, of which he had been a member, would create a memorial so that he could be properly edified. Then she left.

My first reaction to the idea was that it was impossible. It could never happen for the simple reason that Mauch Chunk was a name that was near and dear to everybody. But at the same time, when I spoke to other people in the town, they saw in it a great opportunity to bring the two towns together for the first time. Because, actually you see, we had two towns, Mauch Chunk and East Mauch Chunk. Mauch Chunk in turn was broken down into Mauch Chunk and Upper Mauch Chunk. Each had its own certain degree of pride and there was a rivalry built up. We just couldn't get together on big projects with any success because there was too much pulling apart.

She had agreed to come back at some later date and in the interim, former legislator and strong civic worker, Frank Bernhard, who was impressed by her story, and I decided that when she returned we would discuss it at greater length. By that time, I had a fairly representative group of businessmen and citizens who sat down with her.

Gerry Jackson was in favor of setting up some kind of a youth program—summer camps, possibly even schools whereby young people would be served and which would be a true honor to the memory of Jim Thorpe.

I must say that this provoked a great deal of publicity and as time went on this town got more coverage over this Jim Thorpe story than anything that had ever happened at any time in the past. I think it filled a lot of our heads sky high with dreams and aspirations and things like that.

Then, the residents voted to change the towns' name and Jim's body was brought here. All the schools were dismissed for the day. The school children with flags and flowers lined the curbs from the very end of the town over in Mauch Chunk all the way over to the Evergreen Cemetery. We decided to place his body in a temporary crypt over in the Evergreen Chapel until such a time as we could create a memorial.

Thinking that the National Fraternal Order of Eagles was going to finance this plan, we expected to be contacted soon. Mrs. Thorpe said this was possible because Jim had done a great deal of work for the Eagles, appearing at benefits and affairs of this nature.

Well, time went on and the Eagles were not fulfilling their obligation, if they ever had one. Finally, we believed that something had to be done. We knew none of us individually had enough money to create this memorial so we said we would borrow the money from this industrial fund that we had been raising.

To save money, we did all the site work ourselves. In fact, all of the labor was done by volunteers. So, you see, this money was taken from the fund with the idea that it would be paid back. The agreement Mrs. Thorpe signed and which was signed by the borough council, was that the borough would provide this memorial if the Eagles did not. And of course after two years, our committee felt that we were obligated because all the other preliminary work had been done.

So, we decided, one night after a great deal of soul-searching, that this was the right thing to do and it would be good for the community. We had already gained a great deal by bringing the two towns together so we arranged with the Summit Hill Marble and Granite Company to prepare this $10,000 memorial mausoleum.

We had the dedication of the monument on Memorial Day of 1957. There was very big crowd here that day. Someone estimated their number at 15,000. People came from all parts of the country. Our senators and legislators were here as well as a number of Indians. Jim's three daughters, Joe Guyon, and Pete Calac were in attendance and Al Schacht was the Master of Ceremonies. Also, Mrs. Olivia Herman, in preparation for this, did a great deal of work by training young groups to perform.

I live, believe me, in great hope. I think something good yet is going to come of our plans. We are making more progress now than we ever did before. Jim Thorpe brought these two towns together and gave us our first positive movement in a hundred years. We now have one school district, one council, and a borough manager.

Now this is rather significant; since we became one school, on

231

the athletic line we have won state honors in basketball and football. I think Jim would look back and be proud of this achievement. In addition, we now have boys going away to college on athletic scholarships who would never have been able to afford it.

By bringing Jim here we created a memorial for him and I might say we have never tried to capitalize on his name. You go up there and you are able to see that Memorial tract today exactly as it was when he was buried. We have done nothing in any direction to commercialize on the existence of the memorial. We believed that Jim would like to lie in peace, and that is exactly the way we are doing it.[2]

On the front of Jim's red granite memorial, is engraved the epitaph:

"SIR, YOU ARE GREATEST ATHLETE IN THE WORLD"

KING GUSTAV STOCKHOLM, SWEDEN 1912 OLYMPICS

1888   JIM THORPE   1953

On all four sides are etchings depicting his Indian heritage and his careers in football, baseball, track, and field. Around the mound encircling the structure, samples of earth from places significant in Jim's career have been scattered. Sent by the State of Oklahoma, they were taken from the very spot where the Thorpe farm was located, from Indian Field at the Carlisle Indian School, from the Polo Grounds in New York, and from the track at the Olympic Stadium in Stockholm, Sweden.

Jim's death has not diminished his fame. In the last two decades, there has been a perennial stream of honors and awards keeping his name alive, as well as the constant petition, where only the names of the campaigners are changed, for his exoneration. "It is amazing to me," said Gail Thorpe, "that young people today remember him and his achievements and look at me with awe just because I am his daughter."[3]

Recent honors include naming the NFL's most prestigious award, the Most Valuable Player, the Jim Thorpe Trophy; its first year being 1955. Three years later, Jim was elected to the National Indian Hall of Fame in Anadarko.

His name was placed on the roll of the Pennsylvania Hall of Fame in 1961. Charter membership in the National Professional Football Hall of Fame with George Halas, Sammy Baugh, Red Grange, Wilbur "Fats" Henry, Curly Lambeau, Dutch Clark, Cal Hubbard, Johnny "Blood" McNally, Bronko Nagurski, Joe Carr, Ernie Nevers, Don Hutson, Tim Mara, Mel Hein, Bert Bell, and George Preston Marshall, came in September, 1963. To complement the section of the Hall of Fame exhibition rotunda devoted to Jim and the early days of pro football an impressive life-size statue of Jim, a gift of Jack Cusack, stands at the Hall's entrance.

In 1967, through the efforts of Beth and Homer Ray and other concerned citizens, "Jim Thorpe Day" was celebrated in Yale, Oklahoma. Artist Charles Banks Wilson, commissioned by the state to paint Jim's portrait, which now hangs in the rotunda of the state capitol, was the main speaker. The ceremonies included the designation by the Oklahoma Historical Society of Yale as "The Home of Jim Thorpe." More recently, the home that Jim and Iva owned in Yale has been purchased by the state and is open to the public. Jim's pre-Olympic track medals are on display in the home. The Oklahoma Historical Society is currently designing an interpretive center which will be erected east of the home. The center, financed through appropriations by the legislature, will house Thorpe memorabilia and a history of the development of athletic equipment. It will also contain a research library. The state has erected an official marker in Jim Thorpe Park, and the home is on the National Register.

An impressive collection of Thorpe mementos and items from the greatest athletes of all time are owned by Joel Platt of Pittsburgh. Devoting most of his life to the creation of a national "Sports Immortals Museum," Mr. Platt has amassed more than one million items of such quality that his collection clearly exceeds those found in the major halls of fame.

Olympic gold medals

Courtesy Cumberland County Historical Society and Hamilton Library Association

Along with the efforts of his family, Leon Saperstein of the *Providence Visitor* and baseball's Billy Martin have launched vigorous efforts to revalidate Jim's honors. This time, they will succeed!

"Sixty Years Later, Thorpe's Amateur Status Restored." West Yellowstone, Montana, Oct. 12, 1973—The Amateur Athletic Union Friday restored the amateur standing of fabled Indian athlete Jim Thorpe, who starred in the 1912 Olympics only to be stripped of his gold medals on allegations that he was a professional.

The move clears the way for intercession on Thorpe's behalf by the U.S. Olympic Committee with the International Olympic Committee, which stripped Thorpe of his medals in 1913.

The A.A U. cannot restore Thorpe's medals, but will send a letter to the U.S.O.C. informing the committee of Thorpe's new standing as an amateur for the period of 1909–12.[4]

CHAPTER 15

Retrospect

By Dr. Joseph Alexander

I am probably the only one in the country who ever played college football while being in medical school. Participation in intercollegiate athletics by graduate students was not allowed.

I made the Syracuse University varsity during my junior year but this was also my first year in medical school. Chancellor James Roscoe Day was interested in building up the reputation of Syracuse by virtue of its athletic teams, so when it came to a decision as to whether or not I would play, the football coach was more powerful with the Chancellor than the Dean of the Medical School.

One of my best games was against Rutgers in the Polo Grounds in 1918. I made two touchdowns and intercepted six passes. They had twenty-three first downs to our two, but we won the game 21–0.

I was nineteen, captaining a team that had many 21-, 22-, and 23-year olds. I was scared to death until the whistle blew and I forgot all about being afraid. That was the turning point of my career. I changed from a careless or indifferent player to one who wanted to do well. I was fortunate that Walter Camp and Grantland Rice were in attendance at the game.

My last year, 1920, I was considered to be the All-America center; the previous two seasons, I was an All-America guard. That made me a center with all of the professional teams I played with in my six and one-half year career. That must have been my natural position.

In those days it was a hit-or-miss proposition; one of the exceptions being the Chicago Bears. We never had a fixed team and in fact, switched squads almost every week. Why, at ten o'clock on a Saturday morning, I took the train from Grand Central Station in New York to Broad Street Station in Philadelphia. At that time, the run was about two hours long. So I would get in at twelve o'clock and have a plate of soup, my lunch, in the station. Then I took a subway out to the field and got there at about one o'clock and dressed for the game. After the game was over, I would have to dress in a hurry to get back to Philadelphia to get the six o'clock train to New York.

And from New York, I would take whatever train I needed to get to Chicago, Buffalo, Cleveland, or Akron, depending on where I was going. The trip to Chicago took fifteen hours. So I would arrive Sunday morning around eleven o'clock just in time to catch a taxi and get partly undressed in it and go onto the field and play a game.

Oh, I had a tough time, I lost something like thirty-eight pounds during that first season. This was in 1921, and 1922 was a repetition of the same thing.

By 1923 I began to be organized. I finally admitted to myself that I couldn't travel from place to place and so I played with the Ben Franklin Yellowjackets, which later became the Philadelphia Eagles.

The player who, in his prime, had the greatest effect on the odds of a game was Jim Thorpe. He could do anything a football player is asked to do! He could hit the middle of the line, go off tackle, sweep the ends, or receive a pass. He could tackle and he could block.

He was not spectacular as the men are now, nowhere near as spectacular as a Sayers of Chicago, a professional speed merchant. But remember, in those days the overall speeds weren't so great, and yet Thorpe was a fast man by any standard.

With Canton Bulldogs, 1920

The fact that he was a high stepper made him difficult to bring down. In other words, you could never tackle both legs. You see, you had to hit him around the body. That's the value of a Jim Brown. His stride was long enough and yet he was always well balanced. Jim Thorpe had this same sense of balance but wasn't quite as heavy, weighing only about 200 pounds.

One memory of Jim that I will always look back on with a smile occurred when Thorpe's Indians were playing Brickley's Giants. Later, the Mara brothers bought the team and called it the New York Giants. But before this game with Thorpe, Brickley gave an exhibition of drop kicking. He got into his determined crouch and kicked field goals from the five, ten, fifteen, and from every five-yard line up to the fifty.

Right after Brickley finished, Thorpe went ahead and did the same thing with his free and easy style, from an upright position and after drop-kicking a field goal from the fifty, turned around and kicked one over the opposite crossbars as an extra measure.

When Jim's medals were taken away, every athlete in the country was sore at the Olympic Committee. Everybody wanted him to keep his medals. He was entitled to them; he earned them. Everybody was playing semi-pro baseball or football, and it is important to point out that Jim never played pro football while he was attending Carlisle.

After the Tufts-Syracuse game of 1916, which was played on a Saturday, seven Syracuse men and eight from Tufts played in a professional game the next day in Springfield, Massachusetts. All of them were kicked out of college that evening for playing in that game.

The majority of the violators, of course, were never caught. I played against Dartmouth one year and we beat them 10–0 in a tough game. The Dartmouth coach, a fellow named Hubie Spears, came over between the halves and walked off the field with me. He took me by the arm and said, "Well, I see you've got plenty of experience playing pro out in Ohio." There was a player from Rutgers named Alexander who was playing out there and somebody would use my name just for fun or just to get a better salary.

Most of the time they used different names but if a town wanted to make some money, they would promote the game by advertising the names of the stars. When the news got back to other conference schools, they could protest if they wanted, but most of the time it would be denied. You see, nobody could prove it.

They didn't take too many pictures in those days. This is an important point, because photography has built up since that time. If we saw a cameraman, we would kick him off the field. We used to have a superstition not to be photographed.

And there was a superstition not to go on the field in a clean uniform. Now they have uniforms all the time and are constantly changing them. But back then, if a man came on the field with a clean uniform, his teammates would take him and roll him in the dirt.

We never used to wash the undershirt. It was dirty and sweaty and all different colors because of perspiration and dirt. There was no such thing as a laundry! If we had mud caked on our pants, we would have to wait until it dried and then hit if off with a hammer or with a fist.

The same is true with the shoes. The shoes would never fit and were always nondescript. If you lost a cleat, you were out of luck because nobody, no shoemaker, even knew how to repair a cleat.

The shoulder pads were pieces of leather, tied together with shoelaces, on the front and back, with just flaps on the shoulders. It hung loose and the only thing that kept it on was the sweater. It had to be adjusted after every time you were hit.

Nobody ever wore a hard helmet, always soft leather with one quarter of an inch of felt padding. If you received a blow on top of the helmet, it would transmit directly to the head. The main reason for the felt was to prevent the ears from being torn. There was no protection for the neck.

There was no such thing as a facemask, and noseguards

239

or mouthpieces, got in the way and were seldom used.

We had hip pads made of felt and pressed paper or pieces of wood for the front of the thigh. You can see old pictures showing the ridges.

The best shinguards were made from magazines. I would tear one in half, put it on both shins and pull my socks over the paper. By the time I'd perspire a little it had molded to my leg, forming a perfect shinguard.

I ran into some difficulty when I was practicing medicine at Mt. Sinai and Belleview hospitals because of my football connections, and even after my last game with Syracuse my coach didn't want me to accept a $500 offer to play one game of pro football. I told him I had a $200 second semester's tuition to pay for medical school, and he said not to worry that it would be taken care of; so I didn't play in the game.

He was so much against it because he thought professional football would push the college game into the background the same way professional baseball overshadowed the college brand.

In the late twenties the colleges began to realize that a man wasn't ready for professional competition until he had adequate varsity seasoning. They even passed regulations along those lines. High school graduates or college freshmen aren't ready, especially when you look at how difficult it is for rookies, some of whom were college stars, to make the teams.[1]

By Jack Dempsey

I knew Jim for a great many years and was always a great admirer of his. His knowledge of the finer points of boxing truly amazed me and on several occasions we would work out at the gym. I began to realize, as I watched him spar in the ring, that if he had started as a young man he would have been a great fighter. Yes, he was the greatest of all athletes. He could have excelled at anything.

I have always thought that he was one of the finest persons

I have ever known. Everybody admired the man. Of course, having a little Indian in my own blood I admired him that much more because the hardships that an Indian has to endure in this country are inexcusable. After all, this was their land and we, you might say, infringed upon them. My great-great-grandparents, on both my mother's and father's side, were full-blooded Cherokee Indians. That makes me one-eighth Indian. I didn't get enough. I know that.

This brings to mind the loss of Jim's Olympic medals and trophies. I think this is what started him on the downgrade in his life. I don't think this was the right thing to do, but that is what happened and it hurt him a great deal. The man was broke and he didn't understand the amateur rules. He had to eat! What could he do? He played some baseball instead of farming only because he loved athletics and excelled in them. As far as I was concerned, I was sorry to see it happen. But at the same time, we have got to live up to the rules and regulations of our society. The law is the law and it was his business to live up to it. If he had had the proper guidance, the whole affair never would have happened.

Jim was intelligent, sound, and had good ideas, but he did not have too much of a formal education. My own education in Manassa, Colorado, where I was born and raised, was very poor. I never finished the eighth grade, but my father was a school teacher. As a result, I had a little better opportunity to learn a few things than the average fellow who didn't go to school. My first break came when I fought Jess Willard for the title. I licked every contender and therefore I got the shot at Willard. I was lucky and knocked him out, and that made me the champion.

While there was a social stigma on professional sports in those days, the fight game was not affected as much. Boxing is obviously not a team sport, and as a result the fighters usually did not travel in large groups which would be conspicuous to the public.

At the time of the depression I was just getting out of the fight game. I gave a few exhibitions, refereed fights, and

241

things like that. That kept me busy. It was hard to find work for most people, but I was just lucky that the fight business was booming.

After that I entered the restaurant business, and it has given me a good life. I think the people like me and I like them and we try to serve good food, give good service, and run a really legitimate business. I think that the quality of sincerity is what you need to be a success in anything you do.

When Jim opened a restaurant, in his later years, I think he failed because of a lack of experience and a good business partner. As for myself, I had the experience and a partner, Jack Amiel, who has been in this line of work for a great many years. He looks after all the "restaurant end" of it, like the food and the help. Jim was victimized by shrewd promoters and was not able to protect himself because of his generous and trusting nature. I have had all kinds of things happen to me, different decisions to make, and many things I shouldn't have done. There were periods when I had to work in railroad camps, ditch camps, mining camps, wash dishes, and generally do anything to make a living. But, after all, that is experience and background and it is part of life, and more often than not you learn the hard way.[2]

By George Halas

A lot of footballs have flown between the uprights since the afternoon of September 17, 1920, when the representatives of eleven midwestern professional football teams met in Canton. I was there as coach of the Decatur Staleys.

Looking back over the last half-century, I am still rather amazed that I ever got into pro football in the first place. Baseball was my favorite sport during my high school days at Crane Tech in Chicago, and I also made more base hits than tackles at Illinois. In fact, I played only one full season at right end for the Illini as a senior in 1917. A fractured jaw sabotaged my sophomore year, and a broken leg kept me on the bench most of the 1916 season.

But I batted .350 over three seasons as a right fielder for

Ralph Hay's Garage, 1920

the Illini baseball team, and a scout named Bob Connery recommended me to the New York Yankees. World War I was in progress so I served a fourteen-month hitch in the Navy before reporting to the Yankees' spring training camp at Jacksonville, Florida, in 1919.

I made the team, but in an exhibition game against Brooklyn I came up to bat against Rube Marquard, the great left-hander who set a major-league record of nineteen consecutive victories. Marquard had a dandy curve, but I figured Rube wouldn't risk an arm injury by throwing a curve against a rookie so early in the spring. So I dug in and looked for his fast ball.

It was a good guess. Marquard came down the middle with his fast one and I hit a triple and had to slide into third base. I didn't pay much attention to it until the next batter hit a single. As I ran home, I started to limp with what I thought was a charley horse and so did the trainer.

They gave me a few days rest and I was back in the lineup again, but the pain came back on me and that's the way it was from Jacksonville all the way up to New York. The Yankees sent me to the best orthopedic man, and I managed to start the season against Philadelphia and the Washington team with Walter Johnson. But after playing three or four days, I'd be laid up and that continued until our second trip around to Cleveland.

I asked Miller Huggins, our manager, to send me down to "Bonesetter" Reese who had saved my career twice before. He did permit me, so I got up at five o'clock the next morning and caught the electric down to Youngstown.

I gave my story to "Bonesetter" and he said, "Get on that table!" He felt around and agreed: "Yes, when you slid into third base, you twisted your hip bone and it's pressing on a nerve, but I can fix that."

He went down with those steel fingers of his, grabbed the bone, twisted it and that afternoon I was running like wild! I've always been very grateful for what he did for me.

But I was having trouble with a curve ball, so they sent me to St. Paul in the American Association where Mike

Kelly, the manager, taught me how to hit a curve. Why he was never in the big leagues I don't know, but I really enjoyed playing under one of the greatest managers I've ever known.

That fall I went to work for the C. B. & Q. Railroad here in Chicago in their engineering department. I also played pro football with the Hammond, Indiana, team for a hundred dollars a game, more than twice my weekly railroad salary. Hammond had some of the big college names of the era, such as Gil Falcon, a 235-pound fullback; Paddy Driscoll from Northwestern; Milt Ghee, quarterback from Dartmouth; Shorty Des Jardiens, University of Chicago; Hugh Blacklock, tackle from Michigan State; and a couple of University of Minnesota stars, Bert Baston, an end, and "Doc" Hauser, All-American, who played the end at the other side of the line from me.

It was at this time that Mr. A. E. Staley of Decatur sent up the general superintendent of his company to interview me to see if I would organize a football team to represent his organization.

Mr. Staley owned a prosperous corn products firm and was the most enthusiastic sports fan I've ever met. His company already sponsored a strong semi-pro baseball team managed by former big leaguer Joe (Iron Man) McGinnity. He indicated to me that while I was forming the team I could be learning the business.

Within two weeks, I signed the nucleus of a strong squad, including such standouts as Blacklock; guard Jerry Jones and center George Trafton of Notre Dame; quarterback Walter (Pard) Pearce of Penn; fullback Bob Koehler of Northwestern; end Guy Chamberlain of Nebraska; halfback Dutch Sternaman, tackle Burt Ingwersen, and fullback Jake Lanum of Illinois; Jim Conzelman, a halfback from Washington University in St. Louis, Kyle McWherter, Leo Johnson, George Petty, and Charley Dressen. We had a wonderful record and won the championship that year.

After 1920 there was a bit of a recession, and so Mr. Staley said to me: "George, I'm sorry we cannot have the team another year. I think pro football will succeed in Chicago and I would like you to take this $5,000 to get off the ground, with one condition: that during the 1921 season, you call the team the 'Chicago Staleys,'" which we did do. That was the biggest break of my life and I'll never forget it!

It took me a few moments to comprehend the overwhelming generosity of his offer. He was giving me the Staley franchise. Not only giving it, he was paying me $5,000 to accept it!

Recently, I mentioned this story to a man who is a member of a group which paid more than $10,000,000 for a National Football League franchise. He just shook his head.

Once again we had a good record, primarily because we practiced every day. Now I think that gave us quite a lead over most of our opponents. The following year, I changed our name to the Chicago Bears.

On November 4, 1923, occurred the most memorable incident in my entire football career, and Jim Thorpe was the cause of it. The Bears were playing Thorpe's Indians in Chicago. It was a rainy and muddy day, and, in fact, it poured during the game.

The Indians were threatening to score on us and were deep in our territory when Blacklock hit Thorpe a crusher that shook the ball loose and I recovered on the two. Luckily, the ball had bounced into my hands and I took off—with Jim in hot pursuit.

I knew that Jim in a straight race would be tough to outdistance or better said, would let no man escape him, especially in this case, since he had fumbled the ball away. So I knew my only chance was to pursue a zigzag course and not give him the angle he would need to bring me down.

Jim had a knack or habit or talent, I do not know which word to use to describe it, of never tackling a man from behind. Even more than his great speed was his favorite defensive action, which was punishing and physical and effective.

He had powerful legs and usually wouldn't use a normal tackle. Instead, he would get close enough to sail forward

246

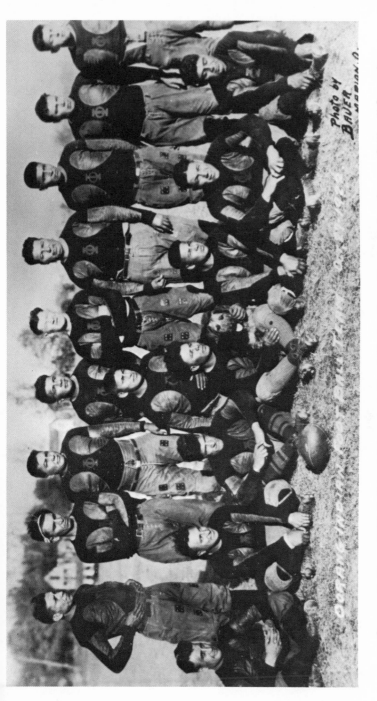

Oorang Indians, 1922. Left to right, seated: Pearl Clarke, Leon Boutwill, Joe Guyon, Stillwell Sanooke, Bill Winneshek, and Bemus Pierce; kneeling: Nick Lasso; standing: Asa Walker, Haskell Hill, Buck Jones, Elmer Busch, Jim Thorpe, Ted St. Germaine, Xavier Downwind, Baptist Thunder, Pete Calac

Courtesy Maxine and Robert Lingo

in the air whip those legs and literally knock the other man's legs out from under him and it was a tough blow too. I knew that and didn't want any part of it!

So by taking a diagonal, crisscross route, ten yards diagonally to the left, then a veering change of direction for ten yards to the right, I knew this was my only chance of escape. To have gone straight downfield would have meant disaster. I was also helped a great deal by the quagmire of a field.

This worked until he nailed me at the eight-yard line and we just floated over the goal line together. It was a touchdown, a 98-yard run officially, but in retrospect, I insist the actual distance covered was twice or maybe three times that because of the zigging and zagging.

Well do I remember that day! We were so tired! I finally got up on one elbow and saw Jim also spraddled out full length in the north end zone.

Taking into consideration Jim's speed and strength as well as his ability to run, pass, kick, and play defense, he was the greatest. I was certainly impressed with his ability whenever we played against his team, because when he put on that football suit, he gave 100 per cent.

As for his sportsmanship; I caught a pass in one game and was tackled from behind. I was still trying to crawl a few more yards on my hands and knees. Jim came up and could have thrown his knees right into my head or shoulders or ribs but, instead of that, he just sat astride me and bore me to the ground. He said: "If you're a horse, I'll ride you."[3]

By Tom Harmon

I met Jim on many occasions, usually at a gathering of football men around the Southern California area and I also remember meeting him in Chicago and New York at this same type of gathering. From my remembrances and the conversations that I had with Jim, he always appeared to be a mountain of a man, a man who seemed to have determination written in every wrinkle or characteristic of his face. He was a very quiet individual, not one who boasted or talked of his own exploits. He was, I would say in category, much better as a listener than a talker. However, his presence, no matter who was in the group, was always overpowering.

At all the times that I did meet with him and talk to him, he was always very articulate. He believed in the common things in life and he was a very down-to-earth person, a man who was very forthright, very frank and he spoke his mind and his opinions as he believed.

I never did see Jim play football. He was ahead of my time in that regard. However, I did, on occasion, see some films of him playing and, of course, had many conversations with men who played with and against him. From the description of these men there would be no question that Jim could have played professional football today. His talent was so tremendous that he would make any backfield, and he certainly was as strong as any man who possibly ever played the game. In his particular greatness, he was obviously capable of not only taking care of himself but several other men at the same time.

His minor infraction of the Olympic rules was not a major crime and, in my opinion, certainly not reason enough to ever take away a man's medals. Heaven knows, today, that by those same standards, every man in the United States who plays collegiate football or collegiate baseball or collegiate basketball is a professional, if you judge a man by taking four or five dollars to play in a semi-pro baseball game and rule him a professional.

The term of amateurism today, possibly could be called "shamateurism" more than anything else because there is no standard; there is no level on which a man can be judged as an amateur. It is different for tennis as it is different for golf, football, basketball, baseball, and what have you.

I think these concepts have changed throughout the years. There is more lenience given to the athlete of today in allowance for his school, books, tuition, room and board, and things of this nature. Certainly football, or any sport, was not refined in the days of Thorpe to the extent of where

249

many men, if any, were given an athletic scholarship for their athletic ability.

To my mind I think this is one of the black marks of athletics today and doubly so in amateur athletics because there should be a set standard kept by all sports. This should be stringently enforced. Number one, there is no such standard. Number two, it is not enforced. Number three, there is no enforcement body and I doubt that there ever will be because the people who run tennis, run tennis. They do not bother with football. The people who run football do not pay any attention to golf and so on down the line.

There is no centralized body that could act as a judge should cases of violation come up. As I say, myself, I think the greatest fault of amateur sports today is the hypocrisy which goes on and which everybody practices. But, by the same token, it is the way of life for a coach. He either has material, and that material is what eventually gives him a winning season, or he does not have a job, and that is very unfortunate.

Thorpe was a man who appeared to me to have been raised in the "school of hard knocks" and possibly with experience he did learn a little bit more about money. But I doubt very much if he ever learned how to take care of it or ever learned its value. He was probably always a very easy-come, easy-go guy and, consequently, I am certain that at the time of his heyday or at the time of his losing the medals there were those who attempted to utilize his name and the story to their benefit. Possibly, they did give Jim a fair break. However, I would assume that he got the short end of most of those deals.

It is hard to define the problems that a person of great renown or athletic ability runs into, because they are all different. Today, as you probably can understand, there is a great deal more of a commercial aspect to an athlete's endorsing certain things. He is able to take advantage of speaking engagements, film work, and all the other by-products of a great name in sports.

I would assume very few of these things were possible at

the time that Jim Thorpe played, because sports had not reached the plateau they are in today. To utilize Thorpe in a football game, taking his name and exploiting him, I am sure Jim probably played a lot of football games where he may have gotten twenty-five dollars for the game, and in some games, when the promoters ran out, he did not get a dime.

It would be a delightful thing to see a man of his ability and his great natural, raw talent come onto the sports scene today. If this had been the case, I think that his life would have been very, very different. By this I mean the cloud of doubt about his professionalism and other things of similar nature; I just do not feel that it would have been necessary for Jim to become involved in a great many things which he got in a problem about, either because of money or prestige or somebody taking advantage of him.

It is just a shame that he did not have the opportunity to play under the modern era, but, as the man said, "You cannot take the clock back. You have to play it as it lies." But I think Jim did a pretty good job of that and, in my humble opinion, I think, regardless of what anybody says, Jim Thorpe could have played on anybody's football team, at any time, and been a very valuable addition to that team.

I only can say that my associations with Jim Thorpe are a pleasant memory to me. I remember him very well. I remember many of our conversations relative to football and the way he used to laugh at how intricate football had become today. But, again, I always had the feeling that I was in the presence of greatness when I was around Jim. Certainly the man is a legend, deservedly so, and it is just unfortunate that possibly he was born fifty years too soon. Had Jim Thorpe been playing in football, today, quite possibly he would have set records that nobody could have touched.[4]

By Burt Lancaster

It was about seventeen years ago when we were doing the Jim Thorpe picture. Jim was kept around the set with the title of technical adviser, but the job was a manufactured one. They really didn't know what to do with him, which is generally the case when you do anyone's life who happens to be alive. The ironic thing is that those making the film want to do it so much better than the guy who actually lived it and, of course, by its very nature a lot of the things are not true. They follow a thin line of truth, perhaps, trying to show the person's best light so that it winds up in a blaze of glory.

I remember at one football practice during the making of the film, Thorpe, who was sitting in the stands watching us, came over and showed me how to kick the ball. He said some very kind things like, "That's fine. You are doing it well."

He was a bear of a man, somewhere around sixty or there-abouts. I wasn't a kid myself either. I was thirty-seven when I did the picture and had to go into a lot of very serious training. You know, I had to learn to play football, and toward the end we had a seventeen day period in which I worked out with all the football players from USC and UCLA. By the end of that time I could actually stay in there and maneuver. I had to learn how to high jump a certain way and learn how to put the shot, the discus, and all those things.

Jess Hill, the former athletic director at USC, who was at that time the track coach, trained me along with a boy called Al Lawrence, who doubled me and later finished third in the American Decathlon.

I was in really wonderful condition in those days. I did roadwork every single day for three solid weeks. I learned to run, learned to hurdle, not that I was particularly good, but I mean I was able to put the shot, the discus, and the javelin very well, that is, with form. You know, we could trick the distances. All I had to do was to look pretty good doing it, you see, and then of course the problem was the acting. The first thing they did was dye my hair black.

Yes, when you talk about athletics, Thorpe was certainly incomparable even by standards of today. He was able to compete in football when he was past forty and was still

Jim Thorpe—All American movie, 1951

quite a player. The stories about him are legend.

On the other hand, if you compare the track and field records and times, Thorpe was head and shoulders above the athletes of his particular day. His weakest area was in the pole vault, but it was true of everybody in those days. A real training program had not been developed, and of course they didn't have the equipment that is available now. He compensated for this with superior speed and endurance, and his weight, not much over 180 pounds, was considerably less than when he was in his prime. Still he was able to put the shot 48 feet.

Even though the athletes today, I think, are much more serious and conscientious about their training, there is no doubt in my mind that Thorpe trained and trained hard. There was a story told to me that Thorpe would often sit down with a bottle of whiskey while he was practicing what we call the "long jump" now, then he would just put the bottle down and jump 23 feet 11 inches which was fabulous in those days. But you see, these are the kind of stories that, by their very nature, sound phony. If you know anything about training, you can imagine the kind of condition you must be in for a Decathlon. It is unquestionably the most grueling and demanding of the track and field sports.

At present, all of the top athletes almost invariably, to begin with, come from colleges where they are brought up in the whole tradition of discipline where their work is concerned. They are bright, intelligent, and have lawyers to advise them and make investments.

They set up, from the very beginning, a financial program over a period of years and plan very much like a businessman does. In those days there wasn't anybody to do that for them or suggest it, and they didn't have the foresight to do it on their own.

You know, this approach is all relatively new. As a matter of fact, it was not until after the Second World War that this began to take place. You read about athletes who made a great deal of money in the old days, fighters particularly, and they wound up broke. Thorpe certainly was a victim of a time when there were not people around to advise him how to handle his affairs or to do it for him. Professional football, too, in his day was a pretty sordid thing as far as the promise of any kind of security in terms of old-age pensions and after-retirement benefits and the other things that all the football players have today.

To complicate matters even further, the depression years hit and there were few jobs. The situation here in the motion-picture business was terrible. You can hear some of these old timers around the studios talk about it. One of the reasons that Hollywood unions are as strong as they are today is because in those days the heads of studios very often had people working twenty-four hours a day for twenty-five or thirty dollars a week. I mean they just kept them going on pictures night and day, and the abuses were awful, and so when the unions came in, they came in with a vengeance.

Now, perhaps, we have the strongest union, in terms of wages and benefits, in the entire country. But at that time, the late twenties to the middle thirties, I was a kid in New York City, and wasn't really affected by it. I do know that grown men with families were working for fifteen dollars a week. I can remember myself standing in line to shovel snow for fifty cents an hour and sometimes we would stand in line all night long. It would get so cold we would have to wrap burlap around our feet, but really, I was luckier than most. My father had a job in the post office which did not pay a great deal but by the standards of the times it was passable. We had all we needed to eat and never suffered in that regard.

By the time Thorpe came out here to California, he really didn't do very much except some doubling and working as an extra in pictures. But there again, as a former professional athlete, he was not regarded as a responsible person.

Aside from this, however, I am sure there must have been something troubling Thorpe. I would venture to guess that this must have been true from the rather haphazard and loose way he lived and his attempting to try his continuance in athletics into a period long past his prime, where he tried to eke out a living in relationship to the figure he had been before. What was a man forty-five years old doing playing professional football and taking all those knocks? He was a rare person, it is true, but he obviously lacked either the attitude or the perception to say to himself at a certain point, "Well, I am going to try to do something else. I have got to do something that has some longevity, some stability to it." He just drifted in his later years, and I think the death of his son had a lot to do with his attitude. But there is no question about it, he never received much encouragement.

Then, of course, earlier he suffered the loss of his amateurism and Olympic medals. I know there was a strong attempt made on the part of Warner Brothers to try to get his medals back. They were hoping to be able to do that as the finish for the picture. It would have been a fact and would have occurred at that time, but they were not able to do it, and the substitute was to put him in the Hall of Fame in the State of Oklahoma.

The whole concept of amateurism, as we know it, is rather silly. There is no such thing as a simon-pure athlete. Amateurism was popular in Thorpe's day for the reason that we talked about before; that is, professionalism was looked down upon. Now, we don't make the distinction, for instance, by saying professional businessman or professional doctor. This is when someone is working, making a living, and receiving some financial benefits.

But the concept of the prize for a prize fight was being put up even before Thorpe's time. The aristocracy, the royalty or the gentlemen of the period would get people very low on the social ladder. They organized it solely for their own pleasure and offered a prize of money to these people. Then, when it became organized into a business-type venture, the prize money became the important thing.

The well-to-do person could always be an amateur because he could control his life. He could take the time to do whatever he wanted in terms of training. He could set up his own program of living and look for his income from other sources either from a business or an inheritance. All athletes are subsidized in one way or another. They come to me and people all over the country as they have done for many years and ask us to make contributions to the Olympic team, and we do.

There is another thing, too. An athlete who is dedicated will very often be much more dedicated because he is getting something like money, rather than a medal. You cannot say that the professional basketball players or the professional baseball players work less hard now that they are professionals than they did when they were amateurs. I would venture to say that they work twice as hard. The rewards are greater and there is more money. The incentive is there. They are better athletes for it. Again, it has to do with an old snobbish socially oriented attitude toward the stigma of professionalism. If a man was a simon-pure athlete, you know, he could raise his head with pride and say, "I am not doing it for money, I am doing it for love." Well, that is just a lot of poppycock. But nevertheless, that was what some people followed. I mean a man like Brundage, of necessity, has to believe that what he did was the right thing because he has been lambasted for this time immemorial. And, I daresay, he acted out of motives that he felt were honorable, you know, puritan motives.

You did not read much about Thorpe after he retired, and added to that, his innate character was one of quietude. He opened up a bar and that would last for awhile. Then it would be another bar and finally it would be a kind of oblivion. There is a tendency for people to forget the athletic heroes.[5]

By Leo V. Lyons

I became interested in football way back in 1906. I was fourteen years of age and didn't have enough money to buy a pair of football shoes. So I went to a shoemaker to have him cut up some hard leather and put cleats on my old shoes. At first, he didn't know what I was talking about because he was deaf and dumb. I tried to show him by making motions. Finally, I went home and got a football picture out of a magazine and imitated kicking a football and he got the idea.

I used the shoes to play some sand-lot football at Reynolds Field but the cleats didn't stay on over five minutes and I had to play the balance of our choose-up game in my stocking feet. Even then I believed someday this game could be a big affair.

In 1908 a school chum of mine was playing with the Rochester Jefferson football club and I said: "Dutch, I'd like to try out for the team." He took me up to a hotel and we went upstairs, climbed a ladder into a blind attic without lights, put on our clothes and walked a mile to the field where we were going to play. From then on, I really got the feeling to pursue it.

We were playing our games at a field on Genesee Park Boulevard and Scottsville Road. The price of admission was ten cents, but most of the crowd would come through the woods to avoid paying the dime. When new homes were spreading out into the area, we moved to Sheehan's Field at the corner of Monroe and Elmwood Avenue and charged twenty-five cents.

The fans, in those days, stood right on the sidelines and since I was the night wire chief for the telephone company at that time, I decided to put a fence around the field. One evening, I persuaded the president's chauffeur, who drove an open Packard, to put some old wire and crossarms into the car and take them out to Sheehan's Field. I borrowed a posthole digger from Joe Sterrell, of the Empire Fence Company and one of our players. When I finished my midnight-to-eight shift, I took a streetcar, with the posthole digger, to the end of the line and walked two miles to the field.

I worked all day digging holes for the new fence, went home about four o'clock to take a nap, went to work at midnight and was out again the next day digging holes for the fence. Saturday morning I had the holes all dug and two of my players, Don Gray and Joe Buckmeyer, came out and helped me. We put the crossarms in the holes, filled in the dirt, packed it down, put the wire on, tied one end of it to the bumper of Don's old Buick to stretch it and then went around the field to staple the wire on. I helped to mark the field Sunday morning and in the afternoon played the whole game. In the first quarter the crowd tore the fence down.

That day the Jeffersons played the Oxfords from what they called the "butterhole" in Rochester. Bill Caulfield, playing next to Jack Slattery, who later became chief of the fire department, heard a commotion on the sidelines and said: "Slatts! Your father's in a fight!" You see, fights were common among partisans from different parts of the city. Well, signals were being called and despite this, both teams joined the fight on the sidelines which was going merrily along until Judge Sheehan's (then Jimmy Sheehan's) mother came out of her home which joined the field, and stopped the fight with a shotgun.

One time we scheduled a game with the Lancaster Iron Works. They were all iron workers and arrived on a special New York Central train. They came out to the field waving twenty-dollar bills in the air confident that they would beat us twenty to nothing or better. Nobody took the bet and they won 20 to 3, but we weren't satisfied with the beating. So later on in December, we scheduled an indoor game with them since it was too cold to play outdoors. I went out to the New York State Armory and marked off a gridiron on the hardwood dance floor. Although the end zones were short, it was long enough for a game.

We played outdoor rules, wearing rubber soled sneaks instead of cleats. I played quarterback in that game and one time when I was running with the ball, I was hit low and high and was sliding across the floor on one eye. After the blood was swept off the floor, they had to take me to the doctor who had to take eleven stitches in me.

Fearful of my wife and mother finding out I was still playing pro football, I stopped up to the *Democrat and Chronicle* on the way home and talked to Charlie Kinney, the sportswriter. When he looked at my head all done up in gauze and cotton, he began to laugh. But I said: "Charlie, this is nothing to laugh about. You have to keep my name out of the line-up." He replied: "Don't worry. I'll take good care of that, Leo." I thanked him and went home.

By the time I got there, it was about one-thirty in the morning. My wife was asleep but when I walked into the bed-room, she turned the light on and screamed when she saw my head. I looked like a Turk wearing a turban. She wanted to know what happened and I said: "You know that iron staircase leading to the front door at the Armory, where we used to go to dances? Well, a drunk came in and I was afraid he would cause some trouble. I tried to keep him from going in but he took a punch at me and I ducked my head and hit my eye on the staircase."

The next day her brother picked up the paper, opened it to the sports page and began to laugh. I winked at him but it didn't do any good. My wife went over and grabbed it and read the lineup. There was the left end, left tackle, left guard, . . . quarterback—Manafraid. I saw Kinney later on and asked: "What did you give me that name for?" He answered: "I gave you an old Indian name because it was short for Man-afraid-of-his-wife."

Our next field, the Bay Street ball park, was the scene of many a hard-fought game and from there we moved to a new area on Norton Street in the year 1917. By that time, we were New York State Champions. We defeated all the teams in the area around New York and beat Buffalo for the championship, 7 to 6.

My Jeffs had played and beaten the available state professional teams and were searching for another opponent. I had read that the Canton Bulldogs were claiming the title of World's Champs. They defeated Wheeling, West Virginia, the week before, 88 to 0, and another team the week before that, 110 to 0. Nevertheless, we thought we were pretty good and so I wrote to Jack Cusack, their manager, for at least one more encounter before the season's end. My challenge was accepted, and the eight-hundred-dollar guarantee seemed to be an attractive offer.

It was to be a professional football game contesting the

championship of the world; a world that stretched from Canton, where Thorpe played on Sundays, to Rochester where I managed and played for the Jeffersons.

The Bulldog backfield was made up of Jim Thorpe, Pete Calac, Joe Guyon, and Greasy Neale, with many another All-American on the team. Therefore, we had only a few weeks to whip our team into shape. We worked out under an arc light on week nights after working all day.

Arranging the game soon became fraught with problems, for as the game approached, a flu epidemic infected upstate New York. Many of the Jeffs succumbed or had relatives stricken. My roster dwindled to ten men who were ready to face the great Bulldogs. Second-line reinforcements, "ringers," were obtained from other pro or semi-pro teams in the area. I gave them instructions for getting to Canton, arranged their complicated fares and went in the opposite direction to Syracuse to buy me some college men. Most pro teams then were made up of about equal parts college men and "non-U" men, like myself. Sometimes the college fellows were still undergraduates. They played "pro" on Sunday, took their fifty dollars, and returned to school on Monday.

Tufts was playing at Syracuse University on Saturday, the day before the game in Canton, and I still had hopes of enlisting some players to give Canton a showing. This meant marching right into the locker rooms after the game. A tackle, Mitchell, and a halfback, Haggerty, were available from the Tufts team and Rip Flannery, a Syracuse halfback, agreed to take the tour to Canton. Can you imagine a pro scout doing such a thing today? In 1917 that was part of our game.

Rip, a future New York State Supreme Court Justice, and the rest of us were almost to the train when he discovered he had forgotten his cleated shoes. He insisted that we, he and I, go back and get them. When we arrived at the locker room, we entered through an unlatched window, got the shoes and were on our way out when the night watchman, a fellow known in those parts as "Big Mike" Porter, fell upon us. He chased us across the campus and even fired a shot at the pair of fleet-footed broken field runners.

My other boys were on their way from Rochester to Canton by the cheapest, though not necessarily the shortest, route. Their itinerary included a train from Rochester to Buffalo on Saturday afternoon. There they embarked on a passenger boat to Cleveland that night. Sunday morning it was the Wheeling and Lake Erie Railroad to Canton and the local street car to the Cortland Hotel.

After a restful night in coach accommodations, the three ringers and myself joined the team on the morning of the game. We numbered sixteen men at this point. Stocking practice began in the ballroom of the hotel. A Billy Bauer practice pass went awry and escaped through an open window of the hotel. Our drill was halted until someone retrieved our only ball.

The Jeffs' arrival at the field of play was marked by a jeering mob of rabid Bulldog fans. They mocked the Rochester challengers and even provided a stretcher in front of our bench, to eventually remove one of us. We stopped for a look at the crowd and a man standing there asked: "Is this your first team?" I said: "Yes." He just laughed and pointed to the stretcher. "We have a guy named Jim Thorpe," he said, "and last week he killed two guys playing against us."

Wherever the Canton team played, Jim would give an exhibition of punting. In this particular game, he stood in the end zone, while a photographer and newspaperman marked the distances. He kicked the old football one hundred yards on the fly twice out of five tries. The other three traveled eighty to ninety yards and bounded over the goal line.

In any event, neither the fans nor the Bulldogs frightened our team, but they did defeat us. With Thorpe, a blurred streak skirting the ends and smashing the line, the Bulldogs romped to 49 to 0 victory, sending my Jeffs back to Rochester, bruised and believing that Canton did have the champions of the world.

One incident occurred just after the opening kickoff that doesn't illustrate Jim's ability as a player but rather his qual-

Thorpe
with Canton
Bulldogs,
1920

ity as a man. Our star running back, Henry McDonald, who could cover 100 yards in 10.2 seconds was knocked out of bounds. Henry, a black, began to be threatened by the Canton tackler with: "Black is black and white is white and where I come from, they don't mix." Sizing up the situation immediately, Jim ran between the two men and with the most fearsome stare I've seen told his teammate: "We're here to play football!" thus preventing a real donnybrook. His word was law!

When we were leaving the field, I half-stepped alongside the great Thorpe and suggested: "Jim, someday this game will draw like professional baseball." He replied: "The boys out here have been talking about it. I'll write to you." This brief conversation could very well have prompted the beginning of the National Football League. It was the only chance I had to talk to him that day and actually the first good look I got at the great athlete. All during the game he had flown past my end position.

Apparently Thorpe realized the difficulties we faced in that game and respected our abilities enough to promise to contact me about the formation of a league. We did correspond through 1919, when Ralph Hay, then general manager of the Bulldogs, called me to Canton for a meeting.

My last effort to stay with the pros occurred in 1925 when I tried to sign Red Grange. C. C. Pyle, his manager, brought him to the Morrison Hotel in Chicago. I had an associate bringing me a certified check for $5,000 that Grange was supposed to receive before each game, plus percentage privileges. The lobby was filled with the smoke of the reporters who had gathered from all over the country, but by the time he got up to my room on the seventeenth floor, Grange and Pyle had already signed with the Bears for $3,000.

In 1958 I was invited to the annual meeting of the NFL by Bert Bell and addressed the owners in behalf of the Jim Thorpe Memorial. And in 1960, I was appointed Honorary Historian. The motion was made by George Halas and seconded by Jack Mara.

My connection with the sport has been a great experience.

I met some wonderful people and time has vindicated my faith in the future of pro football.

I think it is only fitting that I close by saying that I consider Jim Thorpe to be the greatest all-around athlete the world will ever see. I asked him to speak before the Rotary Club one afternoon in 1940. That morning, I took him out to Monroe High School to talk to the students.

As you know, an auditorium in a high school with maybe 1500 or 2000 youngsters is ordinarily like a beehive. But when Jim stood up on the stage, just at a bare desk, with no microphone, you could have heard a pin drop. The kids probably didn't know Thorpe, but their fathers and grandfathers did.

Jim looked out and began: "I think the best way to talk to you boys and girls is to give you the story of my life." They loved every minute of it.[6]

By I. R. "Ike" Martin

I was born right out in the country, in Missouri, and never heard a train whistle until I was nine years of age. Having brothers who went to college, I had a desire to go myself and attended William Jewel College. I played defensive tackle and halfback on the football team.

I played my first pro football game under the assumed name, Johnson. I was coaching at Heidelberg where our games were on Friday. Friday night, I would leave for Fort Wayne, play for the Friars, come back Sunday and be on the job Monday. Since the colleges were opposed to pro ball, I would have lost my job if I were caught, so I was advertised as the "Mysterious Mr. Johnson."

After an important game we pulled out of the fire in Wabash, a little boy about twelve years old, jumped up on the running board of the car and said: "I know who you are! My brother was here from St. Joseph, Missouri, and he saw you play. But I'm not going to tell anyone." I must admit, that was quite a thrill for me.

When I went to work for the Goodyear Tire and Rubber

265

Company, in charge of employees' activities, even they objected to my playing. Sometimes, I had to put adhesive tape over my entire face to hide from my boss. It wasn't until after the war that I used my real name.

In 1919 the American League was formed and I played halfback with Canton for $150 a game, plus expenses. I loved the game so much! I would have played if they didn't pay me anything.

I wore number five and Jim Thorpe was number eight, and I came to know him very well. [In 1920, "Ike" tied Jim for the league championship for most points scored.] He was always full of fun, both on the field and off. I recall the incident of Jim's medals being taken from him. It was done because he had violated the rules. In my way of thinking, it was an awfully little technicality for him to be disbarred, but through the later years of Jim's life when he tried to get them back, Brundage always stuck strictly to the rules.

I've also heard people talk of his drinking, but when he was playing football, I never saw him take a drink. Thorpe was a man who played as hard as he could and hit as hard as he could. I considered myself fortunate that he was on my side and I didn't have to tackle him.

He even asked us to miss a man sometimes so he could hit that much harder. He figured if he hit somebody really hard, the next time, the fellow wouldn't be so anxious to hit him.

One day Bobby Nash, who unquestionably was one of the greatest ends, and the Massillon team were playing against us. Jim went back to catch a punt and told me to let Nash alone and I did.

They both hit like two locomotives and neither one got up from the field. They carried them both off, but that was his theory: "Let them get out of my way!" He wouldn't let a man tackle him at an angle; he would go straight at him. He knocked quite a few of them out but it was all perfectly legitimate.

He was rough but always clean. I never saw him do anything dirty. His high level of sportsmanship was never more evident than when he would grin that big grin of his in appreciation for a good play when someone threw him for a loss.

He took a terrible beating in those early years, with all the defenses keying on him. And those who say he didn't practice are not telling the truth. To my knowledge, he never once missed a practice at Canton. He was always on the job!

You had to be a top man. You must understand that there was somebody looking for your job all the time. Many were All-Americans and even some of them didn't make it, so it was an especially hard game.

Jim was well paid, and rightfully so, but seemed to run through his money awfully fast. He was big-hearted, and people, other than the players, were always borrowing from him.

I was asked at the Touchdown Club to compare Thorpe and Brown. I described a game we played against Dayton to illustrate my point. They had a good club and we were being beat. With very little time left, Thorpe drop-kicked a field goal from the 48-yard line to win the game. Brown couldn't do that and neither could Grange of Illinois even though you could never belittle his running ability.

There's no question about who was the greatest player; it was Thorpe. And I've seen them all because when I quit playing, I went to see all the big games.

You can say this about Jim Thorpe; maybe I've seen better passers, but he could throw as long a ball as anybody who ever lived and accurately, too. He could do so many things that none of the rest could do.

Yes, there were many great specialists: Gus Dorais, Fats Henry, Al Feeney, Horse Edwards, Bo McMillin, Knute Rockne, Charley Brickley, Red Roberts, Pudge Heffelfinger, and many others, but as I've said before, Jim Thorpe was pretty much a specialist in every department both on offense and defense.[7]

By Grace Thorpe

Just as Dad didn't know the Olympic rules, Indian people

even today don't know the rules in terms of the way white people do things. As far as I'm concerned you can be a professional in baseball and an amateur in track. I cannot see what relation they have to one another. Football scholarships at the present time include spending money and allowances for clothes, and I don't see how that is any different than Dad playing ball during the summer.

In his later years, Dad read the newspaper, cover to cover, but as a young man he didn't. I can still see him sitting down reading it and every so often looking up over his glasses to tell me about something he had read. So many of our young Indian people do not read the paper; they'll read the Indian newspapers that have been coming out during the last couple of years, but I doubt very much if they are up on all that is happening nationally and internationally.

A solution would be for more of our people to study the political structure of the U.S. and also to get into the communications field. But as you know, most of our people are very poor, and there are not many poor people who can go into politics.

On the brighter side, I have seen a lot of hope for the Indian in the last five years. I returned to areas where I've been away for that period of time and I can see the difference. In Oklahoma, for example, we now have three-bedroom low-cost housing and that's a delight to see. In Arizona they have a beautiful arts and crafts shop on the Gila River reservation, south of Phoenix. Also I have received notices, not too long ago, describing a modern motel that has just opened up on the Crow reservation and another big convention center in the Warm Springs, Oregon, reservation.

Being here in Washington, I hear all the different things the Indian people are doing and can witness first-hand their strengthening determination. If things continue the way they are going, the Indians will take over the reins of their government and manage it themselves rather than have the Bureau of Indian Affairs do it for them. What has happened to our people all along is that when a change occurs in the federal administration, a new commissioner of Indian Affairs and a new director for the Department of Interior are appointed and we have absolutely no continuity.

Speaking personally for a moment, my sisters and I talked at our last powwow about how we felt Dad's name should be used. His name has been exploited. We've been contacted by people wanting to open up Jim Thorpe motels, trading posts and sporting goods stores, just to name a few. We thought that by forming an organization we could give our stamp of approval to various groups who will do things in Dad's name in a dignified way to help keep our Indian heritage alive.

Most of our Indian people are torn between the two cultures. In my case, the Indian people look at me as a white, while the white people say I'm an Indian. This leads me to believe that more of our Indian people need to retain their culture, language, and indeed, their Indianness. I believe a lot of the frustration of our people, the suicide rate, and the alcoholism problem are based on removing them from their Indian world and putting them into the other without adequate preparation.

Then again, maybe some do not choose to go into the other culture; they want to stay. But because society is changing, and they do not have any money, they become destitute.

I recognize the existence of a cross culture but only going one way, from the Indian into the white. The white coming into the Indian has been tried and it hasn't worked for our people. Let them concentrate right now on their Indian culture because by understanding their culture, they, in turn, could teach it in the public-school system and in the universities. This would provide jobs and I for one have been lecturing at various universities for many years. I think there needs to be more emphasis placed on telling the Indian story to the rest of society. Therefore by selectively using Dad's name, we can be of some help in economic improvements or perhaps legal assistance.

I'm into the legal scene these days. As a matter of fact we've already sponsored the Indian hot line in Shawnee.

Any Indian in Oklahoma can call our lawyer, at no charge, for instant legal advice. He had 500 calls the first month.

I was one of those who was assimilated after I left Indian school. Mother remarried and we went to Illinois and from there I went into the service, was married overseas, and had two children, Thorpe and Dagmar. (Dagmar, a master's graduate from Deganawidah Quetzalcoatl University, is currently a second-year law student at Stanford University and working with the Wounded Knee legal defense counsel.) I returned to a job in New York, and that was where I brought up my children.

In 1967 I wondered what I was doing in New York and decided to work for Indian causes. So I sold my home, sent my resumé to various Indian groups and bunked at my mother's home in California until I got some answers.

I received a call from the National Congress of the American Indian, while I was out on the desert doing some rock hunting, and they wanted to know if I could handle two large conferences, one on the west coast and one on the east. Their purpose was to encourage industrialists to open branch plants on Indian reservations and this had never been done before.

At any rate the conferences were very successful. The N.C.A.I. was able to get several million dollars in economic development programs. Some of it has been good and some bad. The good was that jobs were provided, and the bad was that the air became polluted because of the relaxed environmental regulations. Then too, the government allowed them to pay half-wages for the first year while the Indians were being trained. Some of them stayed just that long and when the year was up, they left. But in some cases it has worked out very well. The Indian people could stay at home and still have jobs.

Then Alcatraz hit and I went over there to help with their public relations, and I've been working on individual land claims since then. Right now, I am a law intern at Senator Abourezk's office and attend the Antioch School of Law.

Thorpe with daughter Grace, 1926

Courtesy Grace Thorpe

The Senator is chairman of the Subcommittee on Indian Affairs and our leading Indian advocate.

My main interest in life is getting surplus land for the Indian people. In 1970 President Nixon announced that the federal government was going to give away 6.8 billion dollars worth of surplus property, and I see no reason why the Indians cannot get some of these properties back. They need them for schools, health clinics, and economic development. Many of them are landless. This is ridiculous but true! Many of these lands should be given back to these landless tribes whose property was stolen from them many years ago.

I hope to get a bill written on Indian land issues and I already have a Senator and a member of the House who are interested in cosponsoring the bill. I'm trying to line up others and hope to be finished in another year. Then I hope to return to Oklahoma to work on this project.

Dad was always fighting for Indian rights. In the thirties, the Hollywood Studios would hire white people for Indian roles. I remember Dad at the time trying to get the directors to hire Indians for these parts. He knew how badly they needed the money, and forty years later the fight is still going on.

I have so many wonderful memories of Dad. One of my first was when I was four or five and a student at Haskell. He was visiting me and agreed to put on a kicking exhibition, along with his friend, John Levi, a great Indian athlete.

The people were jammed around the field and cheering louder with each goal. Since Dad had promised to take me for some candy, I was, frankly, more interested in that than the football stuff.

Stories are told about some of the things I did when I was a little girl. People in the neighborhood would send me into the house to get one of Dad's medals. He had two or three trunks filled with nothing but medals and I didn't know any better so I would hand them out to anyone who asked.

When I was a few years older, I remember the day he put me in my place. He was going to do a show and we were walking up the steps to the radio station in L.A. I was at the age when I thought everybody was looking at me. I was all dressed up and had just discovered I was a girl, was more like it. So I was paying a lot of attention to myself, being very self-conscious, when all of a sudden, he got behind me, put his nails into my ankle and made a sound like a dog. I screamed like you wouldn't believe and he kept walking up the steps acting like he didn't know me.

He was cool, my gosh, was he cool! We took a trip from California to Oklahoma to visit my Aunt Mary, Dad's sister, and you must realize the Indian people don't stop overnight; we don't have the money. He had driven all night over the mountains and by morning was getting tired, so he turned to me and said: "This is as good a time as any to teach you how to drive." I was fourteen at the time and eagerly said, "Okay!"

He showed me where the brake was, how to hold the steering wheel and give it the gas. Then he put it in gear, watched me for a few minutes to see if I was all right with a car coming and climbed into the back seat and went to sleep.

It was a flat desert and even if I had gone off the road, it wouldn't have done any harm. I couldn't shift the gears, so when I saw Albuquerque on the horizon, I woke him up to take over but, by then, he had gotten a nice three-hour rest.

When we'd stay with Aunt Mary, Dad went to bed around nine and would get up before anyone else and go down to the pecan grove and shoot squirrels. He cleaned them and Aunt Mary cooked them and we had fried squirrel for breakfast. It was delightful.

He was a good cook too! He used to do a thing with potatoes, scrambled eggs, and bacon. It was gorgeous! When he went coon hunting or fishing, he would clean them and prepare the most delicious coon or fish stew.

At one time he had about eighteen coon hounds in his backyard. It wasn't very big which didn't make us popular with the neighbors. He always had dogs and, oh, the sound they made when they wanted to get out and run.

He liked to take the boys hunting and fishing or playing ball to encourage them in physical ways. All of his children, boys and girls, have excellent coordination.

Dad was a very graceful man who moved very nicely. He was a beautiful dancer and had really great rhythm. Different times we'd go out in groups and I'd dance with him. One night in Hollywood, we were having a great time, and I heard a woman say: "Well really! He looks old enough to be her father." That tickled me.

Other times we went bowling in Hawthorne, California, and he threw a powerful ball. It didn't matter what side of the head pin he hit because they would all go down and he'd have another 200 game.

Being a good swimmer, he taught the kids, but whatever he did, he did it right. He excelled in anything that took coordination.

He used to sew, too. If there was a rip or tear in any of his clothes, he would go ahead and fix it.

And his approach to problem-solving was very direct. One time he was tied up in traffic in L.A. and the driver behind him kept honking and honking and there was no place Dad could go. So he got out of his car and told the man that he couldn't move.

He no sooner got back in the car when the man started up again. So he got out the second time, lifted up the man's hood and disconnected his horn.

Mother is eighty-two years old, lives in Hawthorne, and still drives a car. The children are spread out all over the country today. Gail is Office Services Supervisor for the Girl Scout National Branch Office in Chicago and has two grown daughters, Lynn and Sharon. Sharon has three children and Lynn is expecting her seventh.

Charlotte works as a night supervisor for the Motorola Corporation in Phoenix. Her eldest son, Michael has recently completed his doctorate in education and another son, John, has just graduated from high school.

Carl Phillip is retired from the military and is living in Falls Church, Virginia. His three daughters are named Carla, Karen, and Teresa. Bill works for an industrial firm in Arlinggon, Texas, and has a son, Bill, Jr.

Dick is employed by the Oklahoma State Senate as chief

of supplies and lives in Shawnee. He is married to an Indian girl and has two children, Larry and Anita. Recently, he was elected to the Council of the Sac and Fox tribe.

Jack has his own business, a Volkswagen repair shop in Shawnee. He married an Indian girl and they have a boy, Gary.[8]

By George Trafton

My football career began during the First World War when I played with Camp Grant. Then I came out of the Army and went to Notre Dame where Knute Rockne was the coach. He was the finest and the most intelligent coach that ever lived. When he was killed in that airplane accident in Kansas City, I know a lot of people said that they shouldn't have let brains of that class fly around in the air. The man was so smart that very few coaches could beat him and none was able to do it consistently.

There's so much to be learned in football. I found that out when I left Notre Dame and went to Northwestern as a line coach in 1922. Shoo-hoo! If Rockne had been up there coaching with me, we would have won the conference title. As it was, we won three games which was something because they hadn't won a game in two years. We beat Purdue, Monmouth, and Beloit and tied Minnesota. Oh we had a big year, and they were all very happy about it.

From there I went into professional football at Decatur, Illinois, with the Staley Starch Workers, or the Decatur Staleys, the forerunner of the Chicago Bears. Mr. Staley already had a fine baseball team, with such stars as Ray Bennett who used to play with the White Sox and a fellow by the name of George Halas, formerly with the Yankees. Then he wanted a football team.

Our first game in that year of 1920 was against Hammond whom we beat. Most of our games were played in Decatur to cut down on expenses, and there were no big payoffs after the game. We were starch workers first and football players second. I received a salary for paddling starch. And

I mean there was no kidding around. I had to work.

When the Staleys became the Bears, I was the highest-paid lineman in the western circuit. I was earning $150 per game back in the days when $100 per game was a lot of money. They had wanted to give me $125, but I said no and threatened to play for Hammond.

You had to be a man in those days because you not only had to lick the guy in front of you but you had to fight your way out. I remember that the average pay was fifty to seventy-five dollars per game. There just wasn't much money because the crowds were very, very sparse. Sparse in all places but one—the one where Jim Thorpe happened to be playing. Our paid attendance averaged about 1,200 before we played against his team. In the two games of 1921 against him there were 6,000 and 8,000 people. Yes, things were rough before Thorpe came along.

He was practically the whole team down there in Canton, and don't forget he played with them when they were World Champions and had nothing but All-Americans on the roster. One of his best games was against Hammond in 1919. Canton was winning the game, thanks to Thorpe's running and kicking, but the score was close and Hammond was threatening in the closing minutes of the final quarter. Thorpe wanted to tackle the ball carrier and try to force a fumble. So he told the tackle to move in and the end to move out. They obeyed his instructions and left a big hole in the line and on the next play Gil Falcon, the Hammond fullback, took the handoff and headed for the opening. Just as he got there, old Thorpe hit him and almost tore him in half. Oh boy! You could hear it all over the ballpark!

Canton got the ball, and Jim, standing in his own end zone, punted the ball out of bounds at the other end of the field on the one-yard line. The kick went all the way in the air.

I played against Thorpe in Shreveport, Louisiana, in 1922. At that time, he was playing for the Oorang Indians, and I was with Bo McMillin's All-Americans. This game was after the regular season because I was still with the Bears. There was not too much strictness in the rules and regulations. So

Canton Bulldogs, 1920 World Champions

Courtesy Pro Football Hall of Fame

I would play the season out up in the North, where it was cold and snowy and then come South where it was beautiful.

They had Thorpe, Calac, and Guyon, and, oh brother, a whole list of Indian stars!

"We'll beat them," said McMillin.

"You'll beat who?" I answered.

"We'll beat these fellows easy!"

"Boy, you just haven't got enough men to hold off those Indians!"

The final score was Indians 36, All-Americans 0.

Rockne used to tell about his encounter with Thorpe. He was playing end for Massillon when Thorpe ran a sweep in his direction. Rockne was there to meet him and nail him for a loss. Thorpe said: "You mustn't do that, Rock. These fans paid to see Old Jim run. Be a good boy and let Old Jim run." The next time Thorpe came at him there was another collision but this time Rockne went down and Thorpe ran 50 yards for a touchdown.

Rockne was still groggy when Thorpe returned to see how he was feeling. Handing him a wet towel, Thorpe smiled and said: "That's a good boy, Rock. You let Old Jim run."

I never had any real conversations with Jim except on the playing field, because he was always the captain of his team, and I was captain of the Bears for eight years until I got sick and tired of having all the abuse heaped on me. But Jim was a very stoical person, not very talkative or sociable.

The guy seldom showed any emotions. You could never tell what he felt like. Even if a game ended adversely, against his team, he would just hang his head and walk off the field.

He did not have a bad temper, but if pushed far enough, he would occasionally get angry. And if you had this 215-pound guy angry at you, you had better get up in the stands. You don't want to get down where he can reach you. Thorpe was one hell of a competitor!

Now they tell me that if he only drank one quart of whiskey the night before a game, Canton would win the next day. If he drank more than a quart, they couldn't win. It is also said that he was a lazy person. Well, both of these judgments are fallacies, because when I met the man, he already had a fabulous reputation and when I played against him he was always in great shape.

No, Jim's difficulties in later life were not caused by drinking or laziness but by his background. If he had asked his mother or father: "Should I play baseball during the summer for sixty dollars a month?" they would have given their approval instead of saying: "No. It isn't all right. You would be classed as a professional."

Now I got kicked out of Notre Dame for the same simple reason. I read about Rockne playing with Massillon when he was playing with Notre Dame so what the hell am I supposed to do? I had a contract to play professional football before I ever got to college. I mean that! If you didn't have any money, you would go out on the weekend and pick up fifty dollars.

One day after the season ended, however, I had just finished basketball practice and returned to my room to find that my roommate had broken into my trunk and stolen all of my money.

He was through anyway because he didn't have any eligibility left, and I have never seen him to this day. So I went up to Chicago to play some more pro football and got caught. They threw me out of school. I took the rap for a couple of other guys who were in the game with me, but nobody said anything. They didn't even ask me if there was anybody else. They had the big guy and that was all they wanted. The losing bettors were unhappy because we had won. It wasn't Chris O'Brien's fault. He was a nice guy about it. He gave me enough money to tempt me and I couldn't help it. I had to buy my mother a present for Christmas and I didn't have any money.

But Thorpe played for what? He sacrificed his entire amateur career for a few dollars and they take his medals away and made a very humiliated person out of him. He had no background, so what the hell. Thorpe was no dummy. The

King of Sweden had told him that he was the greatest athlete in the world, and he was the greatest. Because he played a lousy little baseball he lost everything.

That's the trouble with people who have great ability. They are all taken advantage of to varying degrees. Joe Louis is another example. He was the most abused heavyweight champion we ever had. I happen to know that for a fact because I used to own 10 per cent of him but I gave it back to him right off the bat. I got out of that picture in a hurry!

He was twenty years old when John Roxborough brought him into my gymnasium in Chicago, and it was there that Jack Blackburn taught him how to box. Every day he would practice the same combination, jab, jab, and right hand, over and over again. I did the best I could to help the poor kid because everyone was always hollering at him. Yes, Joe Louis had a bad time of it. They tried to take everything. He got 50 per cent and paid all the expenses. Oh, what a bad deal!

He was not only exploited by his managers but also by the United States government. Yes, the great U.S. government took advantage of him! I never felt so disgusted in my life! A great deal of the money that he owed them came from benefit fights at Madison Square Garden from which he received nothing. He would fight a guy for the benefit of the Marine Corps, the Army, the Navy, or the Merchant Marines and they are taxing this man for money he never received. Why the hell didn't they go to the people that got the money? But they finally threw it out because they were ashamed of what they were doing to the fellow.

People have asked me many times: "Who was the greatest football player you ever saw or played against?"

"Well," I said, "I happened to be very fortunate. I've seen George McAfee and Gale Sayers and I've played with George Gipp and Bronko Nagurski, but the greatest of them all was Jim Thorpe."

"What's the matter with Ernie Nevers?"

"You didn't hear me mention his name, did you?"

"Well he scored forty points against you guys one day."

"That's right. But he had a hell of lot of help!" I played against him maybe twenty times and I never let the man get past the line of scrimmage. Nevers was a great football player but he couldn't compare with Nagurski. Bronko ran his own interference. George Gipp was a hell of a football player. But the Indian just had something better than all of them. All I can say is that I consider and always did consider Jim to be the greatest football player that ever lived.[10]

Appendix

What follows are the athletic records and tributes of James Francis Thorpe, or Wa-tho-huck (Bright Path), May 28, 1888–March 28, 1953.

TRACK AND FIELD RECORDS

100-yard dash	10 seconds
100-yard dash (Exhibition)	9.8 seconds
120-yard high hurdles	15.2 seconds
220-yard low hurdles	23.8 seconds
440-yard race	48 seconds
1,500 meter run	4 minutes 40.1 seconds
High jump	6 ft. 5 in.
Pole vault	10 ft. 8 in.
Broad jump	24 ft. 1 in.
Hammer throw	138 feet
Shot put	47 ft. 10 in.
Javelin	163 feet
Discus	125 ft. 8 in.

OLYMPIC RECORDS—1912
Pentathlon

Broad jump	23 ft. 2-7/10 in.
Javelin	153 ft. 2-19/20 in.
200-meter race	22.9 seconds
Discus	116 ft. 8-4/10 in.
1,500-meter race	4 minutes 44.8 seconds

(Won the Gold Medal with 7 points)

Decathlon

100-meter race	11.2 seconds

Broad jump	22 ft. 2-3/10 in.
Shot put	42 ft. 5-9/20 in.
High jump	6 ft. 1-6/10 in.
400-meter race	47.6 seconds
110-meter high hurdles	15.6 seconds
Discus	121 ft. 3-9/10 in.
Pole vault	10 ft. 7-19/20 in.
Javelin	149 ft. 11-2/10 in.
1,500-meter race	4 minutes 40.1 seconds

(Won the Gold Medal with 8,412.955 points)

MAJOR LEAGUE BASEBALL RECORD

Team	Yr.	Gms.	At Bat	Hits	Avg.	Pos.	Field Avg.
New York Giants	1913	19	35	5	.143	OF	.994 (9 gms.)
New York Giants	1914	30	31	6	.194	OF	.750 (4 gms.)
New York Giants	1915	17	52	12	.231	OF	.933 (15 gms.)
Cincinnati Reds	1917	77	251	62	.247	OF	.959 (71 gms.)
New York Giants	1917	26	57	11	.193	OF	.969 (20 gms.)
New York Giants	1918	58	113	28	.248	OF	.983 (44 gms.)
New York Giants	1919	2	3	1	.333	OF	1.000 (2 gms.)
Boston Braves	1919	60	156	51	.327	OF	.926 (38 gms.)
						1st	.867 (2 gms.)

CARLISLE FOOTBALL RECORD, INDIVIDUAL & TEAM
(During Jim's Career)

October 12, 1907   1st varsity game vs. Syracuse.

September 19, 1908	Played 1st half against Conway Hall, running for five touchdowns and passing for another.
September 26, 1908	Scored winning touchdown against Villanova.
October 3, 1908	3 field goals against Penn State.
October 24, 1908	40-yard run from scrimmage for touchdown and kicked extra point to tie Penn 6 to 6.
November 7, 1908	Completed 55-yard pass play and had a 65-yard run from scrimmage against Harvard.
November 14, 1908	Ran for winning touchdown in 6 to 0 victory over Western Pennsylvania.
September 30, 1911	Scored only touchdown of game with an 85-yard run against Dickinson.
October 7, 1911	28-, 14-, and 67-yard runs for three touchdowns in only half played vs. Mt. St. Mary's.
October 14, 1911	Open field run of 45 yards against Georgetown.
October 21, 1911	Punted 50 to 70 yards on each kick and got downfield each time to grab the ball himself or make the tackle against Pitt. On one occasion, he received his own punt and ran the remaining 20 yards for the score.
October 28, 1911	Kicked a 35-yard field goal and ran for a touchdown against Lafayette.
November 4, 1911	Kicked four field goals of 13, 37, 43, and 48 yards to defeat Harvard.
November 17, 1911	Vs. Syracuse ran for two touchdowns from scrimmage.
November 22, 1911	Only played for first two series of downs and scored twice against Johns Hopkins.
November 30, 1911	Forty-yard run from scrimmage, 27 and 33-yard field goals and estab-

	lished new field record with an 83-yard punt against Brown.
September 28, 1912	Ran for two touchdowns against Dickinson, one for 29 yards, the other for 110.
October 5, 1912	Four interceptions against Washington and Jefferson.
October 12, 1912	Scored three touchdowns against Syracuse.
October 19, 1912	Scored three touchdowns, one for 40 yards, against Pitt.
October 28, 1912	Ran 62 yards from scrimmage for a touchdown and averaged 75 yards punting against Toronto.
November 2, 1912	Scored 28 points against Lehigh, one touchdown covering 110 yards after an interception, and threw a ball 67 yards in the air for a completion to the 1/2-yard line.
November 9, 1912	Set up all four touchdowns averaging more than ten yards per carry against Army. Ran a punt back through the entire 11 defenders for a 45-yard touchdown (an offsides penalty nullified it).
November 16, 1912	Ran 75 yards from scrimmage and threw 15 yards for touchdowns against Penn.
November 23, 1912	Vs. Springfield, scored all 30 points with four touchdowns, three field goals and one extra point; the longest run being 57 yards.
November 28, 1912	Ran for three touchdowns and kicked two field goals; his better runs going for 20, 30, 33, 50, and 50 yards against Brown.

1907

Car.		Opp.
40	Leb. Valley	0
10	Villanova	0
91	Susquehanna	0
18	Penn St.	5
14	Syracuse	6
15	Bucknell	0
26	Penn	6
0	Princeton	16
23	Harvard	15
12	Minnesota	10
18	Chicago	4
267		62

Won 10, Lost 1

1908

Car.		Opp.
53	Conway Hall	0
35	Leb. Valley	0
10	Villanova	0
12	Penn St.	5
12	Syracuse	0
6	Penn	6
16	Navy	6
0	Harvard	17
6	West. Penn.	0
6	Minnesota	11
17	St. Louis	0
31	Nebraska	6
8	Denver	4
212		55

Won 10, Lost 2, Tied 1

1911

Car.		Opp.
53	Leb. Valley	0
32	Muhlenberg	0
17	Dickinson	0
46	Mt. St. Mary's	5
28	Georgetown	5
17	Pitt	0
19	Lafayette	0
16	Penn	0
18	Harvard	15
11	Syracuse	12
29	J. Hopkins	6
12	Brown	6
298		49

Won 11, Lost 1

1912

Car.		Opp.
50	Albright	7
45	Leb. Valley	0
34	Dickinson	0
65	Villanova	0
0	Wash. & Jeff.	0
33	Syracuse	0
45	Pitt	8
34	Georgetown	20
49	Toronto	1
34	Lehigh	14
27	Army	6
26	Penn	34
30	Springfield	24
32	Brown	0
504		114

Won 12, Lost 1, Tied 1

Tributes

1908   Third Team All-American.

1911   First Team All-American.

1912   First Team All-American.

1912   Proclaimed "The Greatest Athlete in the World" by King Gustav V of Sweden.

1912   Presented by the King with the Laurel Wreath, Gold Medal, and Life-size Bronze Bust of the King for Pentathlon victory.

1912   Presented by the King with the Laurel Wreath, Gold Medal, and a jeweled, 30-pound Silver Chalice, lined with gold, in the shape of a viking ship for Decathlon victory.

1919–
1920   Elected and re-elected first president of the American Professional Football Association; later to be named the National Football League.

1922   Granted approval for the formation of an All-Indian Professional Football Team, "The Oorang Indians."

1938   Named to Knute Rockne, Grantland Rice, and "Hurry Up" Yost's "All-Time" All-American Teams.

1943   Named to Clark Shaughnessy's "Eternal" All-American Team.

1950   Voted Greatest Football Player of the half-century by the Associated Press.

1950   Voted Greatest Male Athlete of the half-century by the Associated Press.

1950   Elected to Helms Hall Professional Football Hall of Fame (in addition to previous induction into the College Division).

1951   World Premiere of *Jim Thorpe, All-American* motion picture.

1951   Dedication of tablet monument in Carlisle.

1951   Elected to National College Football Hall of Fame (National Football Foundation and Hall of Fame, New York City).

1912–
1953   Officially honored by government and civic leaders in hundreds of towns and cities and countries

288

throughout the world.

1953 Dedication of Jim Thorpe Stadium, Shawnee, Oklahoma.

1955 NFL's "Most Valuable Player" award named "The Jim Thorpe Trophy."

1957 Dedication of Jim Thorpe Memorial Mausoleum in Jim Thorpe, Pennsylvania, formerly Mauch Chunk and East Mauch Chunk. The high school was also renamed after him.

1958 Elected to the National Indian Hall of Fame in Anadarko.

1961 Voted "World's Greatest Athlete" by the editors of *El Universal,* Caracas, Venezuela.

1961 Elected to the Pennsylvania Hall of Fame.

1963 Enshrined as a Charter Member in the National Professional Football Hall of Fame, Canton, Ohio. Later, a statue of him was dedicated.

1967 "Jim Thorpe Day" celebrated in Yale, Oklahoma; followed by placing of historical markers by the Oklahoma State Historical Society, designating his hometown and house where he lived, and announcement that his portrait will hang in the rotunda of the state capitol.

1969 Through the efforts of the Carlisle, Pennsylvania, Jaycees and Governor Shafer, in excess of 5,000 signatures were collected on "Project Jim Thorpe Day" for the purpose of his exoneration and sent to the United States Olympic Committee.

1973 Amateur Athletic Union announcement restoring Jim's amateur status.

1975 Senate resolution to restore Jim's amateur status introduced by Senator Quentin Burdick, North Dakota; Grace Thorpe is looking for cosponsors.

1975 Enshrined in the National Track and Field Hall of Fame of the United States of America, Charleston, West Virginia.

1977 Named the "Greatest American Football Player in History" in a national poll conducted by *Sport* magazine.

Notes

NOTES, CHAPTER 1

1. "Born the year 1888, 28th day of May, near and south of Bellemont-Pottawatomie County—along the banks of North Fork River. The trading post at that time was Old Shawnee. As there was no post office at that date, I believe Shawnee could claim my birthtown or city. I hope this will clear up the inquiries as to my birthplace. Jim Thorpe." (Jim wrote this note on October 20, 1943, in the office of Fred Grove, the managing editor of the *Shawnee News Star.*)

2. He was christened "James Francis Thorpe."

3. Interview with Charlotte Thorpe Adler, daughter of Jim Thorpe, August 21, 1967, New York City.

4. Bernard De Voto, *Across the Wide Missouri*, 43, 44.

5. Interview with Chief Garland Nevitt, July 14, 1967, Dearborn, Michigan.

6. Letter from Arthur Wakolee, Sac and Fox lecturer, November 10, 1967.

7. Jim Thorpe's personal scrapbook, entrusted to author by Patricia Thorpe, widow of Jim Thorpe, August 19, 1967–November 30, 1967. (According to the files of Grace Thorpe, Jim's father married three times. His wives and children were: No-ten-o-quah: Frank, Fannie, and Minnie; Charlotte View: George, Jim, Charles, Edward, Mary, and Adeline; Julia Mixon: William and Roscoe.)

8. Jim Thorpe's personal scrapbook.

9. *Ibid.*

10. *Ibid.*

11. *Ibid.*

12. Letter from Arthur Wakolee, August 25, 1967.

13. *Ibid.*, January 3, 1968.

14. Interview with Patricia Thorpe, July 24, 1967, Banning, California.

NOTES, CHAPTER 2

1. Letter from Arthur Wakolee, January 3, 1968.

2. Jim Thorpe's personal scrapbook.

3. Letter from Arthur Wakolee, January 3, 1968.

4. *Ibid.*, August 25, 1967.

5. Interview with Elizabeth K. Dunn, librarian at Haskell Indian Junior College, July 28, 1967.

6. *Ibid.*

7. Interview with George Washington, Haskell instructor, July 28, 1967.

8. Interview with Elizabeth K. Dunn.

9. Interview with George Washington.

10. Interview with Elizabeth K. Dunn.

11. Interview with Chief Garland Nevitt.

12. Interview with George Washington.

13. Jim Thorpe's personal scrapbook.

14. *Ibid.*

15. *Ibid.*

16. On page 28 in *The Jim Thorpe Story*, Gene Schoor wrote that there was no baseball for Jim to play at this time, and that the primary reason for Jim's acceptance to Carlisle was his desire to become an electrician. This is not factual.

17. Interview with George Washington.

18. The *Lon Scott News* publication loaned by Joseph Boyle, former editor of the *Jim Thorpe Times-News*, August 17, 1967.

19. Jim Thorpe's personal scrapbook.

NOTES, CHAPTER 3

1. Richard Henry Pratt, *Battlefield and Classroom*, 97.

2. *Ibid.*, 118, 119.

3. *Ibid.*, 119, 120.

4. *Ibid.*, 120.

5. *Ibid.*, 180.

6. *Ibid.*, 122.

7. *Ibid.*, 167.

8. *Ibid.*, 213, 214.

9. *Ibid.*, 221–24.

10. Interview with Mrs. Verna (Donegan) Whistler, former teacher at the Carlisle Indian School, August 14, 1967, Carlisle, Pennsylvania.

11. *Ibid.*

12. Interview with Pete Calac, teammate and lifelong friend of Jim Thorpe, July 27, 1967, Canton, Ohio.

13. Interview with Arthur Martin, August 15, 1967, Carlisle, Pennsylvania.

14. Interview with Mrs. Whistler.

NOTES, CHAPTER 4

1. Interview with Chief Freeman Johnson, Grand Sachem of the Senecas, December 2, 1967, Rochester, New York.

2. Richard Henry Pratt, *Battlefield and Classroom*, 317, 318.

3. Glenn S. Warner, "The Indian Massacres," *Collier's* (October 17, 1931), 7.

4. Glenn S. Warner, "Heap Big Run-Most-Fast," *Collier's* (October 24, 1931), 18.

5. Warner, "The Indian Massacres," *Collier's* (October 17, 1931), 8.

6. *Ibid.,* 61.

7. Warner, "Heap Big Run-Most-Fast," *Collier's* (October 24, 1931), 18.

8. *Ibid.,* 19

9. Warner, "The Indian Massacres," *Collier's* (October 17, 1931), 8.

10. *Ibid.,* 62

11. John S. Steckbeck, *Red Menaces,* 67.

12. Interview with Arthur Martin.

13. Warner, "Heap Big Run-Most-Fast," *Collier's* (October 24, 1931), 19.

14. Interview with Arthur Martin.

15. Interview with Hyman Goldstein, Dickinson's star quarterback (1911–12), August 16, 1967, Carlisle, Pennsylvania. Mr. Goldstein, presently a prominent attorney in Carlisle, was selected as Dickinson College's All-Time Greatest Athlete.

16. Warner, "The Indian Massacres," *Collier's* (October 17, 1931), 7, 8.

17. John S. Steckbeck, *Fabulous Redmen,* 66.

18. Interview with Hyman Goldstein.

19. Interview with Andy Kerr, one of college football's outstanding coaches, October 19, 1967, Hamilton, New York.

NOTES, CHAPTER 5

1. Richard Henry Pratt, *Battlefield and Classroom,* 311.

2. Interview with Mrs. Verna (Donegan) Whistler.

3. *Ibid.*

4. From the files of Elizabeth K. Dunn.

5. Jim Thorpe's personal scrapbook.

6. Charlotte Thorpe Adler's personal scrapbook entrusted to author, August 21, 1967.

7. Jim Thorpe's personal scrapbook.

8. *Ibid.*

9. *Ibid.*

10. *Ibid.*

11 Interview with Arthur Martin.

12. Jim Thorpe's personal scrapbook.

13. *Ibid.*

14. *Ibid.*

15. *Ibid.*

16. Interview with Henry Clune, historian and columnist for the *Rochester Democrat & Chronicle,* October 10, 1967, Rochester, New York.

17. Jim Thorpe's personal scrapbook.

18. *Ibid.*

19. *New York Times,* October 6, 1907, Sports Section, 2.

20. *Ibid.,* October 13, 1907, Sports Section, 2.
21. *Ibid.,* October 27, 1907, Sports Section, 5.
22. *Ibid.,* November 3, 1907, Sports Section, 1.
23. Jim Thorpe's personal scrapbook.
24. *Ibid.*
25. *New York Times,* November 10, 1907, Sports Section, 1.
26. *Ibid.,* November 17, 1907, Sports Section, 1.
27. *Ibid.,* November 24, 1907, Sports Section, 1.
28. Interview with Arthur Martin.
29. Jim Thorpe's personal scrapbook.
30. *Ibid.*
31. Charlotte Thorpe Adler's personal scrapbook.
32. Jim Thorpe's personal scrapbook.
33. Interview with Jim Wood, June 1, 1967, Rochester, New York.

NOTES, CHAPTER 6

1. Jim Thorpe's personal scrapbook.
2. Glenn S. Warner, "Red Menaces," *Collier's* (October 31, 1931), 17.
3. James C. Heartwell's personal scrapbook entrusted to author, July 20, 1967.
4. Interview with Chief Freeman Johnson.
5. Field goals counted four points and touchdowns five points during this era.
6. *New York Times,* October 11, 1908, Sports Section, 1.
7. John S. Steckbeck, *Fabulous Redmen,* 75, 76.
8. Jim Thorpe's personal scrapbook.
9. James C. Heartwell's personal scrapbook.
10. *New York Times.* October 25, 1908, Sports Section, 1.
11. Warner, "Red Menaces," *Collier's* (October 31, 1931), 16.
12. *New York Times,* November 8, 1908, Sports Section, 1.
13. *Philadelphia Public Ledger,* November 2, 1908, 7.
14. *New York Times,* November 8, 1908, Sports Section, 1.
15. Charlotte Thorpe Adler's personal scrapbook.
16. James C. Heartwell's personal scrapbook.
17. *New York Times,* November 22, 1908, Sports Section, 2.
18. Charlotte Thorpe Adler's personal scrapbook.
19. James C. Heartwell's personal scrapbook.
20. Joseph Boyle's personal scrapbook.
21. *Ibid.*
22. Interview with Arthur Martin.
23. Warner, "Red Menaces," *Collier's* (October 31, 1931), 16, 17.

NOTES, CHAPTER 7

1. Jim Thorpe's personal scrapbook.

2. Arthur Daley, *Pro Football's Hall of Fame,* 29.

3. From the files of Vernon Sechriest, editor, *Rocky Mount* (North Carolina) *Telegram,* May 26, 1972.

4. Interview with Grace Thorpe, August 3, 1974, Washington, D.C.

5. James C. Heartwell's personal scrapbook.

6. *Ibid.*

7. Walter H. Lingo, "The Life Story of Jim Thorpe," *Athletic World* (July, 1923), 24.

8. *Ibid.*

9. John S. Steckbeck, *Fabulous Redmen,* 86.

10. Gene Schoor, *The Jim Thorpe Story,* 63, 64.

11. *New York Times,* November 1, 1911, Sports Section, 2.

12. Steckbeck, *Fabulous Redmen,* 107.

13. Charlotte Thorpe Adler's personal scrapbook.

14. Al Stump, "Jim Thorpe, Greatest of Them All," *Sport* magazine (December, 1949), 54.

15. Charlotte Thorpe Adler's personal scrapbook.

16. *Ibid.*

17. *Ibid.*

18. James C. Heartwell's personal scrapbook.

19. Jim Thorpe's personal scrapbook.

20. *Ibid.*

21. *Ibid.*

22. James C. Heartwell's personal scrapbook.

23. Jim Thorpe's personal scrapbook.

24. Daley, *Pro Football's Hall of Fame,* 31.

25. Jim Thorpe's personal scrapbook.

26. Charlotte Thorpe Adler's personal scrapbook.

27. Charles Paddock, "Chief Bright Path," from the files of James C. Heartwell.

28. Glenn S. Warner, "Red Menaces," *Collier's* (October 31, 1931), 10, 11, 51.

29. *Boston Sunday Post,* November 12, 1911, 14.

30. *New York Times,* November 12, 1911, Sports Section, 1.

31. Jim Thorpe's personal scrapbook.

32. From the files of James C. Heartwell.

33. *Boston Sunday Post,* November 12, 1911, 18.

34. Stump, "Jim Thorpe, Greatest of Them All," *Sport* magazine (December, 1949), 54.

35. *Boston Sunday Post,* November 12, 1911, 18.

36. Charlotte Thorpe Adler's personal scrapbook.

37. *Syracuse Post Standard,* November 16, 1911.

38. Steckbeck, *Fabulous Redmen,* 90.

39. *New York Times,* November 19, 1911, Sports Section, 2.

40. A field goal now counted three points.

41. *Providence Daily Journal,* December 1, 1911, 1, 5.

42. James C. Heartwell's personal scrapbook.

43. From the files of the Helms Athletic Foundation, Helms Hall, Los Angeles, California.

44. Jim Thorpe's personal scrapbook.

45. From the files of Grace Thorpe.

NOTES, CHAPTER 8

1. This marked the only time in Olympic history that competition was held at a two-year instead of a four-year interval.

2. This group included George S. Patton, Jr., who was to finish a disappointing fifth in the modern Pentathlon (duel shooting, swimming, fencing, riding, and a cross-country race) but who later became one of America's most skillful generals during World War II.

3. Grantland Rice, *The Tumult and the Shouting,* 229.

4. Gene Schoor, *The Jim Thorpe Story,* 77.

5. Interview with Ralph Craig, January 18, 1968, Waynesboro, Virginia.

6. Interview with Avery Brundage, July 12, 1967, Chicago, Illinois.

7. *Ibid.*

8. James E. Sullivan, *The Olympic Games. Stockholm, 1912,* 69.

9. *Ibid.,* 63.

10. *Ibid.*

11. Interview with Ralph Craig.

12. Jim Thorpe's personal scrapbook.

13. *Ibid.*

14. *Ibid.*

15. *Ibid.*

16. Interview with Ralph Craig.

17. Jim Thorpe's personal scrapbook.

18. Interview with Ralph Craig.

19. *Ibid.*

20. Jim Thorpe's personal scrapbook.

21. Rice, *The Tumult and the Shouting,* 230.

22. James C. Heartwell's personal scrapbook.

23. Jim Thorpe's personal scrapbook.

24. Interview with Ralph Craig.

NOTES, CHAPTER 9

1. Jim Thorpe's personal scrapbook.

2. Interview with Arthur Martin.

3. Jim Thorpe's personal scrapbook.

4. Interview with Ralph Craig.

5. From a tape recording sent by Tom Harmon to author, November 24, 1967.

6. Jim Thorpe's personal scrapbook.

7. *Ibid.*

8. *Ibid.*

9. Interview with Pete Calac.

10. Interview with Dr. Joseph Alexander, "the greatest football player ever at Syracuse University!" . . . Chancellor William P. Tolley, September 2, 1967, New York, New York.

11. *New York Times,* October 20, 1912, Sports Section, 1.

12. Jim Thorpe's personal scrapbook.

13. *Ibid.*

14. *Ibid.*

15. *Ibid.*

16. *Ibid.*

17. *Ibid.*

18. *New York Times,* November 3, 1912, Sports Section, 1.

19. Jim Thorpe's personal scrapbook.

20. *Ibid.*

21. Interview with Pete Calac.

22. Jim Thorpe's personal scrapbook.

23. *New York Times,* November 10, 1912, Sports Section, 1, 2.

24. Jim Thorpe's personal scrapbook.

25. *Ibid.*

26. *Ibid.*

27. Colonel Alexander M. Weyand, *The Saga of American Football,* 101.

28. Arthur Daley, *Pro Football's Hall of Fame,* 34.

29. Gene Schoor, *The Jim Thorpe Story,* 1–4.

30. Interview with President Dwight D. Eisenhower, August 17, 1967, Gettysburg, Pennsylvania.

31. Daley, *Pro Football's Hall of Fame,* 34.

32. Grantland Rice, *The Tumult and the Shouting,* 232.

33. From the files of the Cumberland County Historical Society and Hamilton Library Association.

34. *New York Times,* November 17, 1912, Sports Section, 1.

35. Jim Thorpe's personal scrapbook.

36. *New York Times,* November 24, 1912, Sports Section, 1.

37. Interview with Pete Calac.

38. *New York Times,* November 29, 1912, 12.

39. Jim Thorpe's personal scrapbook.

40. *Ibid.*

41. *Ibid.*

42. *Ibid.*

43. From the files of Elizabeth K. Dunn.

44. Jim Thorpe's personal scrapbook.

NOTES, CHAPTER 10

1. From the files of Charlotte Thorpe Adler.
2. Interview with President Dwight D. Eisenhower.
3. Jim Thorpe's personal scrapbook.
4. *Ibid.*
5. Interview with Ernie Shore, Winston-Salem, North Carolina, May 25, 1972.
6. From the files of Leo V. Lyons, Honorary Historian of Professional Football.
7. From the files of James C. Heartwell.
8. Jim Thorpe's personal scrapbook.
9. *Ibid.*
10. Gene Schoor, *The Jim Thorpe Story,* 112.
11. From the files of Joseph Boyle.
12. Jim Thorpe's personal scrapbook.
13. *Ibid.*
14. *Ibid.*
15. *Ibid.*
16. *Ibid.*
17. *Ibid.*
18. *Ibid.*
19. *Ibid.*
20. *Ibid.*
21. From the files of Elizabeth K. Dunn.
22. Letter from Arthur J. Rooney, president of Pittsburgh Steelers Football Club, October 19, 1967.
23. Letter from Jack Cusack, October 4, 1967.
24. Interview with Grace Thorpe.
25. Interview with Avery Brundage.
26. Jim Thorpe's personal scrapbook.
27. Interview with Ralph Craig.
28. Jim Thorpe's personal scrapbook.
29. *Ibid.*

NOTES, CHAPTER 11

1. Jim Thorpe's personal scrapbook.
2. *Ibid.*
3. *Ibid.*
4. Interview with Patricia Thorpe.
5. Jim Thorpe's personal scrapbook.
6. *Ibid.*
7. Interview with Arthur Martin.
8. Interview with Al Schacht, August 22, 1967, New York City.
9. Jim Thorpe's personal scrapbook.

10. Interview with Al Schacht.
11. Lawrence S. Ritter, *The Glory of Their Times,* 175.
12. Interview with Al Schacht.
13. *Ibid.*
14. Robert Leckie, *The Story of Football,* 45.
15. Interview with Charlotte Thorpe Adler.
16. Jim Thorpe's personal scrapbook.
17. *Ibid.*
18. Interview with Charlotte Thorpe Adler.
19. Jim Thorpe's personal scrapbook.
20. Interview with Grace Thorpe.
21. Interview with Al Schacht.
22. *Ibid.*
23. *Ibid.*
24. Jim Thorpe's personal scrapbook.
25. Interview with Al Schacht.

NOTES, CHAPTER 12

1. Grantland Rice, *The Tumult and the Shouting,* 234.
2. Jack Cusack, *Pioneer in Pro Football,* 3–32.

NOTES, CHAPTER 13

1. Interview with George Halas, August 9, 1974, Chicago, Illinois.
2. Interview with Leo V. Lyons, July 1, 1967, Rochester, New York.
3. Interview with I. R. Martin, July 6, 1967, Aurora, Ohio.
4. From the files of I. R. Martin.
5. Letter from Arthur J. Rooney, October 19, 1967.
6. From the files of Henry W. Clune, Scottsville, New York.
7. *Ibid.*
8. Steve Owen, *My Kind of Football,* 28, 29.
9. Interview with Patricia Thorpe.
10. Jim Thorpe's personal scrapbook.
11. *Ibid.*
12. Interview with Ross U. Porter, July 27, 1967, Shawnee, Oklahoma.
13. Letter from Charlotte Thorpe Adler, November 3, 1967.
14. *Long Beach Press-Telegram,* November 13, 1929.
15. James C. Heartwell's personal scrapbook.
16. *Ibid.*
17. *Ibid.*
18. *Long Beach Press-Telegram,* December 7, 1934.
19. Interview with Slim Harrison, July 20, 1967, San Pedro, California.

20. From the files of the Helms Athletic Foundation.
21. Jim Thorpe's personal scrapbook.
22. *Ibid.*
23. *Ibid.*
24. Frank Scully and Norman Sper, "Jim Thorpe; The Greatest Athlete Alive," *American Mercury* magazine (August, 1943).
25. Jim Thorpe's personal scrapbook.
26. *Ibid.*
27. Interview with Mrs. Harrison Ground, July 4, 1967, Basom, New York.
28. Interview with Grace Thorpe.
29. Jim Thorpe's personal scrapbook.
30. James C. Heartwell's personal scrapbook.
31. Interview with Ray Witter, July 4, 1967, Batavia, New York.
32. Jim Thorpe's personal scrapbook.
33. *Ibid.*
34. *Ibid.*
35. Interview with Luther Buss, July 14, 1967, Dearborn, Michigan.
36. *Lon Scott News,* Tulsa, Oklhoma, August 5, 1953.
37. Jim Thorpe's personal scrapbook.
38. *Ibid.*
39. *Ibid.*
40. *Ibid.*
41. *Ibid.*
42. *Ibid.*
43. *Ibid.*
44. *New York Telegram,* July 21, 1948.
45. *San Francisco Examiner,* August 22, 1948.
46. *San Francisco Call-Bulletin,* August 20, 1948.
47. Jim Thorpe's personal scrapbook.
48. *Ibid.*
49. *Ibid.*
50. *Ibid.*
51. *Ibid.*
52. *Ibid.*
53. Wilbur J. Gobrecht, *Jim Thorpe, Carlisle Indian,* 12.
54. *El Universal,* Caracas, Venezuela, December 13, 1961.
55. *Harrisburg Patriot,* January 26, 1950.
56. Jim Thorpe's personal scrapbook.
57. *Ibid.*
58. *Ibid.*
59. From the files of the Cumberland County Historical Society.
60. *Los Angeles Mirror,* August 21, 1951.
61. Jim Thorpe's personal scrapbook.
62. *Harrisburg Evening News,* August 23, 1951.

63. James C. Heartwell's personal scrapbook.

64. *Ibid.*

65. *Ibid.* (All those who were interviewed and had donated to this cause asked to remain anonymous.)

66. Interview with Patricia Thorpe.

67. *Ibid.*

68. Jim Thorpe's personal scrapbook.

69. Interview with Dr. Rachel Jenkins, July 18, 1967.

70. *Indian Leader,* April 10, 1953.

71. Interview with Patricia Thorpe.

72. Interview with Grace Thorpe.

73. Interview with Charlotte Thorpe Adler.

74. Al Stump, *Sport* magazine (December, 1949), 54.

75. Jim Thorpe's personal scrapbook.

NOTES, CHAPTER 14

1. Interview with Ross U. Porter.

2. Interview with Joseph Boyle, August 20, 1967 and August 24, 1974, Jim Thorpe, Pennsylvania.

3. Letter from Gail M. Thorpe, August 20, 1974.

4. *New York Daily News,* October 13, 1973, 33.

NOTES, CHAPTER 15

1. Interview with Dr. Joseph Alexander.

2. Interview with Jack Dempsey, August 22, 1967.

3. Interview with George Halas.

4. From a tape recording by Tom Harmon.

5. Interview with Burt Lancaster, July 23, 1967, Culver City, California.

6. Interview with Leo V. Lyons.

7. Interview with I. R. Martin.

8. Interview with Grace Thorpe.

9. Interview with George Trafton, member of Pro Football Hall of Fame, July 19, 1967, Los Angeles, California.

Bibliography

Letters

Adler, Mrs. Charlotte
(Thorpe)
Alexander, Dr. Joseph
Bird, Candace L.
Bloom, Rich
Bolger, Tom
Boyle, Joseph
Brodsky, Irv
Brundage, Avery
Bucci, Ron
Calac, Mrs. Pete
Campbell, David
Campbell, James
Chapman, Dennis N.
Clune, Henry
Craig, Ralph
Cusack, Jack
Doser, John
Dunn, Miss Elizabeth K.
Durant, Don
Eisenhower, Dwight D.
Fralish, John
Freeman, Everett
Froland, Vic
Galloway, Robert P.
Gillis, Mary
Gross, Lynda
Halas, George
Heartwell, James C.
Henderson, Joe
Hertzler, Mrs. Mary S.
Kerr, Andy

Keys, Tom
Little, Lou
Lucas, James
Lyons, Leo V.
McCann, Richard
McNulty, Margie
Martin, I. R.
Mehr, Joseph O.
Micheli, Frank
Mitchell, Dan
Owen, Irvin
Paynter, Tom
Platt, Joel
Porter, Ross U.
Ray, Beth
Ray, Homer
Rooney, Arthur
Sangster, Mrs. Candy
Schrader, Lowell
Sechriest, Vernon
Steck, Roger
Thorpe, Gail
Thorpe, Mrs. (Patricia) Jim
Tracy, Sterling
Wakolee, Art
Wardecker, James
Welch, Gus
Weyand, Colonel Alex-
ander M.
Whistler, Mrs. Verna
(Donegan)
Wickman, John E.

Periodicals

American Legion
American Magazine
American Mercury
Athletic World
Climax
Collier's
Columbus Sunday Dispatch
　Magazine
Epic

International Affairs, The
　Commonwealth of Penn.
Milwaukee Eagle
Oklahoma's Orbit
Sport
Sports Illustrated
Sport Week
Veteran Boxer

Newspapers

Albany Knickerbocker
　News
Allentown Call Chronicle
Asbury Evening Press
Baltimore Daily Record
Boston American
Boston Globe
Boston Herald
Boston Journal
Boston Post
Buffalo News
Canton Repository
Caracas El Universal
　(Venezuela)
Carlisle Evening News
Chicago Herald American
Chicago Sun Times
Columbus Dispatch
Daily Oklahoman
Denver Post
Detroit Times
Harrisburg Evening News
Harrisburg Patriot
Hazelton Plain Speaker

Milwaukee Journal
New York American
New York Daily News
New York Telegram
New York Times
New York Tribune
New York World
Pasadena Star News
Philadelphia Enquirer
Philadelphia Evening
　Bulletin
Philadelphia Ledger
Philadelphia North
　American
Pittsburgh Dispatch
Pittsburgh Leader
Pittsburgh Press
Providence Daily Journal
Providence Visitor
Reading Eagle
Rochester Democrat
　& Chronicle
Rochester Times Union
Rock Island Argus

Houston Chronicle
Indian Leader, Haskell
   Institute
Jim Thorpe Times-News
Kansas City Star
Long Beach Independent
Long Beach Press Telegram
Lon Scott News
Los Angeles Daily News
Los Angeles Examiner
Los Angeles Mirror
Los Angeles Times
Miami Daily News

Rocky Mount (N.C.)
   Telegram
St. Peterburg Times
San Francisco Bulletin
San Francisco Examiner
Shawnee News Star
Special Service (U.S. Army)
Springfield Union
Syracuse Post Standard
Toronto Mail & Empire
Vallejo Times Herald
Waterbury Republican
Yale News

Tape-recorded interviews

Adler, Charlotte Thorpe
Alexander, Joe
Boyle, Joseph
Brundage, Avery
Buss, Luther
Calac, Pete
Craig, Ralph
Dempsey, Jack
Eisenhower, Dwight D.
Goldstein, Hyman
Ground, Mrs. Harrison
Halas, George
Harmon, Tom
Harrison, Slim
Heartwell, James C.
Johnson, Chief Freeman

Kerr, Andy
Lancaster, Burt
Lyons, Leo V.
Martin, Arthur
Martin, I. R.
Nevitt, Chief Garland
Porter, Ross U.
Schacht, Al
Thorpe, Grace
Thorpe, Jim
Trafton, George
Washington, George
Whistler, Verna (Donegan)
Witter, Ray
Wood, Jim

Scrapbooks

Adler, Charlotte Thorpe
Boyle, Joseph

Heartwell, James C.
Thorpe, Jim

305

Photographs

Charlotte Thorpe Adler Collection
Avery Brundage Collection
Cumberland County Historical Society and Hamilton Library Association Collection
Dwight D. Eisenhower Library Collection
James C. Heartwell Collection
Maxine and Robert Lingo Collection
Arthur Martin Collection
Allan Peterson Collection
Pro Football Hall of Fame Collection
Beth and Homer Ray Collection
Grace Thorpe Collection

Books

American Heritage Book of Indians. American Heritage Publishing Company, New York, 1961.

Baseball Encyclopedia. Macmillan Company, Toronto, Canada, 1969.

Claassen, Harold. *The History of Professional Football.* Prentice-Hall, Englewood Cliffs 1963.

Collier, John. *Indians of the Americas.* Mentor Books, New York, 1947.

Cusack, Jack. *Pioneer in Pro Football.*

Daley, Arthur. *Pro Football's Hall of Fame.* Quadrangle Books, Chicago, 1963.

De Voto, Bernard. *Across the Wide Missouri.* Houghton Mifflin, Boston, 1947.

Dodge, Col. Richard Irving. *Thirty-Three Years Among Our Wild Indians.* Archer House, New York, 1882.

Douglas, Loretto. *The People We Call Indians.* Vantage Press, New York, 1954.

Durant, John, and Otto Bettmann. *Pictorial History of American Sports, from Colonial Times to the Present.* A. S. Barnes, New York, 1952.

Eisenhower, Dwight D. *At Ease.* Doubleday, Garden City, 1967.

Gobrecht, Wilbur J. *Jim Thorpe, Carlisle Indian.* Cumberland County Historical Society and Hamilton Library Association, Carlisle, 1972.

Henry, Bill. *An Approved History of the Olympic Games.* G. P. Putnam's Sons, New York, 1948.

Heuman, William. *The Indians of Carlisle.* G. P. Putnam's Sons, New York, 1965.

Horan, James D. *The Great American West.* Crown Publishers, New York, 1959.

Jackson, Helen Hunt. *A Century of Dishonor.* Harper Torchbooks, New York, 1881.

Kieran, John. *The Story of the Olympic Games, 776 B.C.– 1936 A.D.* J. B. Lippincott, Philadelphia, 1936.

Leavitt, Dr. Jerome E. *America and Its Indians.* Grosset and Dunlap, New York, 1962.

Leckie, Robert. *The Story of Football.* Random House, New York, 1965.

McCracken, Harold. *George Catlin and the Old Frontier.* Bonanza Books, New York, 1959.

Meiers, Earl Schenck. *Football.* Grosset & Dunlap, New York, 1967.

Meyers, Barlow. *Champions All the Way.* Whitman Publishing Company, Racine, 1960.

Owen, Steve. *My Kind of Football.* David McKay, New York, 1952.

Patterson, J. B., ed. *Autobiography of Black Hawk.* Oquawka, Ill., 1882.

Peterson, Allan. *Thorpe of Carlisle.*

(Selected by) Pratt, John Lowell. *Sport, Sport, Sport. True Stories of Great Athletes and Great Human Beings.* J. Lowell Pratt, New York, 1960.

Pratt, Brig. General Richard Henry. *Battlefield and Classroom, Four Decades With the American Indian,* 1867–1904. Yale University Press, New Haven, 1964.

Rice, Grantland. *The Tumult and the Shouting.* A. S. Barnes, New York, 1954.

Ritter, Lawrence S. *The Glory of Their Times. The Story of the Early Days of Baseball Told by the Men Who Played It.* Macmillan, New York, 1966.

Roberts, Howard. *The Chicago Bears.* G. P. Putnam's Sons, New York, 1947.

——— . *The Story of Pro Football.* Rand McNally, 1953.

Schoor, Gene, with Henry Gilfond. *The Jim Thorpe Story.* Julian Messner, New York, 1951.

Smith, Robert. *Illustrated History of Pro Football.* Madison Square Press, Grosset & Dunlap, New York, 1970.

——— . *Pro Football. The History of the Game and the Great Players.* Doubleday, Garden City, 1963.

Steckbeck, John S. *Fabulous Redmen. The Carlisle Indians and Their Famous Football Teams.* J. Horace McFarland Company, Harrisburg, 1951.

Sullivan, James E., ed. *The Olympic Games. Stockholm, 1912.* American Sports Publishing Company, New York, 1912.

Van Every, Dale. *Disinherited: The Lost Birthright of the American Indian.* Avon Books, New York, 1966.

Verrill, A. Hyatt. *The Real Americans.* G. P. Putnam's Sons, New York, 1954.

Wakolee, Pat, and Art Wakolee. *Moccasin Paths.* Deseret Book Company, Salt Lake City, 1966.

Weyand, Alexander M. *Football Immortals.* Macmillan, New York, 1962.

——— . *The Saga of American Football.* Macmillan, New York, 1955.

Index

309